D0986834

Ancient Peoples and Places

FOOD IN ANTIQUITY

General Editor

DR. GLYN DANIEL

ABOUT THE AUTHORS

Don Brothwell studied zoology, geology, and anthropology at University College, London, and archaeology at the Institute of Archaeology there. After three years of teaching in the Faculty of Archaeology and Anthropology at Cambridge, he took up a research post in the Subdepartment of Anthropology at the British Museum (Natural History). Dr. Brothwell is also Honorary Lecturer in Anthropology at University College, London. An author in his own right, he has, in addition, edited the publications Dental Anthropology *and* The Skeletal Biology of Earlier Human Populations *and coedited* Science in Archaeology *(with E. Higgs) and* Diseases in Antiquity *(with A. T. Sanderson).*

Patricia Brothwell studied languages at Westfield College, London, and, after a period of librarianship, her interest in her husband's researches prompted her to visit museums and sites in Europe and North America with him. Her special linguistic and bibliophilic knowledge has helped, in particular, to maintain a reliable balance of food evidence in this book.

Ancient Peoples and Places

FOOD IN ANTIQUITY

A SURVEY OF THE DIET OF EARLY PEOPLES

Don and Patricia Brothwell

67 PHOTOGRAPHS
42 LINE DRAWINGS
4 MAPS
7 TABLES

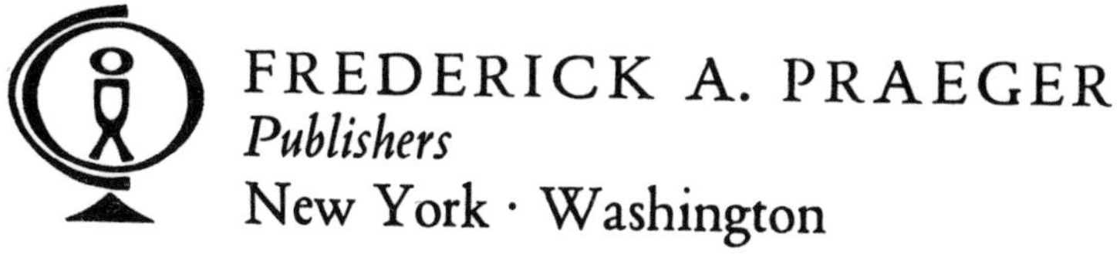

FREDERICK A. PRAEGER
Publishers
New York · Washington

THIS IS VOLUME SIXTY-SIX IN THE SERIES

Ancient Peoples and Places

GENERAL EDITOR: DR. GLYN DANIEL

BOOKS THAT MATTER

Published in the United States of America in 1969
by Frederick A. Praeger Inc., Publishers,
111 Fourth Avenue, New York, N.Y. 10003

Library of Congress Catalog Card Number: 69–19524
Printed in Great Britain

CONTENTS

ILLUSTRATIONS

PLATES

FIGURES

Acknowledgments

A CONSIDERABLE number of individuals, who work in a variety of archaeological, biological and technical fields, have helped us considerably. In particular we should like to thank Dr Kenneth Oakley for initiating the British Museum (Natural History) collection of ancient food debris from various parts of the world—and in so doing setting the seed of our own interest in this subject. We have received help and encouragement, in one way or another, from Mr Eric Higgs, Dr Brian Fagan, Dr William Stearn, Mr Clive Jermy, Mr Raymond Chaplin, Mrs Sheila Dorrell, Mrs Caroline Banks, Miss E. M. Chatt, Dr G. Marrison, Dr J. V. Kinnier Wilson, Mrs Marjorie Firth, Mrs Irene Copeland, Mr H. E. Biggs, Mr L. Matthews, and Dr Brian F. Cook.

We are most grateful to the following individuals or institutions for plates: Dr Kathleen Kenyon (4, 5, 8, 42, 52); Thames and Hudson (9, 25); Mr Eric Higgs (22); Mrs Juliet Jewell (14, 15); Professor Charles Reed (13, 21); Indian Geological Survey (19); Dr C. Higham (12); Mr R. Chaplin (7); Victoria and Albert Museum (26); R.A.F. Institute of Aviation Medicine (29, 30); Dr Jane Goodall (31–33); Trustees of the British Museum (24); New York Metropolitan Museum of Art (34, 35); Paul Elek Productions Ltd., (41, 50); American Museum of Natural History (43–45); Dr E. O. Callen (1–3); Netherlands Institute for the Near East, Leiden (48, 49); Carnegie Institution of Washington (46); Museo Nazionale, Rome (51); Ashmolean Museum, Oxford (55); Museum of Archaeology and Ethnology, Cambridge (58, 60, 61); Dr B. Jørgensen (62, 63); National Museum of Ireland, Dublin (65, 66); The Wellcome Historical Medical Museum (67). All other photographs were obtained from the archives of the Sub-Department of Anthropology

(B.M.N.H.), and are reproduced by courtesy of the Trustees of this museum.

In the case of the figures, we are most grateful for the artistic help of Miss Rosemary Powers. We also wish to thank Mr Eric Higgs for providing Fig. 12; the Council of the Marine Biological Association of the United Kingdom for Fig. 22; and to Professor J. Nenquin for permitting our use of Figs. 39 and 40. Other figures have been adapted and modified from a variety of photographic and line illustrations.

Plain numerals in the margin refer to the bibliography on pp. 193–200.

Chapter I

Introduction

'The history of man from the beginning has been the history of his struggle for daily bread.'
Josué de Castro, *Geography of Hunger.*

THIS BOOK is an attempt to survey briefly but on a world-wide scale, the diets of earlier peoples. If it betrays a certain lack of homogeneity, this is because of the variable nature of the material evidence; whereas there are many large mammal bones available for study, fish, birds, and other vertebrates are scarce, owing to the more fragile nature of the 'hard parts', the hazards of burial, and even the edibility of smaller bones. Similarly, carbonized and dessicated plant remains are not as common as could be desired and thus it is necessary to fall back on literary evidence—with a resulting bias towards the early Mediterranean world. Some topics have had to be treated somewhat cursorily; these include the varied methods of food preservation and cooking, as well as cooking utensils and hunting and collecting methods. Yet again, the culturally determined and widespread ramifications of food taboos could not be dealt with here. As in certain areas today, there is plenty of evidence of food shortages in some earlier communities, affecting either the whole group or segments of it. Our concern, however, must be with the variable and sometimes changing pattern of subsistence in early times, and we shall have succeeded if we demonstrate clearly the diverse nature of human diet in the past.

Strictly speaking, food may be defined as all solid and fluid substances which permit the human organism to grow and maintain its health throughout life. An adequate diet is vital to a population in two basic respects. First, inadequate or abnormal diets open the doors to the retardation of growth, chronic ill health, and a high mortality rate. Secondly, production of sufficient energy, especially in order to maintain an optimum working capacity, depends upon food intake. There is, of course, no such thing as an all-purpose food, and a considerable variety of substances is necessary in modern diet. Bread is rich in carbohydrates, meat in fat and protein, and milk possesses a relatively high calcium content. Thus only a mixed diet caters adequately for our needs, although the combinations can be many and varied and the body will in fact tolerate some degree of insufficiency. Whilst there is no single optimal diet, certain diets are undoubtedly better for body health and performance, and so it is by no means a trivial aspect of archaeological research to attempt to reconstruct the dietary economics of earlier populations.

Whatever range of foodstuffs is consumed, whether they result from a hunting/collecting, or a farming economy, it is essential that the calorific value of the food is sufficient and that proteins, mineral elements and vitamins are included. Of this quadrant of vital components of any diet, sufficiency of calories is by far the most important. Calorie needs vary according to age, sex, and occupation. A child of about five years would need about 1500 calories daily, whereas a fully adult male engaged on heavy agricultural work might need well over 3,000.

THE POPULATION 'EXPLOSION'

Food production as a whole has been increasing ever since Neolithic times and the resulting improvement in man's diet has led to a progressive over-all growth in the world's population.

24 Carleton Coon has recently indicated the size of breeding units likely in Pleistocene man, by reference to data available for modern surviving food-gatherers. He notes that modern 'Stone Age' breeding isolates (small regional groups with restricted contact with other such groups) generally contain no more than 80 to 100 breeding family units, and such figures seem applicable to most pre-Neolithic communities, except perhaps for some of

the final Late Pleistocene groups who were able to slaughter migrating herds of large mammals. There is, however, some difference of opinion, and in a recent population study, Edward 29 Deevey suggests that some kind of social (and sexual) restraint is just as feasible. He estimates that human density during the Palaeolithic period did not exceed 0·04 individuals per square kilometre. He remarks aptly that a 'Palaeolithic man who stuck to business should have found enough food on two square kilometres, instead of 20 or 200. Social forces were probably more powerful than mere starvation in causing man to huddle in small bands.'

Though opinions differ as to why the world remained so sparsely populated during Palaeolithic times, there is certainly general agreement that the Neolithic and Industrial revolutions had a profound effect upon population expansion. Indeed, in both cases there is likely to have been a noticeable jump-up in numbers. Referring again to data by Deevey, the total world population for early hominids of about a million years ago (as exemplified by the Australopithecine group of South and East Africa) may have been much less than half a million. Possibly as a result of the growing efficacy of artifacts and the change to a diet that included more flesh, the population may well have increased to over three million by the end of the Palaeolithic period. Further technological advances during Mesolithic times may not have done much more than cause the steady increase to continue, but with the beginning of village farming and urban development over 7,000 years ago, population figures probably soared within two or three thousand years to over 100 million. This spurt was no doubt the result of a combination of factors, especially the all-the-year-round availability of high-calorie cereal foods and the consequent decrease in malnutrition, and the greater protection larger and more organized social groups offer. *Fig. 1* Of these population 'explosions', by far the greatest has taken place within the past few centuries as a result of industrialization,

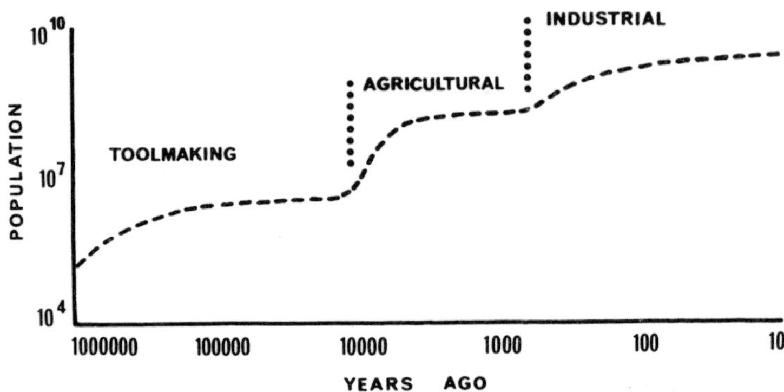

Fig. 1 A population 'curve' (logarithmic scale) showing clearly the presumed relationship between the three major population explosions and levels of cultural attainment. (A simple arithmetic vertical scale in millions of people does not show these changes so precisely)

and even though for many millions nutritional levels are far below a satisfactory standard, there is nevertheless enough food today to keep alive some 3,000 million people.

FIRE AND FOOD

77 Kenneth Oakley has reviewed in detail the evidence for fire-using by Palaeolithic man, and only brief mention of this aspect needs to be made here.

The replacement of at least a part of the diet of raw meat and vegetables by cooked food must certainly have altered the pattern of mastication, digestion and nutrition. The breaking-down of animal and vegetable fibres would have helped to liberate protein and carbohydrate material. Some of the tougher food would also have been made softer, and thus more palatable to the enfeebled and to those without sufficient teeth to chew vigorously. The Neanderthal 'old man' of La Chapelle aux Saints, who had hardly any teeth left (and even those were of no functional value), is a good example of the type of individual who must have benefitted greatly from cooked food.

In Africa, none of the earlier Palaeolithic horizons known indicates the use of fire, but from the Final Acheulian levels and all succeeding horizons in a number of sites in Central and Southern Africa, there is quite positive evidence. From Asia and Europe, there are clear indications that fire-using was a much earlier discovery. The Choukoutien caves, inhabited by Peking man (*Homo erectus pekinensis*) during a part of the Second Glaciation, provide the most ancient example. The evidence included charred bone and antler, which suggests that the fires were not purely for warmth or to frighten away undesirable carnivores. In Europe, fire-using can certainly be associated with Acheulian hand-axe people, as sites in Spain (Torralba), England (Hoxne, Swanscombe), and France (Cagny-la-Garenne) testify. By the time Neanderthal man was established over much of Europe, fire may have been in fairly common use.

Plate 46

Oakley points out that the Lower Palaeolithic groups using fire are likely to have been only *fire-collectors*, but the frequency of Middle and Upper Palaeolithic hearths clearly indicates that most of the Neanderthalers and all the Cro-Magnon and related peoples were *fire-producers.*

A further significant step in cooking foodstuffs must have come with the advent of pottery. At the pre-pottery stage, man would have been limited to softening food by direct exposure to flames or by contact with the hot ashes or stones of a hearth, though it is feasible that by Upper Palaeolithic times, water was heated in leather containers by the addition of hot stones. In pottery vessels, cooked foods could be prepared for eating with less contamination from soil, ash and smoke, and indeed not only would the foods be cleaner, but the taste-range may have changed as well. It must be noted, however, that another aspect of food hygiene, namely, bacterial contamination, may not have been improved. Even with modern washing detergents, the cleaning of early rough-surfaced cooking pots would have been a problem, but how much more so without any form of soap!

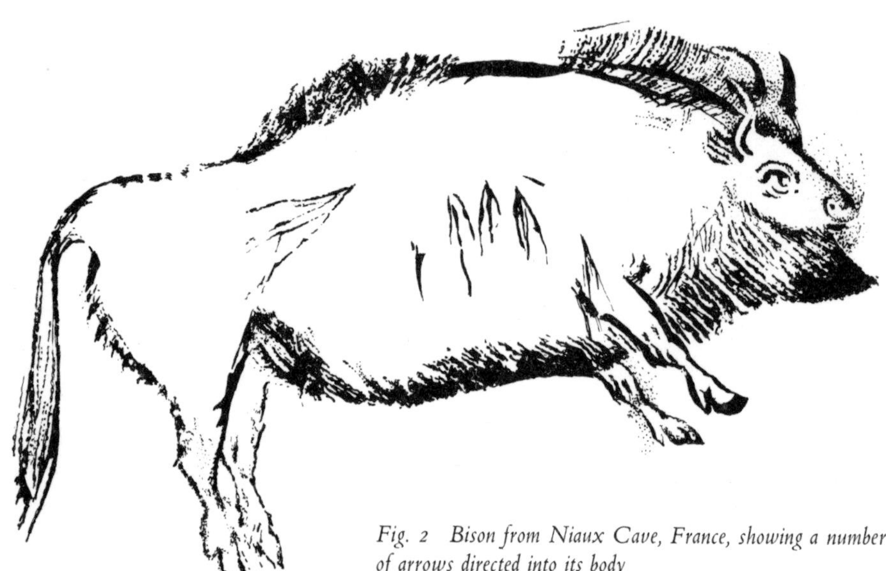

Fig. 2 Bison from Niaux Cave, France, showing a number of arrows directed into its body

SOURCES OF DATA

We may obtain information about ancient diet to a greater or lesser degree from the following sources:

1. Artistic representations of plants and animals in caves, rock-shelters, tombs, monuments, etc.
2. Direct evidence of food remains on living-floors, refuse pits, middens and habitation sites.
3. Written evidence.
4. Analyses of 'stomach' contents in mummies and bog bodies, or coprolites (dried faeces).
5. A study of the habits of modern aboriginal populations (by inference).

By far the most difficult category from the point of view of satisfactory interpretation is artistic representation. There seems little doubt that much of European cave art is concerned directly

Fig. 3

with important food-yielding animals. The wounded bison of Lascaux, the mammoth of Pindal with its vital organ the heart accurately located and prominently displayed, and the bisons of Niaux with arrows piercing their sides, point to an association with hunting. On the other hand, many of these animals were in all probability associated with totem ritual. All in all, however, such representations, whilst no more than a very crude yardstick of the animal-food interests of some earlier human groups, provide evidence that cannot be ignored. Food remains help us both directly and indirectly, though in varying degree, to build up the dietary background of a group. Indeed, the real importance of analyses of, say, shell or animal bones, lies in the relative proportions of those collected together by earlier groups, and in the variations they may demonstrate through space and time. Even so, such specimens can hope to provide only a small part of the total food picture. Insects may have been eaten on the spot; in any event, no traces would normally remain. Only smaller game may have been transported as carcasses to the camp site, *Fig. 2*

Fig. 3 The frequencies of animals in a random sample of 640, as recorded in the Upper Palaeolithic cave art of Europe

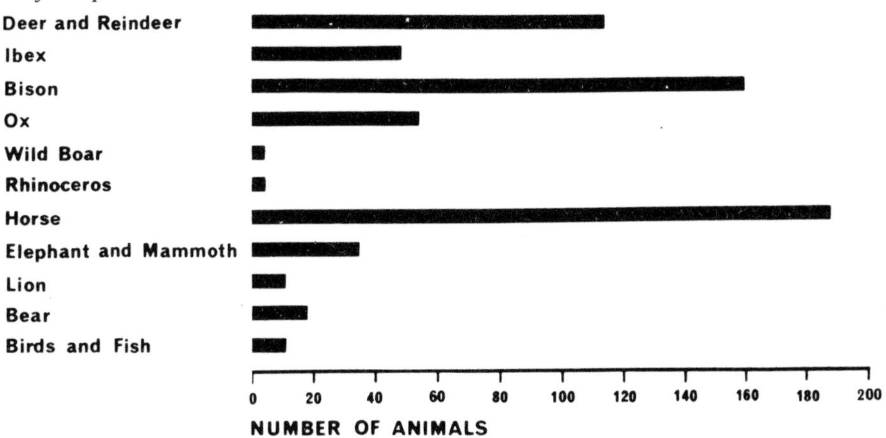

whereas the larger mammals killed some distance away may well have been stripped of flesh and left, for carrion. Where plant foods are concerned, it is only very rarely that any remains are preserved—as at Glastonbury, Jericho and the prehistoric Swiss lake-sites.

Although the intact contents of the human 'stomach' (really including the intestines as well) and coprolites are uncommon materials in archaeobiological research, it may be that a means of detecting such residues more readily may yet be devised. A variety of soil conditions may well be conducive to the preservation of at least some material passing through the alimentary canal, especially seeds, cereal husks, snail shell and crustacean fragments, and it is a challenge to future archaeological excavation to detect such debris in the abdominal soil of skeletons. An instance of the value of special excavation care is provided by the presumed Bronze
109 Age skeleton from Walton-on-the-Naze, reported by S. Hazzle-
Plate 37 dine Warren in 1911. In the position where the viscera had been, a gritty substance was found mainly consisting of the seeds of blackberry, rose and Garden Orache (*Atriplex*), the remains of food eaten just before death. The 'stomach' contents of mummies and naturally preserved bodies offer the most exact—if very limited—evidence of diet. By far the most remarkable example is
50 that of Grauballe man, found in central Jutland in 1952, and dated by C^{14} and pollen analysis to between the third and fifth centuries AD. In all, some 610 cc. of food remains were recovered, appearing as a fine-grained brown mud mixed with larger particles consisting of a large variety of seeds and cereal fragments, and a number of small bone fragments.

At first sight coprolites look very unpromising material, and
15, 16 E. O. Callen of McGill University, who has done much to
Plates 1–3 stimulate interest in this field, recalls that those from the Peruvian site of Huaca Prieta were like lumps of sand and dust. The original texture of such dried excreta can best be restored by soaking them for 72 hours in an 0·5 per cent aqueous solution of
2, 25, 46 sodium triphosphate. In this softened condition the material can

be submitted to detailed microscopic examination, as in the recent Nevada cave studies. In the case of the New World material, it has shown the presence of beans, cucurbit, chili pepper, mussel, clam, snail, fish, crab and sea urchin.

CHEMICAL ANALYSIS

Chemical analysis of the food residues of early man is limited by shortage of material and the present difficulty of drawing firm conclusions from the results. This contrasts with the other aspect of small residue identification where actual structures may be identified. Coprolites may contain food 'residues' too small and digested to be considered except by chemical tests, but also—and these are far more important here—fragments of hair, animal tissue, bacterial structures and plant cells.

Food residues, either intact as solid masses or 'skins', or Plate 8
adulterated with soils in which they were buried, have been reported from sites in various parts of the world; these are dateable to various periods from the Neolithic onwards. In Britain, such specimens have been reported from more than 31 food-vessels and Beakers of the Bronze Age, being described variously as 'greasy earth', 'black carbonaceous nitrogen-rich matter', 'black powder' and 'greasy film'. Recent experimental evidence carried out by one of us (DRB) also suggests that some, at least, of the dark, fairly light-weight 'clinker' associated with cremations from British sites may, in fact, also consist of food debris.

Chemical analysis of altered foodstuffs is by no means a recently inspired line of archaeological research. Bog butter, first reported as early as 1824, was considered chemically in 1881. John Plant, who undertook the study, concluded that the 'bog butter' was in fact a mineral resin produced naturally. This was challenged in the following year by the research chemist, W. I. Macadam, and he analyzed Scottish and Irish samples of bog butter, as well as other fatty materials for comparison. His results 66

	Meat from a bowl	Bread?	Sub-stance from under a platter	Contents of a pot	Crust from inside pot	Meat (untreated with poly-vinyl)	Matter under sheep's bones
Nitrogen	1·7	0·1	2·6	Absent	Absent	2·2	2·2
Total ash	65·1	84·7	56·1	95·2	96·6	62·5	73·7
Chloride as NaCl.	0·9	—	0·7	trace	—	trace	1·9
Phosphate as P_2O_5	13 8	1·2	16·2	2·4	1·5	13·0	20·1
Calcium	11·5	1·7	14·6	34·2	37·6	12·1	19·2

Table 1. Some analytical results on food debris from Jericho tombs. (Figures in percentages)

include data on water, fat, 'insoluble curd', and ash contents, as well as certain physical-chemical data. Also, he attempted to reduce the samples to a basic carbon, hydrogen and oxygen content. Hairs, apparently from cows, were a common factor in these 'butter' samples (and he suggested that the milk was churned in a skin). He demonstrated differences between 'butter' and adipocere (a fatty substance generated in certain dead bodies, and which is resistant to quick decay), although he was rightly careful not to be dogmatic about the true nature of this 'butter' residue. Since then, various other 'butter' samples have been submitted to chemical tests, usually with cautious conclusions as a result.

Plates 4, 5

The excavations by Dr Kathleen Kenyon of burial sites at Jericho have yielded examples of other food remains far more amenable to analysis and, through the nature of the tombs, without much adulteration with the soil. Nevertheless, the analyses were disappointing, and demonstrate that even when conditions generally are most favourable for preservation, bacterial activity may produce marked changes in the foodstuffs to the extent of obscuring the original nature of the funerary offerings.

The work was carried out by a team comprising Mrs Sheila Dorrell, the Laboratories of J. Lyons Ltd, and The British Food Manufacturing Industries Research Association, and the table opposite shows some of their findings.

The low nitrogen values demonstrate clearly that a more fundamental change than simple dehydration of the foodstuff had taken place. This was confirmed by photomicrographic studies which suggest that, in the case of meat, although the specimens had retained something of their original form, the remaining organic matter was most probably that of 'microbial cells and their by-products formed from other microbial cells in a decomposition sequence'. Samples of vegetable origin seem to have stood a better chance of survival in an identifiable form, the silica content of some plant tissue helping to preserve the original condition.

MAN EATS MAN

From the glowing recommendations of recent cannibals, human flesh is known to be tasty to eat, and is certainly no less nutritive than that of other mammals. The number of human beings in existence, particularly in the later stages of man's evolution—say from Upper Palaeolithic times onwards—was certainly sufficiently large to enable the consumption of human meat to be practicable on more than ceremonial occasions. Neither 'lust for human flesh' nor severe protein deficiency are likely to have been principal factors in the evolution of the practice; it seems far more likely that the cycle of events leading to such flesh-eating began with the need to defend group rights to hunt and collect in given territories, any fatal conflicts resulting from such socio-economic clashes being put to good use. When a community is living from day to day on the food resources immediately at hand, it is hardly likely to waste such wholesome meat, whether the deceased is a friend or an enemy!

Such speculations as to the origin and frequency of anthropophagy, are one thing, but what definite evidence have we in fact of man-eating in early populations? A study of cannibalism in various parts of the world during the past century shows it to have been prevalent enough for us to conclude that human flesh made a valid contribution to the food consumed in some groups. But we must beware of assuming that what applies to the present applies equally to the past, and it will be as well to consider some of the claims which have been made in this respect.

Accusations of cannibalism have in fact been levelled against the whole range of hominid types beginning with the earliest known group, the Australopithecines of Africa. Next, in chronological order, to come under suspicion is Peking man. Since 1929 the remains of more than 40 individuals have been found at the site of Choukoutien to the south-west of Peking, seven having skulls relatively well preserved. None of the skeletal remains of this early man showed any evidence of having received proper burial, and in fact the bones were generally broken and scattered. The skull is, in every instance, incomplete; and some of the long bone fragments are stated to be split for the obvious purpose of extracting the marrow. Special attention has been given to the base of the skull, as in every case it is defective, as though enlarged for the purpose of brain extraction.

Plate 9 Similar evidence to that found in China is also forthcoming from Europe as regards the later Neanderthal type of man. Again, among slightly less ancient palaeolithic skulls, those of Solo man from Ngandong in Java are all incomplete, the base of the brain box being missing from most of them.

By far the most convincing manifestation of cannibalism from
Fig. 4 the Palaeolithic is to be seen in an Aurignacian skeleton from Předmost in Moravia. In August 1928, disturbed and fragmentary remains (54 pieces in all) were found, representing the arms and legs of an individual, as well as two teeth. The outstanding bone of this collection is the left femur, which shows not less than

26 transverse cuts, mainly on the front side of the bone. These well-defined cuts, it has been suggested, were the results of a thorough scraping of the bone, presumably during the process of removing the ample thigh muscles. Claims of cannibalism in more recent prehistoric and early historic communities have also been made, but are too numerous to consider here.

Such, then, is the nature of the archaeological evidence available for an assessment of cannibalism in prehistory. There seems little doubt that it was practised among certain early peoples in both the New and the Old Worlds—judging from its distribution in recent times. However, it cannot be too strongly emphasized that the human remains generally presented as evidence of the practice are, for the most part, very far from convincing. All we can say is that cannibalism probably has a very long history, may have been adopted to a greater or lesser degree by a number of ancient peoples and finally, might even have played a useful dietary role in times of a protein crisis.

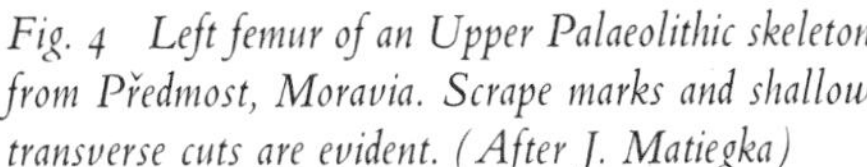

Fig. 4 Left femur of an Upper Palaeolithic skeleton from Předmost, Moravia. Scrape marks and shallow transverse cuts are evident. (After J. Matiegka)

CHAPTER II

The Vertebrates

THE MAMMALS

WHILE THE QUANTITY and variety of vertebrate animal remains, and in particular those of the mammals, show how important protein foods have been to man since his emergence, we can deduce from them far more than this.

There is little doubt that, for food, Palaeolithic and Mesolithic communities made full use of the whole range of mammals, and indeed all animal life, found in their territory. As amongst the Australian aborigines of today, some animals—or parts of them—would, no doubt, have been considered 'delicacies', but in hunting and collecting economies there is no place for a genuine food bias. Even after the Neolithic revolution, wild and easily accessible game continued to be exploited, although produce of the hunt must have become of necessity a much curtailed part of the economy.

In any study of faunal assemblages it is important to remember that what at first sight may appear to be a most uninspiring heap of bone fragments may produce a multi-faceted picture of the food animals. The fauna may reflect not only the general locality, but also climatic and topographical differences (valley, mountain, open veld and so on). The distribution of mammal groups today is of course not necessarily a guide to that of the past, and on this score man himself has markedly altered the spread of some such populations—usually to their detriment, if we except domestic animals. Also, the bone remains at a site need not necessarily reflect the exact proportion of game killed and eaten. This again would vary from period to period (in groups with domesticated stock, the correlation between bones and numbers killed would be greater); also animal size and the non-food value of the carcass would influence the composition of the remains found.

Plate 10

Even in the extremes of hot and cold climates it would still be possible to 'butcher' in the field and take only select pieces back to camp. Low temperatures help to preserve food, the process of putrefaction being retarded. Even among modern Eskimos, a frozen carcass may be picked over more than once, and even after a week or two. In places with high temperatures, especially when the kill was made far from camp, it seems likely that natural drying would be resorted to again and again. The strips of dried meat ('biltong') eaten by some groups in Africa today are the logical sequel to the dried meat with which their Stone Age ancestors must have been acquainted. During the whole history of man, bone marrow has served as food. The result is that at the majority of prehistoric sites, much of the bone debris is in the form of splintered shafts or separated proximal and distal ends of long bones. Even the mandible bodies of larger mammals may at times have been split for their internal organic content, as evidenced for example by French Palaeolithic material. In a similar way, the extraction of brain tissue necessitated the smashing of the bony brain box.

Plate 6

Plate 11

A good idea of the diversity of mammal food consumed by various peoples can be obtained by reference to our diagram where four sites are compared. Each group represents a different region, environment and time period. First, it is clear that some groups enjoyed much larger game resources than others. Secondly, it will be seen that the proportional representation of the major orders (carnivores, primates and so on) can vary considerably. This, of course, depends upon what animals are living near the human group, and how far the climate and topography is conducive to long-distance hunting. Also, the material culture may have been more suited to trapping or spearing some animal forms than others (probably a more important factor where the earlier human group is concerned).

Fig. 5

Taking the quantities per species into account, there is again wide variation in the site samples. This may be due to a number

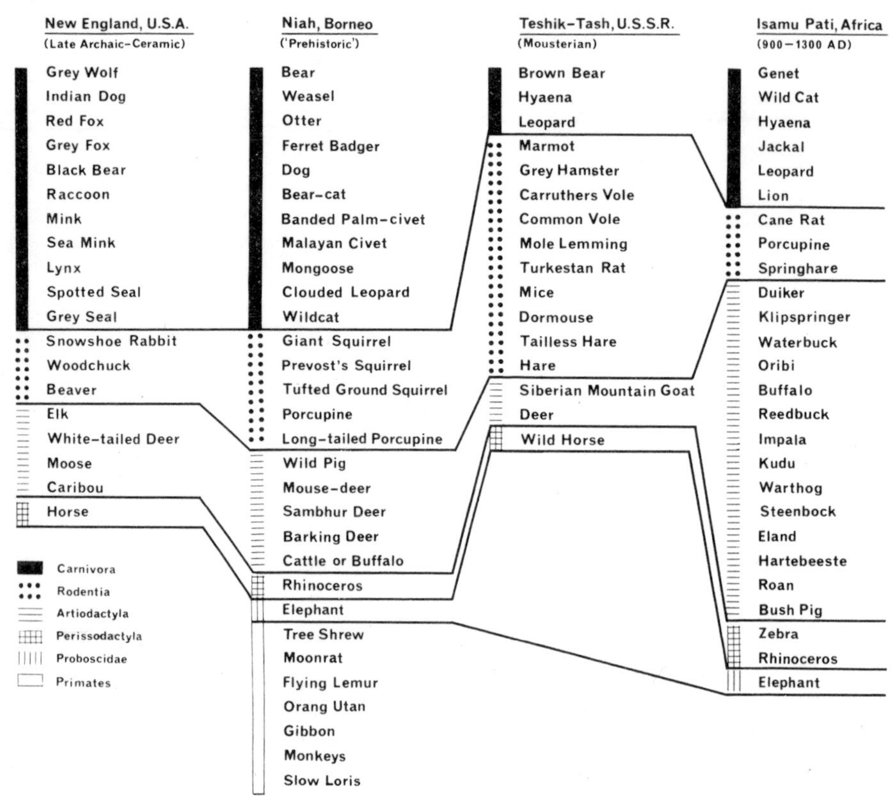

Fig. 5 Species of mammal, of food use, from archaeological sites in four different regions of the world. (Data from Waters 1962, Medway 1958, Movius 1953 and Brian Fagan. Unpublished data on Isamu Pati, Northern Rhodesia)

of causes: some animals are caught more easily, some have a more attractive taste, while the larger mammals guarantee a longer meat supply. The most prolific animal at a site may not of course provide the most meat, and for this reason one must, in food-bone analyses, also consider the amount of edible meat which the remains represent.

In all such quantitative estimates, butchering techniques must
112, 113 be kept firmly in mind. T. E. White, in America, has con-

tributed significantly to this aspect. Let us first consider one site, namely, a fortified earth lodge village 32 ME 15, excavated as part of the River Basin Surveys of the Smithsonian Institution. The considerable amount of bison, deer, and antelope bone was studied in detail by White and the frequency of different parts of the skeleton of these animals recorded. Allowing for accidents of preservation, length of site occupation, and size of population, the following conclusions can be drawn from this type of skeletal sample. First, the methods of preparing the carcass of both large and smaller mammals for food appear to be essentially the same. What minor differences do occur—as in the pelvis and scapula—seem reasonably explained by the greater weight of these parts in the bison and thus a greater likelihood of their being left in the

Fig. 6

Fig. 6 Frequency distribution of the Bison and Deer-Antelope bone from an American Indian site, 32 ME 15. p = proximal, d = distal end of the bone. (Data from White 1954)

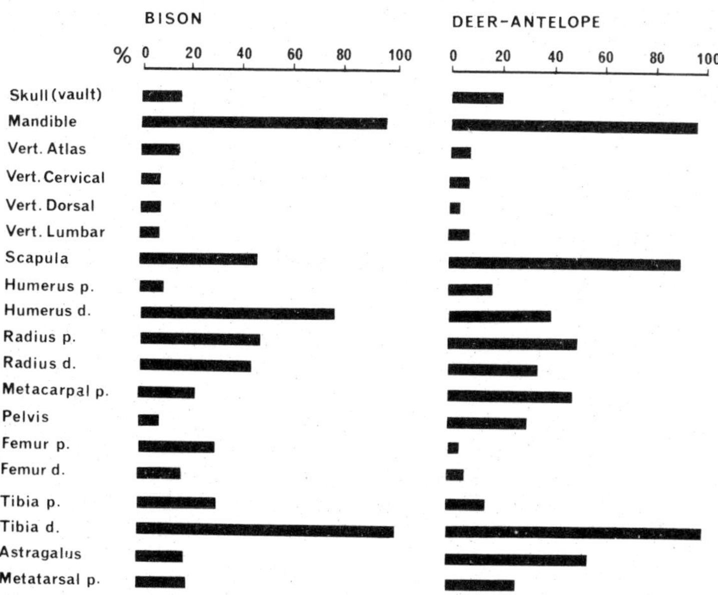

field when the carcass was cut up. On the other hand, the low percentages for some of the smaller limb bones of the combined deer-antelope group might be explained to some extent by the fact that they were fed to dogs. In the case of the skull, it is interesting to note that with large and small game, there were very nearly as many mandibles as there could have been individual animals present. The probable reason for this is that the quickest and easiest way to remove the tongue, a choice cut not to be left behind, would be to smash the ascending ramus of the lower jaw and remove the tongue with the rest of the mandible.

An assessment of animal frequencies at a site is only a very crude indicator of the value of each group to the economy, a few large animals providing a much greater meat weight than many small ones. Indeed, if we base our conclusions on the amount of edible animal meat available, rather than on skeletal numbers alone, we arrive at a more reliable estimate. Referring to White's data again, this time for two sites near Pierre, South Dakota (and divided into four period 'foci'), it was found that the requirements of the group are much greater than the meat supply represented by the bones. Allowing more people per house, the discrepancy of course becomes even larger. Group hunts must often have taken place far from the villages, and it is reasonable to assume that the 'bone-carrying capacity' of the hunters was in inverse ratio to the distance to be covered. In sum, therefore, we may take it that the bone remains represent animals (especially bison) killed locally or retrieved from the river. The weights, incidentally, did not allow for sex differences, a factor which can make a considerable difference to meat weight estimates. The male bison, for example, can have as much as 500 pounds more usable meat than the female, and in some marine mammals the difference between the sexes may be as much as 1,000 pounds of meat.

It should be remembered that large bones were sometimes selected and retained by early hunting groups because they could be put to various uses. For example, at the Upper Palaeolithic site of Kostienki, USSR, large quantities of 'fuel' bones were found. Large animal bones, such as the thigh bones of mammoths and antlers of northern reindeer, were used in building dwellings by the Upper Palaeolithic Russians of Maltá, Buret, and Yeli-seyevichi. Indeed, with the very large mammals and particularly the Pleistocene and more recent Proboscids (elephants and related forms), it is most unlikely that bones were ever carried any distance unless it was intended to use them after the meat had been removed. The Proboscids, incidentally, are a good example of the considerable variation in the distribution of an animal group in Pleistocene and modern times. During the greater part of man's existence, *Elephas* and related genera have been spread over much of Africa, Europe, Asia as far south as Borneo, through North America and well down into South America. As one beast can supply a considerable quantity of edible meat, the killing of one of these animals must have been a great achievement for a group of hunters. The Iberian Pleistocene sites of Cerralbo, Ambrona and Torralba have yielded in all the remains of some 40 to 50 elephants of the species *Palaeoloxodon antiquus*. As many of the bones are smashed, the skeletons incomplete, and human artifacts are contained in the deposits, it is not unreasonable to infer that we have here evidence of extensive—albeit periodic—elephant butchery by a pre-sapiens form of man in Europe. *Fig. 7*

In this connection it is worth noting that in both the New World and the Old World, a number of extinct Pleistocene mammal species, especially from Africa, were much larger than their nearest relatives today. Take, for example, the more southern part of Africa. In the category of herbivores, there were among others the large giraffid *Griquatherium*, giant extinct buffalo *Homoioceras bainii*, and *Bularchos arok*. Giant bush pigs, including *Notochoerus* and *Tapinochoerus* must have provided quite generous helpings of pork. As primates are hunted today by various aboriginal groups—and indeed may be an important part of the meat supply—there is no reason to think that man refrained from Plate 18 eating even 'near cousins' in the past. The giant and plentiful baboon *Dinopithecus*, about the size of a small gorilla, must have been particularly good game.

34 R. F. Ewer has recently emphasized that, considering the richness of fauna in modern African game reserves, earlier Pleistocene Hominids were in all probability even more endowed with potential meat resources. This may have special significance from the point of human evolution; that being the sort of environment in which a large-brained primate might be encouraged to hunt with considerable success. As Ewer says: 'The taste for meat could have been first acquired by eating relatively easily killed things such as tortoises, lizards, porcupines and small mammals like ground squirrels. Driving hyaenas off the remains of the sabre-tooths' kill may also have been an easy way to a good dinner, for, to judge from their dentition, the latter probably did not pick the bones very clean. Newly born buck might provide easy prey now and then and lead on to the idea of hunting the adults. Here a whole series from the smallest, easily killed by a blow on the head if only you are clever enough to cover them, up to the largest and most dangerous, provides a continued stimulus for the perfecting of hunting techniques.'

It would, of course, be wrong to think that only land mammals had been exploited by prehistoric populations. For example, there is every indication that the coastal peoples of Europe and North America in particular hunted seals. In Europe, even
20 allowing for the chance nature of finds, there are many indications of seals at Stone Age midden sites. The earliest evidence of seal-hunting is from Upper Palaeolithic deposits in the Dordogne and at the Grotte de Grimaldi. Danish sites, from the Ertebölle culture onwards, have produced by far the most evidence. In northern Europe, all four major groups, the Ringed, Harp, Grey and Spotted seals, were hunted by Late Stone Age communities, although the finds suggest that the Grey seal was used as food slightly more than the other three varieties. Seal-food continued

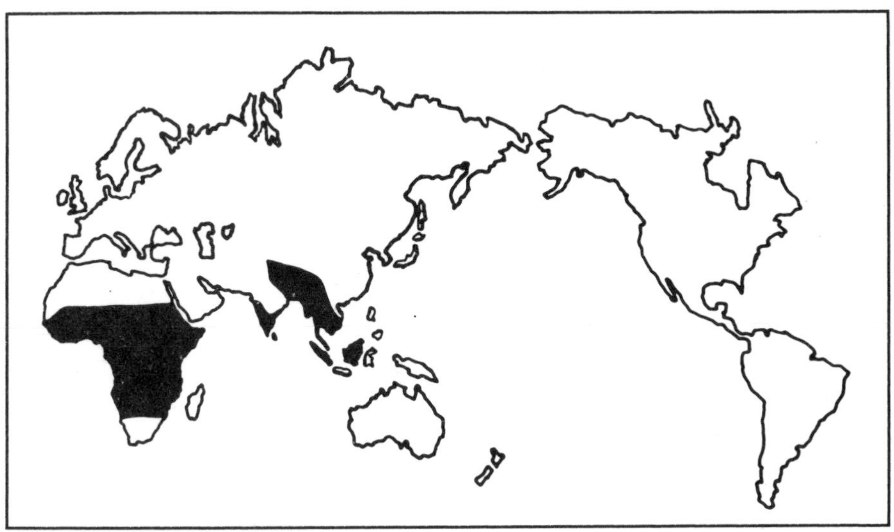

Fig. 7 The approximate distribution of living elephants (above) compared with (below) the probable distribution of Pleistocene members of the Order Proboscidae *(elephants and related forms)*

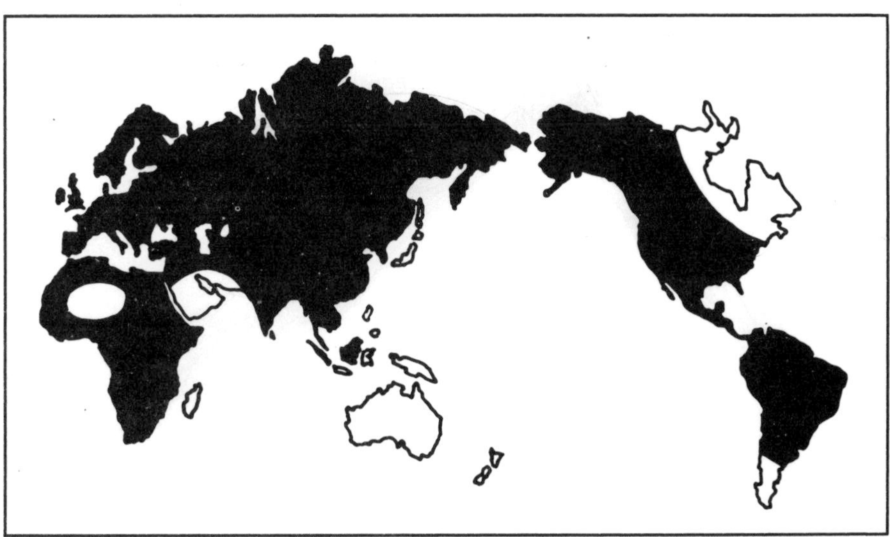

to be valued by some north European groups until recent times, and the Viking settlers of Greenland made good use of it.

The widely held view that prehistoric people resorted to autumn killing of livestock in order to reduce the numbers has recently
54 been critically re-examined by E. S. Higgs and J. P. White. Although it is not unreasonable to suppose that winter fodder reserves might often have been insufficient to support the summer number of cattle, nevertheless it is important to test the validity of this assumption by recourse to the actual material evidence. As Higgs and White state, we can infer an autumn killing—through fodder shortage—only if we can show that an abnormally high number of young animals was killed. What, then, is to be regarded as an abnormal figure? This is still very questionable, and possibly 30/50 per cent is within the range of normality for killings over the whole year. Examining the evidence in Iron Age and Roman material from a site at Old Sleaford, we find that it is very inconclusive. No less than four-fifths of the animals could have been killed throughout the year, and even the remainder—representing 'precisely aged' animals—might have been killed throughout late summer, autumn and winter.

Re-analysis of animal remains from Skara Brae, in Orkney, resulted in similar 'not proven' conclusions, the complications being numerous and the reservations important. First, the sample
Plate 12 numbers at this Orkney site are sadly small. To tell the precise age of animals by their teeth is not in fact as easy as it looks, for there is some variation in eruption times even within a single regional population (and no one can yet say whether prehistoric and modern cattle have similar tooth development times). Also, tooth wear as an age factor is difficult to interpret with exactness, although severely worn teeth must denote the slaughter of fairly old stock. Again, spring births cannot be tied down to, say, a two- or three-week period, but may be spread over as much as two months even in modern cattle. Furthermore, granted that slightly more stock may have been slaughtered in winter months,

might this not be explained by the greater need for animal food supplies in winter owing to the diminution of fruit and vegetable resources at that season? Finally, there is no reliable evidence that during prehistoric times—at least in Britain—there was a shortage of fodder in winter months. Even in the Orkneys, as eighteenth-century cattle numbers show, the environment was well suited for cattle breeding. Thus, before we can state categorically that fodder shortage dictated autumn killing, there are clearly various problems which must be solved in faunal studies.

This has been but a lightning survey of the prehistoric mammals which man has used as food. We have considered in particular the great variety which has been available, and touched on the many problems involved in the study of the bony food debris left behind for posterity. But our troubles do not end here.

DOMESTICATION
15, 75, 86, 87, 117

The domestication of livestock, together with the selective cultivation of certain plants, provided the foundations upon which all other aspects of the Neolithic Revolution must have initially depended. This guarantee of a variety of foodstuffs close at hand, and more certain throughout the year than ever before, must have occasioned considerable mental re-orientation on the part of settled communities and reduced the anxieties inseparable from day-to-day survival by hunting and collecting. One would be in no mood for reflecting upon the great do-it-yourself potentialities of baking clay if the daily need of 2,000/3,000 calories per member of family had to be searched for in the surrounding country.

It is more than likely that a combination of factors brought about a combined 'threshold' stimulus for domestication. This 'threshold' was reached in more than one human population, the aetiological factors involved not necessarily being the same in each case. Also, this process of human intervention and control of wild populations did not take place in all the domestic animal groups at the same time or even in the same millennium. Why did domestication come about? In the case of the dog, the association with man probably began with scavenging, the relationship

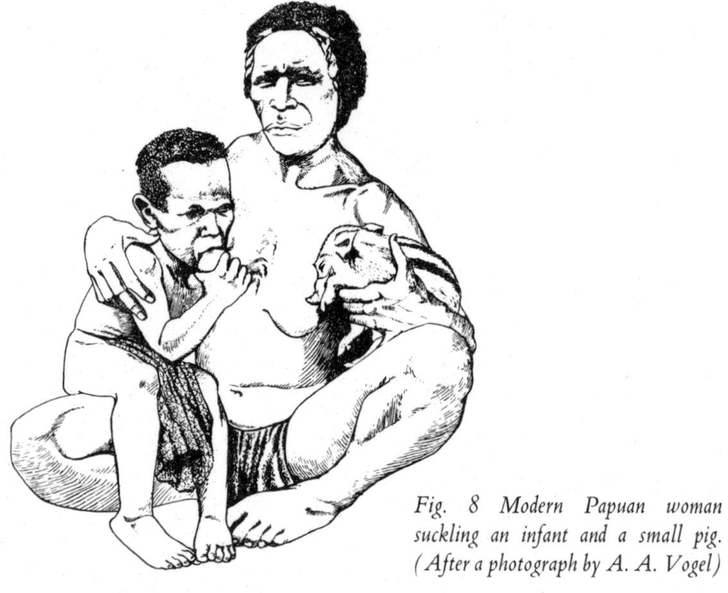

Fig. 8 Modern Papuan woman suckling an infant and a small pig. (After a photograph by A. A. Vogel)

becoming more firmly established by the intentional feeding of disposable offal to wild 'dogs' (wolves). The control of herbivore populations depends in the first instance on the availability of satisfactory plant foods, and it seems most unlikely that cattle were domesticated before plant cultivation was comparatively well organized in Neolithic groups. Considering the evidence from modern primitive societies, it could well be that on various occasions infant wolf pups and piglets, brought back to camp, were suckled by the women. It is easy to imagine that, where a number of young animals were thus allowed to reach sexual maturity, they may have commenced breeding and started domesticating themselves without any human plan being necessary. Finally, as regards the domestication of cattle, it has been suggested by various authors that the motive for capturing and maintaining the aurochs (*Bos primigenius*) in the captive state was to have available for ritual purposes a guaranteed supply of

Fig. 8

this meat. If this was so, early changes in the aurochs population were not intentional on the part of man, but resulted purely from inbreeding and the survival of variants which in unprotected stock would probably not have survived.

A rough indication of the probable time differences involved in domesticating various animal groups is shown in the chart on the opposite page, but of course, this picture may be modified by further discoveries. Although space permits a consideration of only a selection of the total range of animals which have come under the control of man—in fact only those concerned very directly with human diet—it is likely that all were used to some extent as food. The chief domestic value of the horse, camel, onager, ass and mule was for transport and other labour tasks, but their meat was probably utilized on some occasions. Similarly the cat, possibly domesticated in Egypt by Early Dynastic times as a useful pest destroyer and later given special ritual status, no doubt also provided a tasty meal in times of great need. One is reminded of the fact that this animal went into many a stew pot during the Nazi occupation of Europe only two decades ago. *Fig. 9*

Fig. 9 Tentative scheme of domestication periods at present considered critical for the emergence of certain food mammals

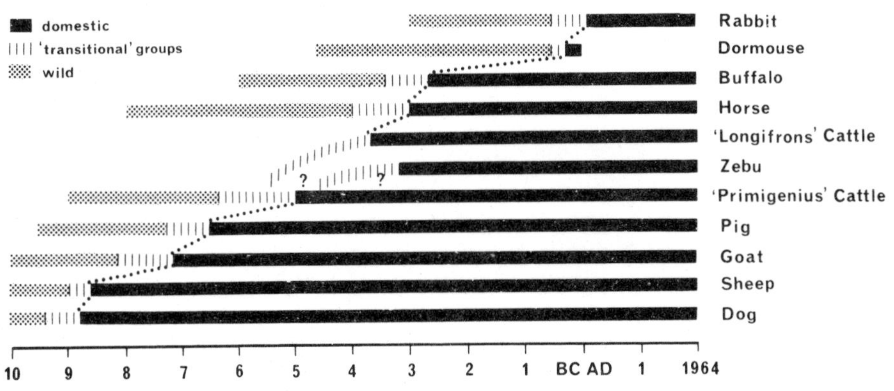

It would, however, be quite wrong to think that the domestic animals known today were the only ones which peoples of earlier cultures attempted to control. It is possible that the striped hyaena was bred in captivity. These carnivores are known to be tameable, and there is evidence from Old Kingdom Egypt that they were *Fig. 11* kept. Indeed, they were not only eaten, but stuffed with food for the specific purpose of fattening, a method applied by the Egyptians even to cranes. There are also other possibilities; both in Egypt and Greece, the flesh of the hedgehog was considered very suitable for eating, and although this is insufficient evidence in itself, one is left wondering whether even this animal was subjected periodically to at least experimental control.

Incidentally, the line of demarcation between early wild and domestic forms is by no means easy to draw. Changes at first must have been extremely slight. Also, it is often forgotten that pre-domestic wild species may well have shown considerable variability, even to the point of being well defined races. The Upper Palaeolithic cave art of France demonstrates, for example, *Fig. 10* that at least two varieties of horse were present in Europe as long ago as the old Stone Age.

Fig. 10 Magdalenian horses: a, from the Niaux Cave, France. It is considered by some to provide definite evidence of the tarpan; b, from Les Combarelles, France. This heavily built variety shows affinities with the modern Przhewalski's horse and large shire horses

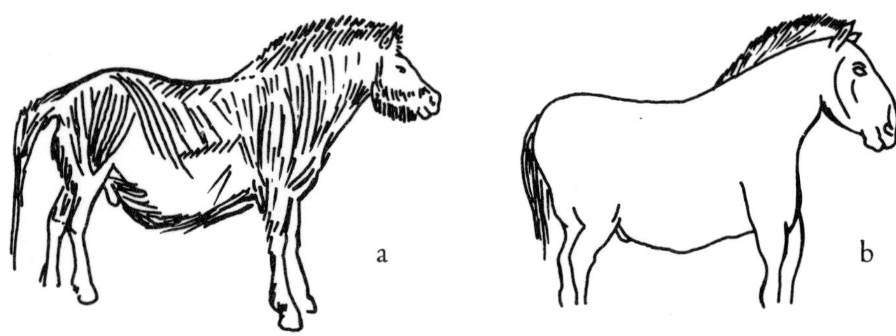

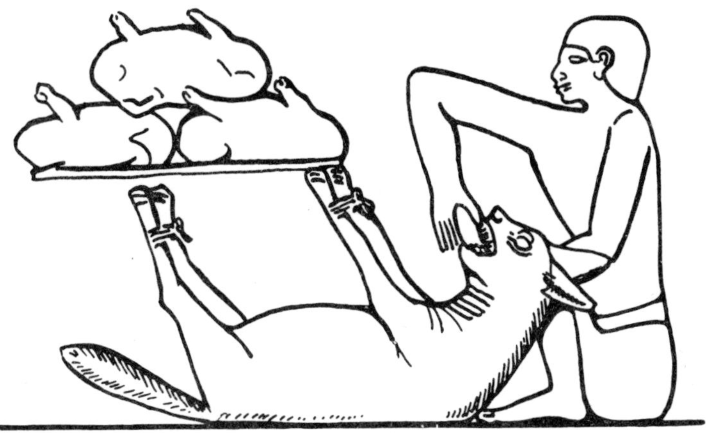

Fig. 11 A striped hyaena being stuffed with food, presumably with the goose or duck. From the Mastaba of Gen-ni-ka, about 2500 BC

DOG

The domestication of dogs, from one or more wild canids, probably commenced earlier than in any of the other domestic groups, though the evidence is very unsatisfactory, and is made even more difficult by an insufficiency of modern comparative material. A wall painting found at Çatal Hüyük, Anatolia (*c.* 5800 BC), shows a hunter with a dog, while unbaked clay figurines from Jarmo, Iraq (*c.* 6500 BC), might represent dogs. At Jarmo, too, were found skeletal remains that could be dog. Claims of a primitive 'dog' from the Belt Cave, Iran (*c.* 9500 BC) and in Natufian levels in Palestine are still very doubtful. Mesolithic 'dog' remains in Europe (including evidence from Star Carr, 7500 BC) suggest also that either Mesolithic communities may have attempted independent domestication from northern wolf varieties, or, alternatively, primitive dogs were 'diffused' into European cultures from the incipient agriculturists in the Mesopotamian area. Various problems must be resolved before the true nature of the emergence of *Canis familiaris* is known. How variable were wild canids and the early domestic dogs, and to what extent did these variations overlap in the two groups? Also, to what extent were early varieties of dog affected periodically by intrusive genes from wild canids (for example by accidental back-crossing with wolf cubs reared in captivity)?

From the beginning, dogs were probably used as food as well
30 as for hunting purposes. Magnus Degerbøl has pointed out for example that, like other food animals, the Maglemosian dog remains from Denmark were very fragmentary and some showed marks where they had been cut. In Egypt, even during Predynastic times, there is some evidence of at least three breeds, and one wonders whether these represent selection for optimal hunting and food varieties. The appearance of the dog in the New World could have been as late as 500 BC, the intrusive mongoloids who took them being of late Mesolithic culture. Various American breeds have been identified, including relatively long-haired and short-snouted types. The Aztecs certainly bred dogs for food, and there is osteological evidence from North American sites to suggest that they were sometimes butchered in the same way as other food mammals.

Turning to the Mediterranean area, it would be wrong to think that the dog had ceased to be eaten by historic times. Soyer's
100 classic book on ancient diets (*Pantropheon*, published in 1853) has this to say on the matter: 'We must beg pardon of the reader for informing him that the dog presented a very relishing dish to many nations advanced in culinary science. To them, one of these animals, young, plump, and delicately prepared, appeared excellent food. . . . The Greeks (we grieve to say it) ate dogs, and even dared to think them good: the grave Hippocrates himself—the most wise, the least gluttonous, and therefore the most impartial of the physicians—was convinced that this quadruped furnished a wholesome and, at the same time, a light food. . . . As to the Romans, they also liked it, and no doubt prepared it in the same manner as the hare, which they thought it resembled in taste.'

On present evidence, the pig may well have been part of a second phase in animal domestication, together with sheep and goat. Unlike the earlier relationship which had developed between man and primitive dogs—a situation which has been of more than dietary value to man—the main value of the pig must always have been for food. PIG

The intensive selection and domestication of the wild boar, *Sus scrofa,* from which all European and most Asiatic pigs are descended, has produced marked changes in body size and shape. This includes changes in tooth morphology and especially skull shape. Plates 14, 15

The earliest definite evidence of a domestic variety of pig is from the village-farming community of Jarmo. Pig teeth from various levels at this site show metrical differences which may well be indicative of domestic and wild varieties. In particular the third molar dimensions varied in the preceramic and ceramic levels, the latter having a smaller over-all size. The samples are admittedly small, but the differences are such as to strongly suggest that we are dealing with two distinct varieties of pig. The apparently 'sudden' replacement of one type by the other at Jarmo points to the domestication of this animal having taken place in another region at an earlier time. The evidence from Tash Air, in the Crimea, suggests that pig domestication may have been taking place in the Mesolithic, and might indicate the original area of pig-breeding by man. Plate 13

By Predynastic times, there is some evidence of a domestic form of pig reaching Egypt, especially at Badari and Toukh. In northern Europe, there was a relative abundance of pigs in the Neolithic era, and indeed it was an important protein source, but later prehistoric times saw a marked falling-off in this area—possibly related to vegetational and economic changes. Probably more than anywhere else, the pig has been valued in eastern Asia. From numerous sites in China, there is abundant evidence of its key position in the provision of animal protein, and during the

Neolithic, *Sus* and *Canis* were by far the most common domestic genera. As is shown by bones and representations in art, early domestic varieties of pig retained much of the appearance of the wild boar, and the modern relatively hairless and bulky breeds are the result of comparatively recent selective breeding.

5 Various parts of the pig were utilized by the Romans, as Apicius so well demonstrates. The preparations included sow's udder, liver, stomach (cleaned out with salt and vinegar and stuffed), kidneys, ham, and at least fifteen methods of using sucking-pig. Of interest is a method of enforced feeding, attributed to the time of Apicius. Sows were stuffed with dried figs and then killed.

THE CAPROVIDS

Goats (*Capra*) and sheep (*Ovis*) may conveniently be considered together. They represent the first ruminants to be domesticated, and may have come under the control of man at about the same time. The goat, being more tolerant of harsher environments such as thorny scrub and mountainous regions, must have proved the better of the two in areas where pasture was scarce. Before the cow became an important source of milk in the latter part of the Neolithic, goat milk must have been an important asset; but on the other hand the sheep will have provided a more tasty and tender joint, and the fat and hair was more valuable.

A complicating factor of goat and sheep studies is that it is not always easy to tell whether a bone is that of a sheep or a goat, and some osteo-archaeologists combine the two for the purposes of statistical analysis.

As yet, the most reliable evidence of goat domestication comes from pre-pottery Neolithic levels at Jericho (*c.* 6–7000 BC). Unlike the wild bezoar goat of that area, the horns were scimitar-shaped, reaching massive proportions in the male. Similar horn
Plate 21 shapes were also in evidence in the pre-pottery period of Jarmo.
Further evidence of early goat, it has been claimed, is provided by the Belt Cave (Iran) dated to *c.* 6000 BC. As the Neolithic continued, this form of early domestic goat appears to have spread

into other parts of the world, and by the third millennium BC art representations clearly indicate other domestic breeds.

The earliest evidence of domestic sheep comes from the site of Zawi Chemi Shanidar (Iraq), and projects their history back to about 9000 BC. The bones showed that this early community was killing a large part of each year's young for food and skins before the end of each year. From faunal studies at Haua Fteah, Cyrenaica, it is clear that domestic caprovids had moved westwards as far as this site by *c.* 4800 BC. This change from wild to domestic stocks—by replacement—is shown clearly by a metrical analysis *Fig. 12*

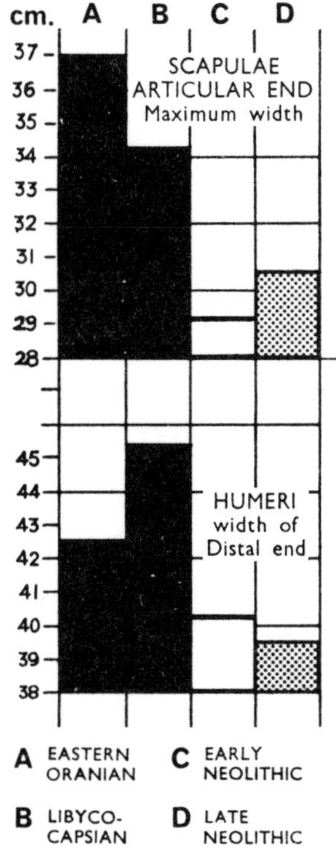

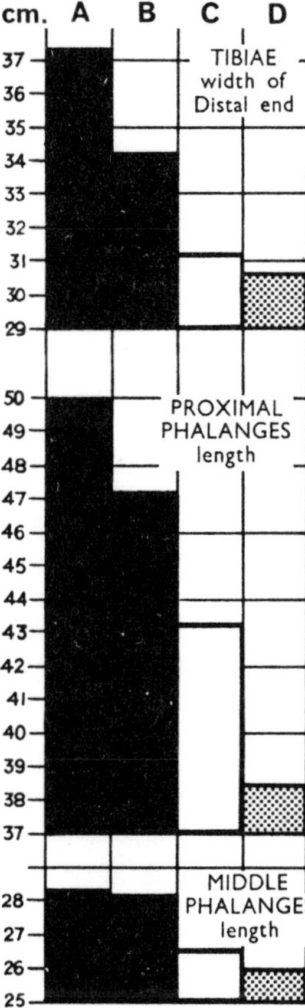

Fig. 12 Differences in mean measurements of Caprovid bones in relation to cultures, Haua Fteah. (Data from E. S. Higgs)

Fig. 13 a, Early Egyptian sheep on a tomb relief of the Fifth Dynasty, about 2500 BC. The long tail and corkscrew twisting horns are clearly shown; b, sheep and goat on part of a plaque of Ur-Enlil, Nippur, about 2000 BC. The long-haired goat has a small beard and upturned tail but horns similar to the Egyptian sheep

of caprovid bones from the site. By about 2000 BC, a number of
Fig. 13 domestic varieties are in evidence in Mesopotamia (F. E. Zeuner
117 gives five), and probably all were derived from wild urial sheep.
As well as the urial stock, the Asiatic moufflon sheep appears to have been domesticated at times. Farther east towards India and Tibet, the domestic sheep again appear to be of basically urial stock, but some breeds may be influenced by—if not derived from—wild argali sheep.

Although there is no evidence as to the antiquity of the practice, it is interesting to note that in the Faroe Islands some 300 years ago, mutton fat was stored against times of need. A seventeenth-century writer recalls that 'The tallow, principally obtained from sheep, was cut in pieces and allowed to rot awhile; it was then rendered, and cast into large pieces, which they dig and put in earth to keep it, it growing the better the longer it is kept, and, when it is old and is cut, it tasteth like old cheese.' This procedure is similar to that for bog butter, and seems likely to represent a far more ancient practice of preserving fats, at least in cooler climates.

CATTLE

59, 75, 117
Plate 22

Although there is evidence in the Upper Palaeolithic Cave Art of Europe that there was considerable variation in the wild form of *Bos primigenius,* the remains of cattle from the Halafian site of Bandahilk (Iraq) seem very likely to be of a domestic stock and not a small wild population, suggesting that the domestication of this animal took place at least 7,000 years ago.

b

The classification of cattle from Pleistocene to recent times, is by no means as clear as it could be. Nevertheless, the tentative 'genealogy' shown below will serve as a useful indication of cattle relationships.

			Hornless forms (by mutation)
			B. longifrons
Bos primigenius	Variants	*Bos. p. taurus*	*B. brachyceros,* hybrid varieties
	of		Long and 'lyre'
	the same		horned types
Bos namadicus	species?	*Bos p. indicus*	(Zebu) hybrid variety

Table 2. Tentative scheme of cattle relationships

Bos primigenius, in its original massive horned and large-bodied form, became especially prevalent in the European area by late Pleistocene times and lingered on until at least the seventeenth-century AD in some parts of eastern Europe. On the other hand, the Indian variant *Bos namadicus* appears to have a longer Pleistocene history, and indeed is more likely to represent an early established geographical race of *B. primigenius* than a separate species. The recognition of a short-horned and long-foreheaded variety, known as *B. longifrons,* results from the study of European

Plates 19, 23

a

Neolithic and Bronze Age material. On the present evidence, it is reasonable to suppose that the *longifrons* variety was derived from the larger horned *primigenius* type, but at what date and in what area is not known. Also, to what extent the differences between these two varieties result from evolutionary processes operating on wild populations, and to what extent they represent 'interference' by man, still remains to be ascertained. *Longifrons* cattle may well have been emerging in Western Asia by at least 3000 BC.

The zebu or humped cattle, now having their main distribution from India to Africa, form a further debatable group. Their origin seems more likely to have been nearer to India, and a
Fig. 14 derivation from the *namadicus* stock has been suggested. Again, it is not easy to decide whether the characteristic zebu features result from domestication or otherwise, and a few authors have suggested that the hump is the result of special selection for religious reasons. From art evidence, it is certain that zebu cattle were being bred in Mesopotamia by about 3000 BC, and at Mohenjo-daro, north-west India, both *primigenius* and zebu varieties had been domesticated by *c.* 2500 BC. Both the Greek and Roman worlds were familiar with zebu cattle.

Fig. 14 a, Zebu bull on a vase from Tell Agrab, Mesopotamia, considered to date from about 2800 BC; b, slightly damaged Greek statuette from Smyrna, Asia Minor, probably second century BC. The 'Zebu hump' is well defined

Hornless cattle, probably the result of intensive breeding from natural mutants, are also clearly in evidence, the bull on the tomb of Akhet-hetap (Fifth Dynasty) at Saqqara being an early example.

In post-*primigenius* herds, reduction in body size is a trend which is probably common to all. This may not have been brought about intentionally, but may be due to natural selection under poor environmental conditions. On the other hand smaller (and younger) carcasses are likely to have been tenderer, and one is left wondering whether the 'tender joint' is not altogether a preference of modern civilized communities.

Although selective breeding during the past millennium must have changed the form of most original stocks, a few herds remain which are relatively pure-bred and still represent pre-medieval varieties. In Britain, the famous white Chillingham herd is a long-horned variety thought to have been brought from Italy by the Romans. With the collapse of Rome, these became feral in the forests, and were not enclosed again until the thirteenth-century.

It may be noted that blood was not only utilized as food when beasts were slaughtered, but that in all probability the drawing

Fig. 15 Part of an Egyptian kitchen scene at Thebes (tomb of Rameses III) showing blood being caught in a bowl for use in cooking

Fig. 15 of blood from live animals was practised by some earlier cultures. This procedure is well known today among some cattle-breeding tribes of Africa, and is also practised by Tibetans.

DORMOUSE In order to satisfy his palate, if not his protein needs, man has favoured at least three smaller mammals. The edible or 'Fat' Dormouse (*Glis glis*) is found wild from Spain through Europe and into south-west Asia. Like the rabbit, it does not seem to have been considered worthy of domestication until Roman times, when its culinary reputation was so high that wealthy Romans initiated the construction of *gliraria* in order to secure easy supply of this tasty rodent. These enclosures, in use by the latter part of the second century BC, were made to simulate the animal's natural habitat, and the occupants were fattened up on a diet of walnuts, acorns and chestnuts. Such restricted breeding populations of dormice, perhaps with periodic 'weeding-out' of defective ones not fully suitable for the table, would have been an ideal environment for domestication changes to have taken place.

Fig. 16

In at least some cases, the final fattening would appear to have been undertaken in special earthenware pots, which restricted the movement of the rodents. Indeed, this may represent the beginning of the indoor 'battery' system of today!

Fig. 16 Special container with holes and internal ridges, used by the Romans for fattening dormice. (After O. Keller)

The preparation of the dormouse for the table could be quite elaborate, as Apicius so well describes. He recommends that it be stuffed with a mixture of minced pork and dormouse meat, pepper, pine-kernels, asafoetida, and *liquamen*; then placed in a small oven to cook.

RABBIT

The fact that the rabbit was domesticated long after most other domestic species is probably due to the limited distribution of the wild form in the post-glacial period. This appears to have been common only in the extreme south-west of Europe, though it had begun to spread by Roman times. Unlike hares, rabbits are quite amenable to enclosures, and reproduction would not be hampered. However, both hares and rabbits (family *Leporidae*) were reared in the Roman *leporaria*, this method of enclosure continuing through into medieval times. But only the rabbit survives as a domestic animal.

GUINEA PIG

Compared with the Old World, the New World has remarkably little to offer in the way of animals domesticated specifically for food. Although the domestication of the llama and alpaca may have helped to ensure meat supplies, it is clear that their main value was for transport (llama) and wool (alpaca). Thus we must look to a much smaller mammal, the guinea pig, for evidence of domestication with the sole purpose of providing meat. Probably the chronic lack of animal protein in the Andean mountain region triggered off the domestication of this rodent by pre-Inca natives, although surprisingly, it was not until after the Spanish Conquest that the domesticated guinea pig spread beyond the Inca Empire.

DAIRY PRODUCE

Milk and milk products are perhaps best considered in this survey of the vertebrates, being a corollary to the domestication of livestock. Because such foodstuffs are perishable, their history is especially patchy, depending for the most part on literary, ceramic and art evidence.

MILK

Plate 25

Early representations of milking include that in a frieze at Ur (*c.* 2900 BC), and on the sarcophagus of Kawit from Deir el-Bahari (Eleventh Dynasty). It is conceivable that milking was early established in Neolithic communities, although techniques for stimulating milk 'let down' may not have been discovered until later. Probably cow and goat milk have been the most generally used by early communities, although the ancient Greeks used only goat and sheep milk, and even then in diluted form. Surprisingly, Pliny recalls that camel's milk is the sweetest, and also notes that Sarmatian tribes commonly mixed millet meal with mare's milk or with blood from a horse's leg vein. Herodotus, again referring to mare's milk, notes that the Scythians skimmed off the cream as the best part. Reindeer milk has been used by the northern communities who have brought this animal under control, and also the elk was at times milked, as a Scythian representation demonstrates. The milk of yaks and asses has also been used in restricted areas. However, there is no evidence to show that the llama was used in this way by New World peoples.

MILK PRODUCTS

The use of butter, sour milk and cheese must have quickly followed the regular milking of animals, for by accident alone these milk products must have occurred again and again. Butter would be very easily produced merely by the action of transporting milk from place to place in containers, and its advantages could not have passed unnoticed. The extent of its use in early Egypt is not known, although a fatty substance found in some mummies has been claimed to be butter. Certainly in Mesopotamia it was of great importance. The milking scene from Ur demonstrates the method used by the shepherds: a man is seated rocking a large narrow-necked jar lying on its side, and to his left two men are straining the resulting liquid in order to take off the butter. The Old Testament has many references to butter beginning with Abraham (*c.* 1500 BC), which suggests that the people of those early days were well acquainted with it. Some doubt, however, has been cast on the use of the word 'butter' and later translators have substituted 'curds' as a more accurate description of the product thought to be indicated. The Hittites with their sheep, goats and cows were also butter-makers and evidently used it widely and in quantity, for the price appears to have been just half of that of oil.

Plate 25

The Greeks and Romans of Classical times hardly knew butter, probably because of the abundance of olive oil in their region. It was chiefly known to them as a choice food of the 'barbarians'. The north European tribes did indeed use it a great deal and their cooler climate was certainly more suited to its production; it was among the Germanic peoples that the methods of salting and making harder pats were developed.

Soured milk or curds have surely been consumed by many peoples from the earliest Neolithic times, but little remains as direct proof of this. They were fairly certainly used in Mesopotamia and Palestine, and possibly in Egypt, and Pliny later mentions their production by 'barbarian' tribes. Nevertheless the Greeks and Romans also used soured milk, and three distinct kinds are mentioned: *oxygala*, which, according to Columella, must have been fairly solid, as the whey was drawn off three times before salt was added and the jar sealed; *melca*, which was obviously more liquid as milk was poured directly into jars containing boiling vinegar and kept overnight in a warm place; and *schiston*, an invention of the physicians of Pliny's day. *Melca*, however, was definitely a dish in itself, for even Apicius includes it in his book and recommends serving it with pepper, *liquamen* or salt, oil and coriander.

Cheese-making is the natural result of soured milk, and an obvious practical means of preserving surplus milk when it could not all be distributed or used, or when the animals were away from
33 the villages in summer pasturage. The Egyptians certainly made cheese, as evidenced by the little pots of it found in the Second
Plates 48, 49 Dynasty tomb at Saqqara, and by Old Kingdom lists of funerary offerings. In Mesopotamia cheese-making was an important task, and some cylinder seals found there depict the shepherd with his flocks, and rows of little circles probably representing cheeses. Numerous cheese-moulds were found in the dairy of the Palace of Mari (third millennium BC). The Hittites not only ate cheese but used it with bread as an offering in religious rituals.

Fig. 17 Pottery cheese-strainers of Neolithic and Bronze Age date in Greece and Crete show that cheese-making began very early there. On the island of Therasia actual remains of what appears to be cheese have been discovered, dating from the Late Bronze Age. The Greeks indeed appear to have been very fond of milk and cheese dishes and Homer twice mentions a particular pottage composed of barley-meal, honey, Pramnian wine and grated goat's milk cheese. By Roman times, cheese satisfied both the
Plate 24 appetite of the peasant and the refined tastes of the gourmet, the methods of production and the different kinds of cheese being many and varied. Smoked cheeses were much appreciated and, in addition to their own specialities, the Romans also imported foreign varieties. Cheese was eaten freshly-made or preserved, and either with bread or as a part of other dishes; in particular, it was an important ingredient of their fancy cakes or breads.

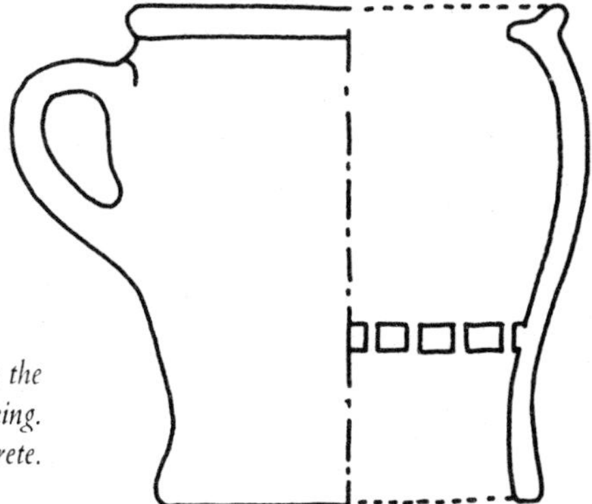

Fig. 17 Jar with perforations in the base; probably used in cheese making. From a house at Palaikastro, Crete. (After R. C. Bosanquet)

BIRDS

Compared with hunting and fishing, fowling has perhaps always been of less importance. Prehistoric fowlers probably relied only to a limited extent on bringing down birds in flight, and most of the catches may well have been by snare and trap; also by direct clubbing and seizure, especially when moulting impeded escape. By direct methods the Great Auk was hunted extensively, not only by Upper Palaeolithic and more recent groups but even by the Neanderthalers. A similar easy catch was the New Zealand giant Moa, slowly hunted out of existence by the Maoris, with the result that there had to be a re-orientation of food-getting habits with fish replacing bird. Although it would be out of place to discuss in detail the wild varieties identified from early sites—they are very numerous and vary according to climate, and geographic position—statistics from one or two regions will help to show their value. From New England sites (Archaic-Ceramic) over ten varieties have been identified, from Lagore Crannog (seventh–tenth century AD) over twenty, from Teshik-Tash (U.S.S.R., Mousterian) at least nineteen, and from Ust'-Kanskaia (U.S.S.R., Mousterian) twelve species. In the case of the latter two Russian sites, only four of the total nineteen genera were common to both, a clear indication of the diversity of fowling which occurred even within a single culture. 20, 117

Fig. 18 Detail of offerings (hare, ibex and ? pelican eggs) in the tomb of Haremhab, Thebes, about 1420 BC

Birds' eggs were, of course, an equally valuable foodstuff, in both early hunting communities and more recent cultures where the domestication of birds occurred. In Egyptian art, bowls of ostrich and other large (pelican?) eggs are depicted a number of times, and the ostrich egg in particular would have been of special value in that its volume is about six times that of a hen's egg. It is well known that by Roman times eggs were preserved,

Fig. 18

Fig. 19 Early evidence of fowls in Egypt. Drawn from a painting on a sherd in the tomb of Tutankhamun, about 1350 BC

using a number of methods, and it was customary for Roman meals to begin with an egg course. Plate 50

Our knowledge of the early domestication of birds is still very meagre. It is likely that the red jungle fowl (*Gallus gallus*) was the main ancestor of the domestic fowl, being indigenous to northern India. Fowls were known to the early Indus Valley civilizations, and they are represented for example on seals from Mohenjo-daro. They continued, with increasing distribution and favour, into historic times. Presumably through good trade contacts with Asia, the fowl appears in Egypt by the fourteenth century BC, *Fig. 19* and is shown on Assyrian seals by the eighth century BC. It was economically important to the Romans and there was a variety of ways of preparing it for the table.

The guinea fowl had reached Greece, probably from North Africa, by the fifth century BC, and was part of the upper-class Roman menu by Varro's time. In contrast to the domestic fowl, however, it made no great impact on the Mediterranean world. Goose domestication was probably a follow-on from the fattening-up of captured fledglings. Domestication probably began in the Neolithic, and the goose was certainly well known in Greece and Rome, and in Egypt by Old Kingdom times. Although the duck has also come under the control of man, both in Europe and Asia, evidence from the past is scanty. Pliny recalls that fattening peacocks began about 70 BC and became a profitable business.

Fig. 20 Egyptian scene depicting the preparation of fish, no doubt prior to salting. (After Wilkinson)

REPTILES AND AMPHIBIANS

Compared with other vertebrates, reptiles and amphibians are relatively uncommon at archaeological sites. Frogs and small lizards of various kinds provide useful food for some human groups today, and are not so difficult to catch. Indeed, the general lack of archaeological evidence probably results to some extent from the fragile nature of the bones of such animals, and perhaps from softer bone being often eaten with the flesh. Tortoises, especially giant varieties, and turtles provided very tasty meat for earlier populations in widely separated parts of the world. At least three varieties of turtle have been identified from New England sites, and the remains of these and similar creatures have also been found for example in prehistoric levels at Niah Cave in Borneo and Gua Cha in Malaya. Prehistoric food debris from Vardaroftsa, Macedonia, included the tortoise. Snakes, of course, have not been overlooked as a source of meat and in China they have been salted and pickled. Celsus recommends vipers as wholesome! Crocodiles are still valued for their flesh and eggs, and Herodotus speaks favourably of these giants of the Nile.

FISH

Remains of fish from archaeological sites present by far the most difficult problems of analysis of any vertebrates. Often only fragments of vertebrae remain, and even where there are plenty of good artistic representations—as for example in Egypt—identification *Fig. 20* is still far from easy (the giant Nile perch, *Perca nilotica*, being one of the exceptions). Even so, there is an increasing amount of *Fig. 21* information about early fish as food. 84

The importance of fish to prehistoric communities of Europe has been well reviewed by Grahame Clark. During Upper Palaeolithic times fishing in this area seems to have been restricted to inland waters and coastal margins. Probably the inhabitants were well aware of seasonal as well as all-the-year-round fishing potentialities. It seems likely that spearing, line-fishing, and clubbing were all employed. During the Mesolithic, improvements in the material culture added to fishing efficiency. From

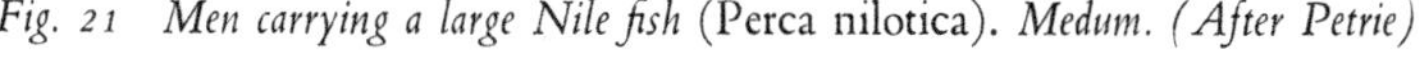

Fig. 21 Men carrying a large Nile fish (Perca nilotica). *Medum. (After Petrie)*

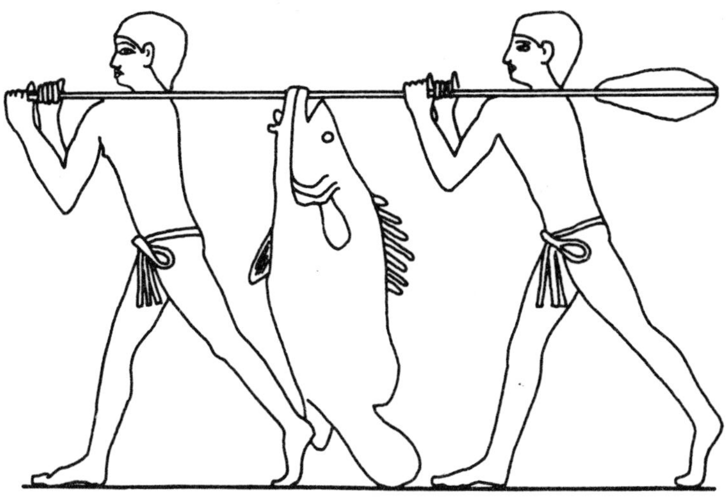

Neolithic to Iron Age times technological improvements continued (barbed hooks, better nets with heavy net-sinkers, and more developed coastal line-fishing from boats). Fish identified in northern Europe between the Upper Palaeolithic and Iron Age include pike, bream, pollack, perch, tench, cod, dog-fish, flounder, eel, haddock, mackerel, coal-fish, whiting, wrasse, and tunny. The final phase of sea-fishing was not complete until early medieval times, when for instance the herring industry became established.

Plate 26

The Romans have left particularly good illustrations of the fish they caught. Surprisingly, one of the most highly thought-of fish was the wrasse, a variety which is certainly not considered so tasty today. Their knowledge of the breeding habits of fish was considerable and fertilized eggs were collected and placed in special lakes or *vivaria.* This resulted in a considerable trade in the sale of young fish for stocking waters. The Assyrians also maintained an ample supply of fish in dams and *vivaria.* Indeed fish-egg trading seems to have been established early on a wide scale, as similar evidence from China suggests. To the Greeks, the tunny was of special interest and it seems that they were very early aware of its multitudes and migrations. Fish were widely dried and salted.

Other fish remains include a variety of species from the New World, as well as accounts of fish food debris and types of fishing tackle from early sites in Africa, Eastern Asia and as far south as Australia. The data are, however, very scattered and incomplete, and perhaps we should be wise to restrict our review of fish food to Europe and the Mediterranean world.

CHAPTER III

The Invertebrates

MOLLUSCS

VERTEBRATES ARE generally quite difficult animals to catch. Admittedly, slow and somnolent lizards need little more than disturbing from their long siestas; and a mere scuffle among a flock of moulting birds would guarantee a dinner or two. The quick-witted mammals, however, necessitated cunning, stealthy hunting, and often considerable physical endurance if a wounded animal had to be followed until its strength bled away and it could finally be approached for the kill. How refreshingly simple and useful it was, therefore, to be able to rely on some animal food by the easy process of picking snails off bushes or, at low tide, pulling mussels away from their rocky moorings. There is certainly plenty of evidence that prehistoric men took full advantage of this high protein food, and if each animal was small, given enough time the total harvest would be rewarding.

A very considerable number of sites throughout the world have yielded shells, both of terrestrial and marine molluscs. When found, they may be crushed, complete, artificially perforated or worked in other ways. An immediate difficulty to be resolved by those undertaking the analysis of shell debris is to determine which varieties of shell do in fact represent food remains. In each case, it is necessary to decide whether the shells were collected (1) for artifacts, (2) for decorative or utilitarian purposes, (3) for food contained in them, or (4) whether they were adventitiously incorporated in the deposit but not collected by man.

The problem of determining the reason for the variety of shells at a particular site is demonstrated well by the recent analyses of shells from early levels at Jericho, undertaken by the malacologist 7
H. E. Biggs. In this sample, the majority were clearly collected for their decorative value, although some, to be described shortly,

were clearly of value as food. In view of the great amount of shellfish used by man, at least during the last 50,000 years of his evolution, largely because of the universal availability of these foods, it would seem best to consider mollusc-eating at a few special areas or sites rather than attempt a general review. We will begin in the New World, moving round to the Far East and completing our brief survey in Europe.

When considering the uneatable remains of shell food, it is, of course, important to try to translate these into the quantities of
23 edible food which they represent. S. F. Cook and A. E. Treganza made an important first step when they proposed certain ratios between edible food and bone and shell remains.

	Weight of edible flesh	*Weight of remains preserved in site*
Mammal and bird bone	20	1
Mussel shell	1	2·35
Clams	1	4·25 (2 samples)

Table 3. Ratios between edible food and bone and shell remains

72 The recent analysis by Clement Meighan of a site on Catalina Island, California, dated to *c.* 3500–4000 BC, shows how much information can be deduced from midden material. In all, twenty-two species of shell were identified. Of these *Mytilus* (mussel) and *Haliotis* (abalone) predominate. Of special interest is the fact that in the lower levels of the site there is a four to one predominance of *Haliotis* over *Mytilus*, whereas in the upper levels quite the reverse situation is found. This cannot be explained by any natural environmental change, and it is reasonable to agree with Meighan that it most likely resulted from over-exploitation of the favoured shell-food until numbers were considerably depleted. As he points out, 'There is considerable theoretical significance to this picture of over-exploitation in view of the

	Bone and shell for 11 Column Samples (1,232 cubic inches)	*Bone and shell for total site (720 cubic yards)* Projected from column samples	*Flesh weight for total site* Projected from column samples
Shell:			
*Mytilus**	3·666	92,738	39,758
*Haliotis***	3·063	78,070	20,542
All other shell	0·733	18,683	6,228
Bone:			
Fish, mammal, bird***	0·197	4,921	98,423

* shell/flesh ratio = 2·35 to 1
** shell/flesh ratio = 3·80 to 1
*** bone/flesh ratio = 1 to 20

Table 4. Meat weights estimated from the Little Harbor (Catalina Island) Site (data from Meighan, 1959). All weights in Kilograms.

opinion sometimes expressed that primitive man was in a sort of balance with his environment. This example shows that in at least some cases primitive man worked his environment for all it would yield of a favored resource, ignoring less desirable foods until forced to utilize them' (pp. 402–3). Although the total meat resources for the site, as shown in the Table above, can be but rough approximations, they nevertheless enable us to visualize in terms of the actual food substance, the availability of animal proteins to these earlier peoples. As can be seen, nearly half the flesh weight was of shell food.

The excavations at Niah in Borneo, directed by Tom Harrisson, have yielded a considerable number of edible mollusc shells. There is clear evidence that shellfish were eaten at Niah throughout

its entire history, spanning more than 40,000 years. However, shells are particularly numerous within the 12–36 inch level below the present surface of the Great Niah Cave, representing perhaps the last 5,000 years. A recent study of Niah shell food by Lord
71 Medway has revealed some significant preferences and differences. The shells presumed to be food debris are all aquatic (although in fact some land snails in the cave could have served as food as well). At least eight species were represented in the food category, three being estuarine and five true freshwater varieties.

The extent of the shellfish at the site is demonstrated by the fact that during the 1958 season alone some 14,632 whole shells were counted. Freshwater varieties were found to be more abundant throughout, although in the central sector of the excavations estuarine shells are proportionally higher. This greater use of the freshwater shellfish appears to be the general rule at every stage. In the case of the freshwater shells, Medway has made a most revealing comparison between the cave shell debris of earlier Niah people, a recent midden, and the frequency of the shell varieties available in a near-by stream today. The results, set out in the Table below, are by no means what one might be led to expect.

Table 5. Edible shellfish from the Niah area

Shell genus	Prehistoric Niah (central area)	Recent Niah (midden *c.* AD 1800)	Freshwater survey Stream sample (1960)
Clea	5,303 (1)*	57 (5)	78 (3)
Neritina	2,769 (2)	436 (2)	301 (2)
Bellamya	562 (3)	82 (4)	2,018 (1)
Rectidens	28 (4)	3,014 (1)	23 (4)
Pila	14 (5)	282 (3)	5 (5)

* numbers in parentheses show the order of shellfish preference as food.

Although *Bellamya* is the commonest form in the stream sample, it is in fact not the most pleasant to eat (the unborn young of this genus may be found with well-formed shells which renders them less palatable). Its third and fourth place as food is thus understandable. *Pila*, although it has the most meat, is tough and does not appear to have been particularly sought out by earlier Niah peoples. The two most palatable varieties, *Clea* and *Rectidens*, show surprising differences in the relative frequency in the prehistoric and recent Niah samples. This might indicate a biological change in the relative frequency of these forms in the Niah area, but seems more likely to reflect changes in shell-food preferences.

Borneo is, of course, not the only territory in Australasia to have yielded archaeological shell remains. The frequency of molluscs at prehistoric sites in New Caledonia suggests that shell food had been a principal source of protein. In Yap and Fiji they have also clearly been used as food. Australia is no exception, and at a rock shelter site at Fromm's Landing, South Australia, dating back to at least 4800 BP, shells were found at all levels.

Europe and south-west Asia provide by far the most varied evidence of the use of shellfish in the past. That molluscs were a source of animal protein by at least early Upper Pleistocene times is demonstrated clearly in these areas. Neanderthal man of Gibraltar, as shown by the limpets and mussels recovered from the Devil's Tower site, was certainly making use of them. From the Mount Carmel sites of Tabún and Skhúl, the marine shells *Cardium, Laevicardium, Ostrea* and *Pecten* seem most likely to be food debris. Late Pleistocene groups in the Mediterranean area, both in North Africa and Europe have left evidence of their food interest in shellfish. One of the best documented instances of their use by Mesolithic Europeans is seen in the shell mounds excavated in the region of Mugem in Portugal. These extensive deposits consist mainly of marine shells, principally cockles, oysters, whelks, scallops and razor-shells.

88 Charles Reed, in a recent stimulating discussion of snail-eating in antiquity, mentions that between about 15,000 and 7,000 years ago the snail *Helix salomonica* was certainly used in Iraq for food, though in more recent times it practically disappears from the archaeological record. Even during that period, however, he thinks *Helix* was not a major food source, especially since it can generally only be gathered during or following rain. The proximity of a group to water also clearly affects their mollusc-eating habits. Reed points out that in a site at Tepe Asiab, Iran (*c.* 10,000 BP), which is near a permanent stream, *H. salomonica* is very rare, but the perhaps more tasty clam *Unio tigridis* was a major protein source.

From the Pre-Pottery Neolithic to the Bronze Age at Jericho there is also evidence that at least two varieties may have been used
7 for food. H. E. Biggs cites the species *Helix prasinata* and *Levantina spiriplana* as being numerous and large enough to suggest that they were collected for eating. The former, incidentally, is very similar to *Helix salomonica* eaten by the Jarmo people of Iraq around the same time as did the Jericho Pre-Pottery folk. The fact that the shells from neither site show any sign of burning indicates that the shell food was not roasted. Also, as most of the shells are intact, the animals must have been put to death before removal. Either they were drowned or killed by boiling, and although the latter alternative seems more likely, it poses another question as regards the type of container used in Pre-Pottery times.

By far the best known Neolithic shell mounds in Europe are those excavated in Denmark. These 'kitchen-middens' are enormous refuse heaps consisting mainly of shell debris. The most abundant species are oyster (*Ostrea*), cockle (*Cardium*), mussel (*Mytilus*) and periwinkle (*Littorina*), but at least nine other species have been identified. One interesting feature was that a number of these species were on average noticeably larger than those found today in the same region. This appears to be another instance where intensive mollusc collection by man has had an

Fig. 22 Above, Ostriaria beneath a bridge connecting two buildings. One oyster is attached to each rope. Roman vase; below, Ostriaria and buildings near Baiae. Three oysters are attached to each rope. (After Günther. Courtesy of the Council of the Marine Biological Association of the United Kingdom)

effect upon some natural (as opposed to domesticated) species of an area.

The beginnings of mollusc culturing is lost in antiquity, and although it has been suggested by some that the Chinese were the first to cultivate oysters, it is to the Romans that we must look for good evidence. Indeed, there seems little doubt that their energies in cultivating both oysters and snails had an important bearing on the food interests of later peoples in these molluscs. Pliny credits Sergius Orata in the first century BC with being the originator of oyster culturing on a lucrative scale. Structural details of these Roman *ostriaria* are best known from drawings on *Fig. 22*
vases, described in detail by R. T. Günther. These suggest that 42
the hanging culture method, still practised today, was employed

by the Romans. The ropes to which the oysters were attached are seen suspended from horizontal wooden supports. This method enabled oysters to be cultivated in rich but sheltered waters. The consumption of oysters not only in Rome, but also in various parts of the Roman Empire including English settlements, is clearly evidenced by the shell debris. Oysters and other shellfish were eaten with quite elaborate sauces. The constituents of one such sauce, as given by Apicius, are: pepper, lovage, parsley, dry mint, bay leaf, malabathrum, plenty of cumin, honey, vinegar, and *liquamen*. On the other hand, an alternative sauce was used for mussels consisting of pepper, celery-seed, rue, honey, *passum*, *liquamen*, a little oil, and cornflour. Mussels were also sometimes fried or served boiled with salt, oil, wine, chopped fresh coriander, and peppercorns.

In contrast to this marine culturing is the cultivation of land snails, so well described in Varro's *Rerum Rusticarum*. Special 'snail-beds' were prepared in a suitable environment and surrounded by water in order to restrict the movements of these snail populations. Varro recognizes several varieties of snail which were eaten, 'small white ones brought from near Reate, the big ones from Illyricum, and those of middle size which come from Africa. Not but what they differ in these places both in distribution and size; for instance, very big snails come from Africa, called *Solitannae*, which are so big that eighty *quadrantes* can be put into their shells . . . [this has been translated as three gallons, which must be a gross exaggeration or a mis-translation]. When large islands are made in the enclosures, they (the snails) bring you in a big haul of pence. They are, I may add, fattened usually in the following way. A jar for them to feed in having holes in it is lined with a mixture of *sapa* and spelt' (translation by Storr-Best, 1912).

A final remark on snails takes us, surprisingly, to the Institute
8 of Aviation Medicine at Farnborough. Recently, J. Billingham
has emphasized the potential value of snails not as flesh food but

for the fluid they contain. Desert survival has been a factor of interest in both World Wars, and there is no doubt that it similarly occupied the minds of earlier peoples, especially those wishing to cross desert environments to more favourable territory. This must at times have been a considerable problem to migratory groups in the past, for without water, survival in true desert conditions has been estimated at about four days (assuming a maximum daily shade temperature of 40° C). Research at Farnborough on a
snail called *Eremina*, found plentifully on desert scrub in Northern Plates 29, 30
Libya, has shown that the fluid (haemolymph) it contains would be sufficient if taken in quantity to enable survival while moving for several days across a desert area. Thus, early migrant groups desperate for water but well acquainted with natural resources could quite conceivably have been aware of snails as more than a source of shell-meat.

INSECTS

Although of the boneless animals, molluscs provided the greatest extra source of animal food, this by no means constituted the only group of invertebrates that was eaten by primitive man. Acting on the principle that he should avail himself of everything edible,
he consumed the myriads of insects, adults and larvae, winged 9
and terrestrial, which are never far from human habitation. Indeed, how better to eliminate these beasts which scourged crops and disturbed noon-day peace than to eat them! By observing the insect-eating habits of certain present-day primitive aboriginal groups we may deduce what those of prehistoric peoples must have been; we should do well, therefore, to consider these first. Although in the drier parts of Australia most insects are abundant only during the rains, ants and termites are available during the whole of the year, and so is honey. Generally speaking, Australia abounds in a great variety of insects, and they and their products are eaten with relish in one or other part of the continent. For

instance, a type of manna is found in some areas on the leaves of Eucalyptus plants. It consists of the white coverings of the larvae of psyllid insects, the covering being a glutinous secretion from the larvae. This secretion may be noticeably sweet, and even though each leaf contains but a small quantity, a diligent collector can obtain a substantial amount of this sugary substance if many plants are involved. The so-called 'honeypots' of Sugar Ants are also a much sought-after food, likewise because of their sweetness. The abdomen of this ant, *Melophorus inflatus*, is remarkably distended by honey, and can be conveniently bitten off and swallowed. The honey of the wild bee, to be dealt with later, is another much sought-after food. The Bugong moth (*Euxoa infusa*) and even the adult Ghost Moth may be eaten. The famous Witchetty Grub is probably a group term and although the caterpillars of the Ghost Moth are the most important representatives, it seems likely that other large caterpillars and perhaps even some common beetle-larvae have also been regarded as witchetties. Some groups collect a variety of locust, which is roasted and eaten without the wings and legs. Even termites and their larvae are sometimes eaten, but here their dietary importance is far less than in certain parts of Africa.

Fig. 23

From a cursory inspection of a handful of yellow creamy grubs, or of locusts shorn of their appendages, there may appear to be little to commend them, or suggest their food value. Analyses of such insect foods, however, have provided some quite surprising results. Termites, lightly fried as eaten in the Belgian Congo, contained 44 per cent fat and 36 per cent protein matter, and their superiority over some other animal foods is demonstrated by the fact that 100 grammes have a calorific value of 560. They are also rich in phosphates. Silkworm pupae, eaten in some silk-growing parts of the world, contain 23 per cent protein and 14 per cent fat. Analysis of dried locusts has revealed percentages of up to 75 per cent proteins and about 20 per cent fat; 100 grammes of locust, when analyzed, showed the presence of 1·75 mg. of riboflavin

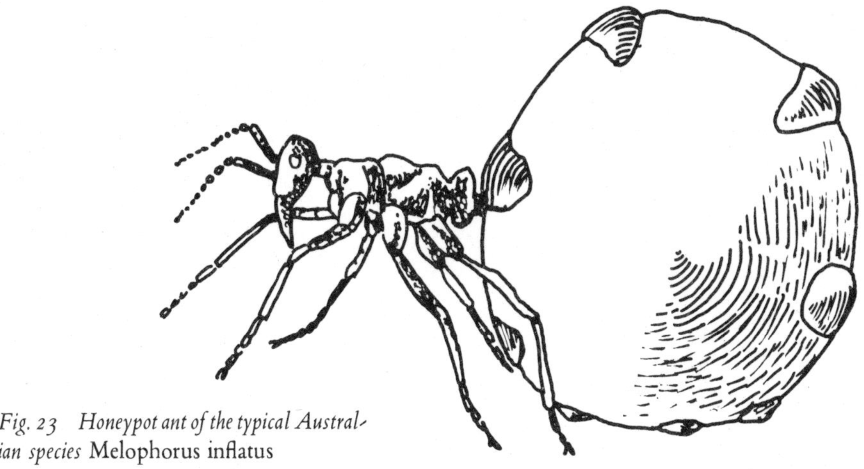

Fig. 23 Honeypot ant of the typical Australian species Melophorus inflatus

and 7·5 mg. of nicotinic acid (vitamin B_2 complex), demonstrating that they are also of value for their vitamins. There is thus no reason to doubt the food value—and at times even survival value—of insects both now and in the past.

Some primates other than man make great use of insects, as, for example, the East African *Cercopithecus* monkey. Chimpanzees have recently been shown to have a taste for termites, and it is thus within the bounds of possibility that the australopithecine hominids of Africa might similarly have appreciated the palatability of insects. If, as some think, these early man-apes tended towards an omnivorous diet, insects could have been a valuable protein source, especially in times of meat shortage. Indeed, it has even been suggested that one possible reason why early stone tools were produced was in order to open termite hills!

Plates 31–33

In later Stone Age times, a remarkable illustration of the interest of early man in insects—or more strictly in this case in their products—is the honey-hunting scene depicted in a cave at Araña, Spain. Further evidence is to be seen on a bone fragment from the Magdalenian site of Les Trois Frères, in southern France, which depicts a grasshopper.

Fig. 24 Part of an Assyrian scene showing men carrying pomegranates and locusts

From early historic times, there is ample evidence that some Mediterranean peoples ate insects. Aristotle records that the larvae of the cicada group of insects taste best when they have attained full size, and the adult females are best when full of eggs. We are led to believe from the writings of Plutarch, however, that in Hellenistic Greece they were regarded as sacred and not generally eaten.

Since the earliest phases of the Neolithic Revolution, locusts have been a particularly serious threat to some human com-

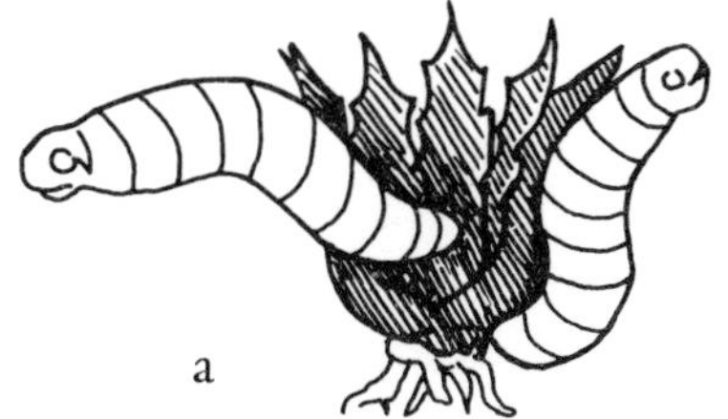

Fig. 25 Drawings of Mexican insects eaten by the Incas: a, caterpillar from the century plant; b, the Corn Ear Worm; c, grasshopper. (All after Suroga, fifteenth century AD)

munities. Locust plagues are described in early Mesopotamia, and ancient locust prayers beg for protection from them. Nevertheless, their abundance in some areas, their pleasant taste, and the relative ease with which they can be captured makes them an obvious and easy source of food. In Assyria they were not purely a food of the poor, for at the palace of Asurbanipal, Nineveh, *Fig. 24* they were served up at royal banquets. Diodorus describes an Ethiopian community of *Acridophagi* (locust-eaters) and recalls that this group attempted to preserve the locusts in salt for times of scarcity. The New Testament mentions that St John fed in the desert on locusts (see also p. 138) and honey (an excellent combination of proteins, fats and sugars!). The Bible also states that other insects are palatable. 'These of them ye may eat: the locust after his kind, and the bald locust after his kind, and the beetle after his kind, and the grasshopper after his kind' (Leviticus, XI, 22).

Aristophanes mentions the sale of 'four-winged' fowl in markets; in fact they were grasshoppers and were apparently purchased cheaply by the poorer classes. Similarly, Pliny discusses the use of large oak grubs by the Romans, and indeed these *cossus* grubs were so coveted by them that they fattened them up with flour. While somewhat debatable, it seems very probable that the larvae referred to belong to the genus *Cerambux*, which although uncommon would have made a tasty titbit.

Except for the written word, there is as yet little direct evidence of insect-eating by earlier peoples. What information we have, however, shows this to be a very promising field, and points to the value of painstaking analyses of archaeo-biological remains. For example, coprolites from three areas of the New World have produced a number of insect varieties, although some were certainly not eaten as food. Faecal remains from a Bluff Dweller
108 site in the Ozark Mountains of Arkansas and Missouri is the
first published example. A detailed examination revealed the presence of beetle larvae of the family *Nitidulidae*, a species of mite, part of an ant, and a number of lice. Coprolites from Kentucky caves contained seeds and pieces of bone, as well as grasshopper
Fig. 25 and beetle fragments. Mexican sites have also yielded coprolite
15, 16 material, and analysis has shown the presence of parts of grass-
hoppers, bees, wasps, ants, mites and termites. Some of these insect fragments may well be adventitious, being swallowed with fruit or other food, but the size of some of them and the variety contained in comparatively few coprolites strongly suggests that some were eaten as food.

CHAPTER IV

Sugars

HONEY

AS A FOOD, honey has much to recommend it. Plants and 9, 38, 39
animals, whilst used as food by man, are not foods by their very nature; honey is. It is produced by the bees specifically as a food. Milk also is a wholly natural food and it is interesting that the two are so often coupled together in myth and religious rite. Milk and honey are frequently mentioned as offerings to gods, or as food of the gods, which indicates how important they were to the ancients. Honey is probably the best natural source of energy available to man, and this is, of course, owing to the pure sugar content which is very easily assimilated by the body. Its powers in this respect must have been recognized by early man, as indeed they are today by modern primitive peoples. The Masai warriors of East Africa, for example, on their long expeditions would take no other food with them but honey. In addition to pure sugar, honey also contains small amounts of calcium, phosphates, iron, sulphur and a certain amount of Vitamins C and B (including the B_2 complex). However, by far the most important item is, of course, the sugar content which is very high, as shown by the following analysis: dextrose about 34·0 per cent, laevulose about 40·5 per cent, sucrose about 1·9 per cent, dextrins and gums about 1·5 per cent. The total of the three basic sugars thus amounts to 76·4 per cent, and although the amounts of dextrose and laevulose are variable the total sugar content usually remains fairly constant.

Although somewhat difficult to date, the earliest direct evidence of human interest in honey occurs in the famous stone-age cave painting from southern Spain, of a man robbing a wild bees' nest. *Fig. 26*
Professor Bodenheimer states that in this part of Spain bees still make their nests in the rocks, and compares the method depicted

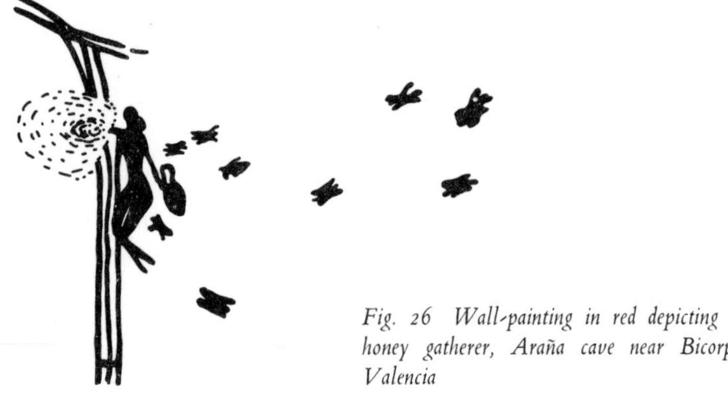

Fig. 26 Wall-painting in red depicting a honey gatherer, Araña cave near Bicorp, Valencia

with that of modern Vedda honey-hunters. The equipment too is much the same. African pygmies use ropes, baskets or bags, and often an axe, so it seems that methods of honey-hunting have not changed much, nor no doubt have the ends to which people would go to obtain this precious food. The extent to which prehistoric peoples used honey is strongly suggested by the ethnographic evidence for modern primitive groups.

Almost all the world over, people have made use of this natural form of sugar; most often they eat it just as it is found, together with the comb and sometimes the larvae. The Australian aborigines will cover miles of territory to discover a bees' nest, usually killing the bees by smoke and then taking the honeycomb, called by them the 'sugar-bag'. It is usually eaten on the spot, though if there is a great amount some will be taken back in baskets. Among the primitive groups in Africa, including Masai, Pygmies, Hottentots, Zulus, and several others, the use of honey is widespread, as also is hive-keeping, however primitive in form. In Madagascar too, the gathering of honey is one of the chief occupations of the forest tribes, and they even have a primitive type of press for the extraction of the honey from the comb. Throughout Asia, in India, Arabia, Indonesia, Ceylon, Burma, Siam and Malaya, honey is used extensively and here as in other countries there are many and varied superstitious practices and rituals connected with the gathering of it. With the Veddas of Ceylon, honey-hunting is the master art, the most highly prized variety being that of the bambara bees who nest high in rocks.

In the Americas, the European honey-bee was unknown before its introduction in the seventeenth century. Prior to this, however, the domestication of the native stingless bees was well under way in both Central and South America, and the Spaniards on their arrival found highly developed bee-keeping already in practice in several places. The Guayaki Indians of Paraguay are a particularly interesting group in this respect. They neither cultivate the land, nor do they know methods of trapping animals, but rely for their existence entirely on gathering what they can and on very primitive methods of hunting and fishing. Honey is their basic food, the foundation on which their entire culture rests. Like the rest of the world, Central and South America have their share of superstition and ritual regarding honey-hunting; the Ancient Maya of Yucatán had more than one type of bee-ceremony, and tributes in honey (which also feature often in Ancient Egypt) were paid to the Aztec king.

It is fairly easy to see from the usage of modern primitive peoples how bee-keeping came into being. A stage intermediate between honey-hunting and fully domestic hives is to be seen among some recent groups, who hang artificial hives made from hollow tree trunks, planks or bark, in trees or near the habitat of wild bees, in the hope that the insects will occupy them, and thus render the process of gathering the combs much easier. Another method is to cut down hollow trunks containing nests, and to take them to the village. However, the actual catching and hiving of a swarm is rarely practised. One factor common to all primitive groups is the knowledge of the powers of smoke in overcoming the ferocity of the bees and forcing them out of the hive.

The earliest portrayal of bee-keeping in ancient Egypt shows us something well-organized and apparently long-established. It comes from a relief in the Fifth-Dynasty temple of Ni-weser-re (2560–2420 BC) at Abusir. On the left, the smoker is in use to subdue the bees prior to taking the combs. It appears to be made of pottery and the bee-keeper is blowing the smoke through into the hive. To the right of the scene, the honey is being extracted from the comb, then filtered and finally packed. The hives are cylindrical pipe hives piled up in rows one on top of the other. This type of hive has not changed in Egypt since the time of this relief, and similar hives can still be seen there today. The scene is completely orderly and suggests that bee-keeping was no new thing in Egypt even as early as the Fifth Dynasty. Indeed, the bee symbolized Lower Egypt and from the very first dynasty when Upper and Lower Egypt were united, this area was referred to as 'the land of the bee'.

There are numerous references to honey in inscriptions and papyri after this. Rekhmire, vizier to Tuthmosis III (1486–1450 BC), collected tributes in kind from Upper Egypt, which included honey from several places. The Nineteenth Dynasty kings rated honey highly and it is listed among the gifts of Ramesses III to the important temples, the amounts noted down being really quite remarkable (thousands of jars in all).

It is from Rekhmire's tomb that the next representation of bee-keeping comes. Again we see the same type of hives, and the honey is shown going through all the processes of extracting, being poured into jars and sealed. In the much later tomb of Pa-bu-sa at Thebes (seventh century BC) we find another bee-keeping scene with the familiar pipe hives attended by a bee-keeper and, above, honey is being poured into a jar.

Plate 34

Honey is frequently mentioned in the Old Testament and from this one gets the impression that it was a regular article of diet. During the famine when Jacob sent the 'best fruits in the land' (Gen. 43.11) to exchange for corn from Egypt, these included honey. When the Israelites in their wanderings came across manna, they likened the flavour to 'wafers made with honey'

(Ex. 16.31). The Book of Ecclesiasticus, representing a much later period, makes the importance of honey quite clear, saying, 'The principal things necessary for the life of men are: water, fire and iron, salt, milk, and bread of flour, and honey, and the cluster of the grape, and oil and clothing.' In spite of the considerable use made of honey there is nothing to suggest that bee-keeping was practised, even though the Israelites were in contact with Egypt; but as they were a chiefly a nomadic people, it is unlikely that they would take up such a settled occupation.

In early Mesopotamia, honey was apparently known but not
used so widely as date syrup, and bee-keeping does not seem to
have been practised. True, there is a text telling us that Shamash-
resh-uzur, governor of Sukhi and Ma'ar, did introduce bee-
keeping there (about 3,000 years ago) but his valiant attempt
appears to have been an isolated instance. It seems highly probable
that these bees were brought in from the land of the Hittites, for 43
it is a known fact that here was a people who were ardent bee-
keepers. The Hittite word for 'honey' is closely related to the
general word for 'sweetness', and honey is frequently mentioned
in documents along with beer, wine and water, as well as being
an important factor in religious ritual. The Law Code found at
Boghazköy gives a more precise reference to honey. This Code
was evidently compiled from already existing laws probably some
time between 1500 and 1460 BC. Here we find that the fine for
stealing a swarm of bees has been reduced, which may imply that
bee-keeping had now become more widespread, so that swarms
would perhaps be worth less than before. Honey is also listed
amongst the agricultural produce along with butter, oil, barley,
wine and other things, the price being given as 1 'zipittani' of
honey—1 shekel.

It is thought that bee-keeping in Greece is an inheritance from early contacts with Egypt. Certainly, when the Greeks came to rule Egypt in the Ptolemaic period they did much to make apiculture there more flourishing than ever. The bees now found in Greece and also in Cyprus, Palestine and Crete are identical with the Egyptian bee. Honey figures prominently in Greek mythology: the young Zeus, for example, was rescued from his father Cronus and brought up secretly, being fed by the nymphs Amalthea and Melissa, on milk and honey. We can gauge the importance that the Classical World attached to honey by the fact that so many people wrote about it. In Greece, Aristotle (384–322 BC) is the earliest writer on bees whose work has come down to us. By his time, however, bee-keeping had long been an established practice. Hesiod, in the eighth century BC makes mention of it, and other writers in the fourth and fifth centuries are reputed to have treated the topic.

Both Theophrastus and Aristotle discuss the different qualities of honey produced in various parts of Greece, rating Attic honey best of all, followed by that from Salamis, Leros, Calymna and Hybla. The honey from Pontus was notorious for its toxic qualities, for the flowers visited by the bees there were a species of rhododendron containing a bitter poisonous substance. Honey was the chief sweetening element in Greek cookery and special honey-cakes were made which, as in Ancient Egypt, were deemed worthy offerings for the gods.

In Rome, of course, bee-keeping was a highly scientific and important pursuit. Most farms kept bee-hives and the majority of books written on agriculture have a chapter devoted to bee-keeping. Perhaps the best-known treatise on bees is Virgil's Fourth *Georgic*; here he is shown to be a small farmer who both knew and loved his bees. It was more usual, however, to give over the care of one's bees to a man, known as the *apiarius*, who would be solely responsible for them and who for preference would even live in a little cottage on the spot. Varro, too, in his *De re rustica*, devotes a section to bees, and states that careful consideration must be given to the positioning of the hives, stressing the importance of the nearness of water and recommending the most suitable plants to grow. Like Virgil he notes that thyme provides the best honey, but also suggests growing roses, poppies, peas, beans and a number of other flowering plants. He gives his opinion of various types of hive and points out in particular the value of regular inspection, fumigation and cleansing, as well as keeping a watch on the numbers of 'kings' in the hive (the sex of the queen bee having not been determined by the ancients). Ready-made food for the bees is, he says, also essential, so that they do not feed on the stores of honey wanted by the bee-keeper. Varro lists three different recipes for it, two for sweet cakes and one for a syrup. Honey was collected three times a year. The success of bee-keeping in early Rome is clearly shown in an anecdote related by Varro about the two brothers Veianus who, inheriting from their father about one acre of land, turned it over to bee-keeping and made their fortunes.

Columella regarded bee-keeping as a serious topic to be treated in an orderly and practical manner. His chapters on bees are very detailed and for long bee-keepers relied on what he had to say.

As we have seen, the preferred honey of the Romans was thyme honey; in this they differed from bee-keepers today, who prize heather honey. Neither this variety nor granulated honey was much appreciated by the ancients. Pliny says that honey which crystallizes is poorly rated, whereas today connoisseurs often prefer the natural granulated form. The Roman bee-keepers must, therefore, have gone to some trouble to keep their honey liquid, as except for a few varieties, all honey will crystallize in time. Of course, having only honey as the chief sweetening element in their cookery, the Romans would have found it far easier to extract from the jars in a liquid form and far more versatile in use.

In Ancient Rome honey must indeed have served a great many purposes. It was used not only for cakes and sweetmeats, but as a preservative for all kinds of things. The first chapter of the *Roman Cookery Book* (attributed not to Apicius but to Apuleius) includes methods of food preservation, for meat as well as fruit, by this means.

From Apicius' cookery book we learn little about cakes and sweets, the edition, as it has come down to us, being singularly lacking in such recipes. However, there is a mention of honey cakes in the first chapter and later there are some recipes for home-made sweets. These latter include stuffed dates fried in honey; various recipes involving bread or wine cakes soaked in milk, then baked, with honey poured over afterwards; a mixture of nuts, honey and other ingredients served up with chopped toasted filberts; and a kind of egg custard. The last-named is a surprisingly simple recipe requiring five eggs to one pint of milk, previously mixed with honey, the mixture being placed in an earthenware pot and baked over a slow fire. Bakers made all kinds of confectionery and sold various honey dainties each with its own name, *liba*, *spira*, *savillum*, and a number of others. The Romans also indulged in eating *dulcia* or sweets made chiefly of honey.

In sauces and dressings, so essential a part of Roman fare, we find honey an important ingredient, whether the dressing be simple or elaborate, and whether it was to be served with vegetables, fish and shellfish, meat and game, or with fruit. Honey is also recommended as a glaze for ham, the skin being removed, the fat scored in a criss-cross design and honey then rubbed in—a process used to this day. Honey quite obviously had the same wide use that sugar has now, and perhaps an even wider one, for the Romans liked to mix the sweet and savoury probably to a far greater degree than is generally practised today.

OTHER SOURCES OF SUGAR

Whilst honey was undoubtedly the most common and popular sweetening substance before the advent of refined sugars, it was not the only one, and in some cases probably not the cheapest. In Egypt, the carob was associated with the word for 'sweetness', but whether it was used as a sugar substitute is doubtful. Fruits which did serve that purpose are the date, the fig and the grape.

Of these, perhaps the most widely used in ancient times was the date. To the Assyrians, who were probably not bee-keepers, it was, in the words of Herodotus, their 'food, wine and honey'. Fig-syrup was also used in Assyria, and Egypt had its own sycamore fig which had a very prolific yield. Whether this was used as a sugar substitute by the Egyptians we do not know, but it is not likely to have gone unnoticed.

The grape was a very important source of sugar, and any country cultivating vines could not fail to realize the value of grape juice as a sweetening substance. Egypt with its vast practice of viticulture can be expected to have exploited the possibilities of grape-syrup—indeed a jar was found in the tomb of Tutankhamun bearing the inscription 'unfermented grape juice'. Certainly when we come to Roman cookery, there is mention of a number of different sweeteners derived from grape-juice, while must was used like honey in preserving fruit. Depending on how much the must was boiled down, *caroenum*, *sapa* or *defrutum* resulted. There were differences of opinion as to how much the juice should be reduced; Pliny tells us that *sapa* was must boiled down to one-third the quantity, and *defrutum* to a half. *Defrutum* was usually used in sweetening sauces as also was *passum* made from dried grapes and must or wine. This was very sweet and differed in flavour from the other three.

In any chapter on sugar and its substitutes one cannot overlook manna, the bread of life to the Israelites during their wanderings
in the Sinai Desert. Their particular kind of manna was probably 62
that formed by the secretion of a small insect on the twigs of the tamarisk; it is still found in that region today and gathered by the Bedouin. Just as the Israelites did, they gather it early in the morning, before the ants have a chance to get to it, and seal it in pots. In good years it is said that a man can collect 4 lb each morning; this would be sufficient to stave off his hunger, and as it will keep indefinitely when carefully packed, one can understand why it was called Bread of Heaven. It must indeed have

seemed heaven-sent to a tribe of undernourished people. The Bedouin makes a kind of purée of it and as such it is a very acceptable addition to their usual diet. This particular tamarisk also occurs in Persia, where the manna is shaken from it and made into cakes with honey and flour. There is no actual proof of this having been done there in ancient times but it is a possibility, in view of the use made of it by the Israelites in by-gone days and by the Bedouin today. In India a different species of tamarisk provides manna, and in his *History*, Herodotus tells us that the people of Lydia, in a town called Callatebus, carried on the manufacture of 'honey' from tamarisk syrup.

Many other trees throughout the world have sugary sap which can be used as a sugar substitute, but they are not referred to by ancient writers. Pliny does mention what he calls *elaiomeli*, a rich sweet oil from palms in coastal regions of Syria; though this may only have been employed as a medicine. The manna ash is indigenous to the Mediterranean area, and exudes manna for which it has since been cultivated, but none of the references to it amongst the early writers has anything to say about this property. Perhaps by this time, in more culturally developed areas, the properties of some plants and trees had already been neglected and forgotten. The use made by recent aboriginal groups of such exudations from the eucalyptus of Australia and species of pine in America suggests that early man might have tapped the sugary sap from a number of trees, which were later neglected as civilization (and also bee-keeping) advanced. The maple also has a sugary sap but Theophrastus does not speak of it in his comments on the tree. The best variety, the sugar maple of America was, however, very well known to the Indians who made great use of its sweet liquid. In Chile too, the sap of the little coconut is boiled down to a sort of treacle and used as sugar in food preparation.

Theophrastus, Pliny and Herodotus all agree that the papyrus of Egypt yielded a sweet juice. Theophrastus links it with two others, 'sari' and 'mnasion', and declares these three to be the most useful of all the sweet plants of Egypt. However, this appears to have been only a sweet-meat and was not used in cooking to replace honey or other syrups.

It seems strange, when one considers how commonplace they are in the modern kitchen, that both cane and beet sugar are comparatively recent introductions. Sugar cane was only just beginning to be known to the western world in the last two or three centuries BC and by Pliny's time it was still merely a medicament: 'It is a kind of honey that collects in reeds', he tells us, 'white like gum and brittle to the teeth, the largest pieces are the size of a filbert. It is only used as a medicine.'

In India, where it originated, there is evidence of sugar cane
from way back in prehistory. Honey was initially the chief 83, 89
sweetener, but although it continued to be used along with sugar until about the third century AD, sugar had by then been equally popular for about seven hundred years. After the third century AD honey was used only in ritual and matters of etiquette. It seems always to have been gathered from wild bees; indeed, having sugar, the early inhabitants of India were not dependent on hive-keeping as many other peoples necessarily were. Philological studies show that the Dravidians already knew how to make *guda* (or treacle) from the sugar-cane and it is thought that they learnt the art from their predecessors, the Proto-Australoids. By the middle of the first millennium BC, there was already a machine for extracting sugar-cane juice and sugar is believed to have been made: 'crystal sugar' was included with spices as a flavouring for a milk-curd recipe called *payasyā*.

The date of the introduction of sugar-cane to Europe is uncertain, but it was being cultivated in Spain after the arrival of the Moors in the eighth century. It seems to have remained a medicine for a long time, and not to have been used generally as a sweetener for food. In England the demand for it became appreciable only when the drinking of tea and coffee grew popular. It is believed that the Venetians were the earliest refiners in Europe, round about the fifteenth century. Beet sugar was not discovered until 1747!

A noticeable feature in early writings which mention sugar substitutes is that they are nearly always called honey; thus, Herodotus talks of date 'honey', tamarisk 'honey', artificially manufactured 'honey', and Pliny says sugar is a 'kind of honey'. This surely demonstrates how high a place honey occupied as a sweetener in the life of earlier man. Dates, figs, grapes and other plants may have provided substitutes but to the Greeks, Romans and Egyptians at the very least, honey remained their main source of sugar.

CHAPTER V

Fungi

THE HUNTING and collecting economies of both early and recent stone-age cultures were of necessity generally geared to utilize every sort of edible plant. In the search for roots, berries and fruits it would have been surprising if fungi had been overlooked. Although some varieties are well camouflaged, sometimes appearing as stones or dead leaves, many fungi readily draw attention to themselves by their colour or size. The *Russulae*, for instance, come in many varied and eye-catching shades, while the *Boletus* group can reach large and very noticeable proportions. Moreover, many fungi have quite an attractive odour, and their taste is distinctly pleasant. Quite the opposite effect is produced by others, and one can imagine that early communities would have instantly rejected these on account of their repulsive flavour and smell; indeed a number produce a violent burning sensation on the tongue when tasted raw. There is no hard and fast rule, however, and several pleasant-tasting varieties no doubt caused severe stomach upsets or periodic mortality; for example, the most deadly mushroom of all, *Amanita phalloides*, the Death Cap, has no particular smell and is said to be mild in flavour. 57, 85, 93

The number of true species of fungi has been put at a little under 40,000 and it thus seems more than likely that at least some of these fungi would have been eaten (regularly) by early man. What vast quantities of edible fungi can be gathered, at least in some of the forest areas of Europe, is shown by the sales of home-grown wild mushrooms at the turn of the century in the Munich market alone. The total sold in a year amounted to 850,000 kilos (about 1,850,000 pounds), in the proportions shown in the Table on the following page.

In making out a case for the importance of fungi as a food in the past, it must also be remembered that they occur in all kinds of places and at almost all times of the year. Although in Europe the summer and autumn months June to November are the most abounding in fungi, offering Field Mushrooms, Ceps, Orange-Cap Boleti, Chanterelles, Parasol Mushrooms, Blewits and many other good edible varieties, spring has its share of good fungi too.

Species	Quantity
Cantharellus cibarius (Chanterelle)	70,000– 90,000 kilos
Boletus edulis (Cep)	300,000–350,000 kilos
Boletus scaber (Rough-stalk boletus)	150,000–180,000 kilos
Russula alutacea ,, *cyanoxantha* ,, *vesca* ,, *virescens*	30,000– 35,000 kilos
Psalliota campestris (Field Mushroom)	80,000–100,000 kilos

Table 6. Analysis of a sample of wild mushrooms sold in the Munich market at the turn of the century

Winter is the least productive season, as fungi flourish most when conditions are warm and moist. However, a number continue to grow until frost sets in. The Buttery Agaric is often abundant in November and December, and Larch Hygrophorus and Fir-wood Agaric will grow under snow. The Spring Hygrophorus is said to occur as early as mid-January during a mild winter in France, and the Oyster Mushroom and Velvet-stemmed Agaric or Winter Mushroom can continue right through the season.

As fungi need for their growth ready-made organic substances created by both animals and plants, it follows that they can be found in widely differing environments, the varieties depending on the type of humus (which in turn depends upon the type of vegetation), and other varying factors such as the degree of humidity, temperature, and exposure. Woodlands, for instance, have a great variety to offer, such as *Boletus, Lactarius, Russula, Amanita*; some particular species of these prefer deciduous woods, others will be found in pine woods, while beech woods have their own special varieties including species of *Cortinarius, Russula* and *Marasmius*. Indeed many fungi form a mycorrhyzal association with the roots of certain trees, so that they are rarely found far from the tree in question: *Boletus elegans*, for example, is closely associated with larch trees. Other kinds of fungus are even to be found in bogs, fens and sand-dunes, and, of course, growing on living trees or tree-stumps. It seems more than likely that such associations would have found their place in the plant lore of some earlier peoples.

With the change from the Palaeolithic methods of food collecting to that of the Neolithic policy of burning and clearing, there would also have been a change but not a diminution in the fungal flora; the grassland fungi would increase at the expense of the woodland varieties, and there might even have been a marked increase at that time of species which thrive on areas where wood has been burnt.

All this suggests that in fungi earlier communities had a useful and possibly fairly constant source of food. That they probably made full use of them in their diet is surely borne out by the important role fungi play in some primitive economies today.

Darwin, in his *Voyage of the Beagle* (1839), gives an account of his visit to Tierra del Fuego, and remarks particularly on the use of a certain fungus there as a main feature of the Fuegians' diet. 'In Tierra del Fuego,' he says, 'the fungus in its tough and mature state is collected in large quantities by the women and children and is eaten uncooked. . . . With the exception of a few berries chiefly of a dwarf arbutus, the natives eat no vegetable food besides this fungus.'

The Australian aborigines relish a certain fungus known as 'blackfellow's bread', and there are numerous references to the use of fungi as food in Central Africa, India, and the Solomon Islands. The North American Yosemite Indians shredded and dried them, afterwards boiling and eating them with salt or making a mushroom soup. In New Guinea and Papua, species of *Agaricus* and *Auricularia* are eaten.

Japan and China both have an established fungus tradition; the Japanese cultivation of *shii-take* on logs of wood in shaded parts of the forests is thought to go back some 2,000 years. The Maori too were well acquainted with mushrooms before they became influenced by modern civilization, and used several kinds, including one (*Auricularia polytricha*) which they did not enjoy eating but would nevertheless resort to in times of scarcity. It is interesting to note that the Maori recognized one species as poisonous when raw, but realized that it could be rendered edible by cooking, their method being to wrap the fungus in leaves and bury it in hot ashes for a long time. This is particularly significant, for it suggests that earlier stone-age peoples may well have made similar use of a variety of fungi which, whilst inedible or even poisonous in the raw state, can be turned into satisfactory and sometimes tasty food by careful processing.

However, it is not always man's aim to suppress the poisonous or intoxicating properties of plants, and it is worth recording here that some groups single out certain varieties of fungi for use as a narcotic or as a stimulant. The Koryak tribes of Kamchatka use Fly Agaric for the latter purpose, as do the Dyaks of Borneo and the native inhabitants of New Guinea other varieties of mushroom. The use of 'teonanacatl' or hallucinogenic fungi is considered by some to have been important in certain early Mexican cultures, and in fact these fungi are still used today in a few villages. The stone effigies known as mushroom stones, some of which perhaps date back to 1000 BC, have been put forward in support of these special fungal uses in early Mexico, and the existence of such cults clearly suggests that these peoples had been able to distinguish the various kinds of mushroom for many centuries.

Fig. 27

The calorific values of fungi are within the range known for vegetables, although smaller than for meat and fish. On the other

Fig. 27 A 'mushroom stone' from Guatemala, dated AD 300–600

hand, the nitrogenous values are higher than those in vegetables. The vitamin content of mushrooms varies, some containing more than one type others none. Chanterelles in particular are quite rich in Vitamin A; Vitamin B_1 is more frequently found in fungi than B_2; Vitamin C is not to be found in any great amount; Vitamin D occurs in at least four common varieties.

The food value of fungi, then, really lies in the nitrogenous substances, which are to us the indigestible factor. Nevertheless, taken in conjunction with other food, it is not unreasonable to suggest that primitive man could have tolerated fairly large quantities. Indeed, this raises the very debatable issue of how similar the digestive abilities of earlier peoples were to ours. It is a fact that the stresses of civilized society cause digestive upsets which are unlikely to have occurred commonly among our early ancestors; but there is also the possibility that adaptations occurred to varying dietary regimes, for there is no reason to think that the complex mosaics of physical change which have occurred in human evolution missed out the digestive tract. Certainly there is room for further research in this field. Animal experiments have demonstrated that the food value of fungi can in certain circumstances be considerable. For instance, tests carried out on laboratory rats showed that those given mushrooms as their protein put on 30 per cent more weight than those being fed cheese; also, fungi have been successfully given as fodder to pigs and poultry to replace fish-meat.

Whatever we choose to believe about their nutritional value to prehistoric man, it is an undisputed fact that fungi were well known and used by various peoples throughout recorded history.

The early Mesopotamians knew both poisonous and edible mushrooms as well as truffles, which are still found abundantly in the area and seem to have been appreciated there at least as early as 1800 BC, as letters found in excavations at Mari show. There are numerous references to fungi in the writings of Greek and Latin authors. According to Pausanias, Greek legend had it that Mycenae was so called by Perseus, after his thirst had been quenched with *mykes* or mushrooms on the site where the city arose. The earliest classical mention of fungi occurs in Euripides (480–406 BC) and Hippocrates (460–*c.* 377 BC), who both refer to cases of poisoning by mushrooms.

It is Theophrastus (*c.* 300 BC) who first makes some attempt at describing mushrooms but he does not go into any great detail. Subsequent references by Nicander (185 BC), Dioscorides (second century AD) and Diphilus (third century BC) all betray great suspicion of fungi, although the latter did admit that they could be 'tasty and nourishing'. Athenaeus was very sceptical and says merely that 'few of them are good and most produce a choking sensation'. It would seem then, from the writings at least, that the early Greeks were not very enthusiastic about mushrooms. Their reluctance may be due to the fact that Greece was, and still is, very poor in natural fungus; moreover, from a remark by Plautus, where he mentions that mushroom consumption was included amongst the expensive eating habits of the wealthy Greeks, one may deduce that they were imported from Italy at a rather high price. However, the fact that they were imported at all suggests that not everyone in ancient Greece was so mistrustful of fungi as the writings indicate; how else can one explain the attempts at cultivation described by Dioscorides? He relates that some people used to take the bark from the black and white poplar, cut it into small pieces and scatter it over areas where there was dung. This practice was said to produce edible fungi at all times of the year. Later in the *Geoponika*, a compilation of works on husbandry produced about AD 900 but whose actual contents come from much earlier authors, there is another suggestion for growing mushrooms on burnt ground, which had to be well-watered after the fire.

If the writings of the Greeks convey the impression that for the most part they were sceptical of fungi, those of the Romans give a vastly different picture. There is as usual little reference to the everyday habits of the lower classes in Rome, but from Ovid (*c.* 43 BC–AD 19) we do get a hint that fungi were used by them in his description of the daily routine of a peasant woman, which included the gathering of *fungos albos*, presumably field mushrooms. Horace (65–8 BC) also mentions fungus-gathering and comments that it is better to use only the fungi which grow in the fields as those in the woods are not to be trusted. Most Latin references to fungi, however, are connected with the luxurious eating habits of the Roman upper classes, who were on the whole self-indulgent and over-fond of food and drink, and very partial to certain fungi. The most popular variety was undoubtedly that known as *Amanita caesarea* (the 'egg mushroom' of present-day Italy, where it is still highly appreciated), and referred to by the Romans as *boletus*. It was in a dish of these, his favourite *boleti*, that the Emperor Claudius was indulging when he was poisoned by his wife Agrippina. They were so highly thought-of, that special cooking vessels known as *boletaria* were used to heat them in.

Plate 35

After *A. caesarea*, in order of preference, came what we know today as *Boletus edulis,* the Cep, which the Romans called *fungi suilli.* But they were not so acceptable as the former, as we can see from an epigram of Martial (AD 43–104), disgruntled because at a dinner he was not served with the best fare:

Sunt tibi boleti : fungos ego sumo suillos. (*Ep. iii. 60*)

Truffles were also widely appreciated as a delicacy and in one of his satires Juvenal (AD 65–185) puts them on a par with *boleti* (at the same time mentioning that the fashion was for the rich to prepare these fungi with their own hands, not leaving so delicate a task to the servants!).

To show how great a great delicacy fungi were for the Romans, we need only turn to Apicius' *Roman Cookery Book.* He gives recipes for *fungi farnei*—tree fungi (what these actually are is unclear), for *boleti* and for truffles. One of these makes use of *boletus* stalks, the part of the mushroom usually somewhat scorned by modern cookery books; these are chopped up and placed in a 'new shallow dish' with pepper, lovage and a little honey, mixed with *liquamen* and cooked with a little oil added.

Although *boleti* and *suilli* loom large in Roman literature, Pliny, that great student of natural history, discussing fungi at length, mentions several others including one which is generally taken to be the Shaggy Ink-cap, owing to the fact that he likens the shape of the cap to the head-dress worn by the priests known as Flamens. He also recommends another variety, now tentatively identified as *Lactarius deliciosus* or alternatively *Russula alutacea,* which is still apparently well known in Italy under various common names. The earliest known picture of a fungus is generally considered to be of *Lactarius deliciosus* and occurs in a fresco at Pompeii.

TRUFFLES

Truffles, although treated as a delicacy by both Greeks and Romans, were also something of a puzzle to them. Mushrooms they could in their own way understand as they had both stalks and 'roots', but truffles just appeared buried in the earth with no clue as to their origin. According to Pliny the most prized truffles came from Africa; Juvenal, more precisely, mentions Libya as the source of the best truffles, though Martial considered them to be still second to *boleti*. It is to Apicius again that we must turn to see how truffles were eaten in ancient Rome. He recommends first scraping, then boiling, and afterwards grilling them lightly on skewers; after this they are to be returned to a pan for boiling, this time with *liquamen, caroenum,* pepper, wine and honey. When the sauce has thickened, he says, they can again be grilled wrapped in a sausage skin, and then served as they are. In addition, Apicius gives three sauces for serving with them and another recipe for cooking them. The Romans may not have known much about the origins of truffles but they certainly had ideas about preparing them for the table.

CHAPTER VI

Cereal Crops

OF VERY SPECIAL importance to man, from the inception of their domestication, have been the carbohydrate-rich cereals. Whereas the control of certain animal species guaranteed easily available meat and dairy produce, cereal crops were particularly durable foodstuffs, provided they were protected from rodents and fungal attack, and could be utilized in a variety of ways. Cereal 'porridges' and 'grits' were established early in pottery cultures, and must have been very useful in feeding both the very young and the very old.

The study of cereal remains is by no means a recent feature of
27 archaeo-botanical research. Alphonse de Candolle initiated
45 studies in 1855, and Oswald Heer demonstrated clearly the
wealth of botanical information to be obtained from archaeological sites in his work on Swiss 'lake-dwellings' (1865 and later). Unfortunately, although pollen studies have increased considerably, as yet relatively little work is being done on early
47–50 food plants. Of special exception are the researches of Hans
67, 68 Helbaek in Denmark and Paul Mangelsdorf in America, both
having a special interest in the development of cereal crops in their own region of the world.

Cereal remains may be identified in various forms, all contributing useful information though not necessarily in the same detail. In conditions of extreme aridity, as in some Egyptian tombs, a natural 'mummification' may take place, every detail even to the fine hairs on the kernels may remain, and the starch will react to the iodine test. It must be emphasized, however, that these grains are dead, the viability of such mummy wheat being a myth. In contrast, peat bogs are also conducive to preservation because of the anaerobic environment and presence of humic acid. As a result, bodies found in the peat bogs of Denmark and northern Germany still have their stomach contents intact. Carbonized grain results from accidental fire or over-parching. Plates 36, 38 39, 42 From earliest times some grains were parched in order to release them from less edible attachments. Temperature regulation seems to have been difficult even in Roman times, the result sometimes being scorching or complete carbonization. Similarly, of course, bread was sometimes charred or burnt. Plate 40 The ash of habitation sites can also remain in identifiable form. Similarly, cereal 'skeletons' may be obtained by crushing pottery. It is well known that casts of grain imprints on pottery can reveal a surprising amount of detail, and similar impressions can be found in wall and floor material.

One should not underestimate the versatility of earlier peoples in utilizing grain crops. Bread was clearly a basic cereal food, the size, shape and ingredients varying with period, country and possibly social strata. At certain periods, particularly in times of need, the flour was increased in bulk in some regions by the addition of ground acorns, chestnuts, and sometimes other plant material. The somewhat flat Roman loaf was square in shape or Plate 41 round, with notches cut into it, whereas early Egyptian loaves could be triangular and in long rolls. Plate 49 In Rome, the best bread was of wheat flour, but barley bread was commonly eaten. Both in Egypt and Rome, cakes and pastry were of all shapes and sizes. Probably the Egyptians were the first to experiment with yeast-fermented doughs, and were responsible for the earliest leavened bread. Both literary and art sources show that the ancient Egyptians kneaded dough with their feet—at least in the larger bakery—for millers and bakers were professional by *c.* 2000 BC. Pliny comments that the quality of bread depends upon the goodness of the wheat and fineness of the sieve. He says, moreover, 'Pound the wheat grains with sand to remove the husks, the grain then being but one-half its former measure. Then twenty-five per cent gypsum is added to seventy-five per cent of this meal and mixed, and the flour is bolted.' By further sieving a very fine flour is produced. One wonders, however, to what extent fine sand particles remained in the flour, and indeed it is possible that some stone dust from querns was also regularly incorporated in the bread. It has been suggested that the severe wear found on the teeth of some earlier populations may have resulted from the abrasive properties of this 'intrusive' powder, but in fact this can only be one of a number of contributory factors.

That cereals could be put to a variety of other uses is demonstrated clearly by Apicius. Barley soups (boiled crushed barley with other ingredients), barley with pork, mussels with crushed spelt, and spelt stuffing for chicken or sucking-pig, are a few combinations he gives.

Cereals have been cultivated independently in both the Old and New Worlds, most cereal types originating in Europe and Asia—though not at the same time and in the same place. The cereals of major importance to earlier populations are outlined in the Table opposite.

Although numerous forms of wheat have been developed by recent agriculturists, only a few major variants are significant in the study of earlier cultures.

Taking Emmer wheat first, Jarmo, in Iraqui Kurdistan, has provided grains strikingly like the wild ancestral form, a fact which suggests that the region taking in this site was at the very earliest stage of plant husbandry. In Egypt, from Predynastic to Roman times this was the predominant species, although club wheat was probably on the increase by the end of the first millennium BC. Emmer has also been found in various early horizons of Palestine, Syria and Asia Minor. It was well in evidence too at the Swiss prehistoric lake-sites, and indeed, in most Neolithic European cultures emmer appears to have been supreme. Probably the basic movement of emmer was westwards, moving down into Egypt and northwards into Europe. By Bronze Age times, the wheat pattern was changing and it was meeting more serious competition with barley in northern Europe, club wheat

CEREAL	WILD ANCESTOR	EARLY CULTIVATED VARIETIES
Wheat	*Triticum dicoccoides*	*T. dicoccum* (Emmer)
	T. dicoccoides x ?*Aegilops*	*T. spelta* (Spelt)
	T. aegilopoides	*T. monococcum* (Einkorn)
	Aegilops x ?Emmer	*T. vulgare* (Bread wheat)
		T. compactum (Club wheat)
Barley		*H. distichum* (two-row)
	Hordeum spontaneum (two-row)	*H. hexastichum* (dense-eared') *six-row*
		H. tetrastichum ('lax-eared')
Millets	*Setaria viridis* (Green millet)	*S. italica* (Italian millet)
	Panicum callosum (Abyssinian millet)	*P. miliaceum* (Common panicum)
Rye	*Secale montanum*	
	Secale ancestrale ?	*S. cereale*
Oats	*Avena fatua*	*A. sativa*
	Avena barbata	*A. strigosa* ('Bristle-pointed')
Rice	*Oryza sativa*	*O. sativa* (Common rice)
	breviligulata	*O. glaberrima* (Sudan–W. Africa)
	perennis	
Maize	*Zea* (? species)	*Zea mays* (Indian corn)

Table 7. Some major cereal varieties known in early cultures

and barley in southern Europe, and club wheat in Asia Minor, Syria and Palestine. In northern Europe emmer lingered on until the third century AD in Denmark and the sixth century AD in Britain.

Club wheat has been identified at a Mesopotamian site dated to 3000 BC, and in a slightly earlier context in Egypt. By the third millennium BC it is present in Kurdistan and by 2000 BC was of obvious importance to people in this area. It was also present with emmer and einkorn in some parts of Europe during the earliest agricultural phase (*c.* 2700 BC), being certainly prized by the people of the Michelsberg culture. Club and bread wheats largely replaced emmer in much of Europe during the past millennium. There is still much to be learned about the early distribution of spelt, although finds from Switzerland, Germany, Poland, England, Denmark, Sweden and Italy provide some clues. It appears on both sides of the Alps by the earlier part of the second millennium BC.

Einkorn, unlike the other mentioned wheats, developed independently of *Triticum aegilopoides*, not being derived from *T. dicoccoides.* Outside of Turkey, the evidence suggests that einkorn was not an important cereal, and it may never have been grown as an individual crop in much of Europe. Carbonized einkorn grain has been identified at Jarmo (*c.* 6700 BC) in association with emmer, and at Çatal Hüyük in Anatolia.

BARLEY

Barley and wheat are the cereals that occur most persistently in Mesopotamian and Egyptian archaeological sites, and they appear to have been introduced into Europe together. Although detailed study of anatomical variation is beyond the scope of this survey, it should be noted that there are two main groups of barley, 'two-row' and 'six-row' types. Six-row barley is divided into 'dense-eared' and 'lax-eared' forms. In all cultivated forms there are also 'naked' varieties (the result of mutation in a cultivated hulled form). There has been much debate as to the possible wild ancestor or ancestors of cultivated barley varieties. It still seems most reasonable, however, to derive both the two-row and six-row types from the wild two-row barley of the Near East (*Hordeum spontaneum*).

From Jarmo there is good evidence of the two-row form, but no six-row barley, and it is significant that the variety present was very similar to the wild *Hordeum*. It is likely that two-row barley did not penetrate far into Europe until classical times, being present in Greece by the third millennium BC, and grown in

Italy in Columella's day. More is known of six-row barley, the lax-eared form being present in the earliest sites of Mesopotamia and the dense-eared form equally long ago in Cilicia. The lax-eared six-row form was definitely in Egypt by the third millennium BC, and it is of special interest that previous to this—in the fifth millennium—a mutant variety occurred with both dense and lax six-row characteristics. Although in the Neolithic of central Europe dense-eared barley predominated, more northerly regions such as Britain and Denmark are distinguished by a predominance of the lax-eared variety.

One particularly important form, naked barley, occurs in the north European Neolithic, but is mainly cultivated in the countries of southern and eastern Asia. It promises thus to be a useful cultural 'marker'. There has been some confused identification of naked barley, and there is a need for special consideration of this variety in future archaeo-botanical investigations. Following the establishment of agriculture in western India by 3000 BC, barley assumed great importance. Indeed, barley and rice became the 'two immortal sons of heaven'. Vedic literature (*c.* 2000–800 BC) refers to barley cakes, and to parched barley ground up with juices, curd, or ghee.

MILLETS

From various European archaeological sites, both the common panicum and Italian millets have been found from the end of the third millennium BC onwards. Considering the number of imprints found, there would appear to have been an increase in its use during the first millennium BC. In particular, the panicum variety appears to have been used in the north, with Italian millet more in evidence in southern Europe. Surprisingly, neither variety has yet been identified in Britain.

In contrast to the noticeable use of this cereal in the European area (even during the first few centuries AD) there is very little evidence of its use in the Near East, although what isolated data we have range in date from 3000 BC to the ninth century AD. There is a complete absence of millet in Egypt. In recent times, millet has become an important cereal crop in the Far East, and indeed, ancient Chinese texts indicate that it has been cultivated there over a long period. The *Fan Shêng-Chih Shu* (*c.* first century BC) not only mentions varieties of millet, but also discusses the best methods of growing and storing such crops.

RYE

As Helbaek points out, rye and oats seem best considered as 'secondary' cultivated plants. Although of importance in modern times, their economic history has been short, and their appearance in early fields appears to have been first as a weed rather than a worthwhile foodstuff. In view of its greater resistance to winter cold, it seems likely that rye would have competed favourably in some higher and colder northern habitats, and what may have been at first regarded as a nuisance by early cultivators in time came to be more predominant—through the natural process of survival—and at this stage was selected for separate cultivation.

In Germany, rye appears during the first millennium BC. By Roman times, it had certainly progressed beyond being a weed, and was cultivated in central Europe, Hungary and Britain. It was also grown in some Mediterranean countries and Turkey, but was not of importance. It is still a major crop in the cold temperate zone through Europe and Asia, and North America.

Although the wild ancestor of rye has not been identified as yet, it is likely to have features in common with wild Afghanistan varieties (*Secale montanum*) and especially with *S. ancestrale* of the Turkey/Afghanistan region.

OATS

Two varieties of oat have assumed economic importance to man, both commencing their association with him as field weeds. The bristle-pointed oat of western Europe is derived from *Avena barbata* which is indigenous to the region from Armenia along the Mediterranean to the Iberian Peninsula. The more widely eaten form, *A. sativa,* is derived from the wild *A. fatua,* indigenous to parts of North Africa, eastern Europe and western Asia.

Early in the first millennium BC, oats were at least present in Germany, Denmark and Switzerland. It was probably during the La Tène expansions that oats became a more common European food, although it seems unlikely to have been a separate crop in Britain until Anglo-Saxon times. Pliny indicates that it was used, at least in central Europe, both as a bread-stuff and in porridge form.

Populations of the Near East appear to have ignored it as a potential food source, and Greek and Roman authors of the second century BC indicate that it was then more valued as a fodder plant.

RICE

This cereal is by far the most important food crop in Asia. It is principally a tropical plant, requiring a fairly high temperature and humidity for its growth, although it is successfully cultivated today in more moderate climates.

It seems reasonable to suppose that the first attempts at rice cultivation would be in forest hollows where a steady water supply could be relied upon from stream or river (though it will tolerate less well watered places). It is unlikely that the construction and maintenance of healthy paddy fields occurred until a fairly advanced stage in Neolithic organization had been attained. Probably the first great rice granaries were established in eastern China and India, the stimulus to cultivate wild rice being triggered off by contact with the eastern margins of the cultures developing wheat and barley crops.

It is claimed that rice was well established as a crop in China by 2800 BC, although Piggott believes it to have been earlier cultivated in India, moving eastwards during the Chinese Bronze Age. The earliest definite evidence is in carbonized paddy grains from an archaeological site at Hasthinapur (Uttar Pradesh), dated to *c.* 1000–750 BC. Rice specimens have also been claimed from the Indian site of Adicchanallur (*c.* 3000 BC), and an excavation in Khotan, Turkestan, of the fifth century BC. In the *Susrutha Samhita*, an early medical compilation (*c.* 1000 BC), the different varieties then existing in India are identified, being classified according to such factors as water requirements and nutritional value. Following Alexander's invasion of India in 320 BC, the Greeks mention the rice crop as being indigenous to India. Moreover Aristobulus, writing about 280 BC, notes that rice was grown in Babylonia, Bactria, and Lower Syria. Surprisingly, although the environment could have been made suitable, there is no evidence of rice in Ancient Egypt, although some consider that the cereal was sent there during the process of trading. What little evidence there is has been used to suggest that movements were also taking place eastwards, and that it spread with South Chinese immigrants into the Philippines before the first millennium BC and to Japan by the first century BC.

As the present facts in no way show a relationship between the common Asiatic rice *Oryza sativa* and the variety found in the Sudan and West Africa, *O. glaberrima*, it has been postulated that the African form arose from an independent source; but again one is left questioning to what extent this African rice cultivation was encouraged by the spreading knowledge of other cereal crops.

It is a great pity that so little is known of this extremely important cereal food, especially from the point of view of dating and the extent to which it was cultivated. Satisfactory cereal yields must have helped considerably to depress the mortality rates and increase population numbers in eastern Asia. Indeed, the mongoloid expansion and consequent movement of other peoples in that area during late prehistoric times might conceivably be linked with the developing cultivation of this critical foodstuff.

MAIZE

Unlike other cereals, the numerous maize kernels are firmly attached to a rigid axis, the cob, and instead of being covered by floral glumes (i.e. 'chaff') as in other cereals, the entire ear is enclosed by modified leaf sheaths. This communal rather than individual protection has the great disadvantage of impeding grain dispersal, and the domestic form we know today is in fact dependent upon man's intervention for its continued survival. Although the only New World cereal to have markedly affected the economy of early indigenous populations, maize is by no

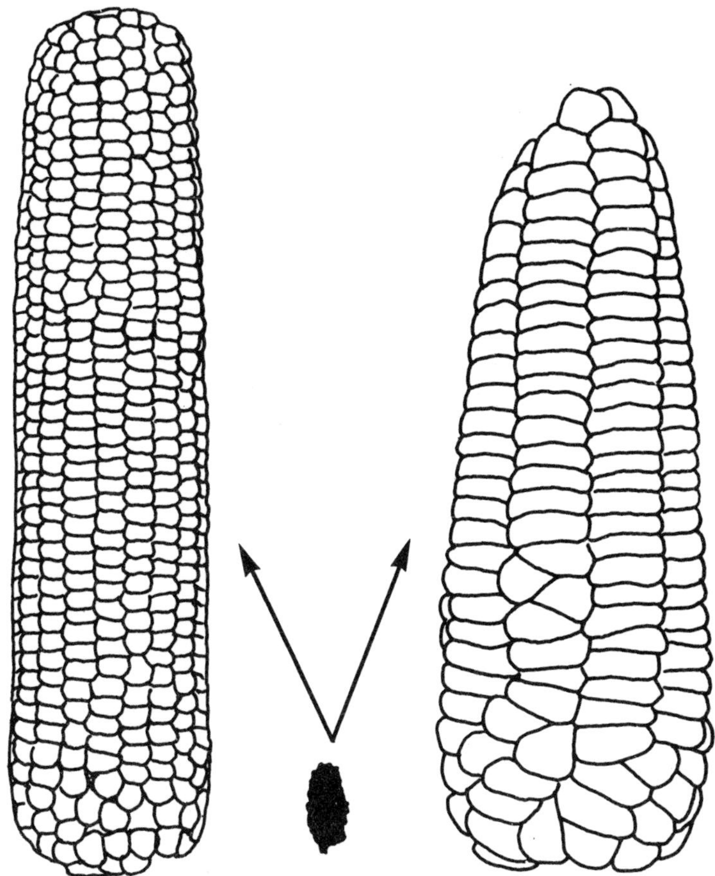

Fig. 28 A primitive maize cob (centre) from Bat Cave about 5500 BC, compared with a modern ear of Cornbelt dent (left) and a large-seeded Peruvian flour corn (right). (After P. C. Mangelsdorf)

means the poor relative of the Old World group. It is in fact potentially the most productive of all, and whereas record yields of wheat seldom exceed 100 bushels per acre, the maximum yields of maize can be more than 300.

The earliest examples of cultivated Indian Corn known so far *Fig. 28*
come from southern Mexico. Until the detailed field work there 68, 81

of R. S. MacNeish and his colleagues in 1960, the Bat Cave in New Mexico had revealed the earliest evidence of maize (*c.* 4500 BC). These large-scale field studies of many occupation sites in the Mexican valley of Tehuacan now enable us to follow the early use and sowing of wild maize in the El Riego Phase (*c.* 7200–5200 BC), the true cultivation of maize during the Coxcatlan Phase (5200–3400 BC), and successive periods of population expansion and increased agricultural organization.

It seems clear therefore that maize has developed as a crop within the last 7,000 years, and the wild ancestral form appears
Plates 43–45 to have been a primitive species of *Zea*, and not a wild corn relative of *Tripsacum* or teosinte. A more advanced form of maize is a not uncommon representation in Peruvian pottery and sometimes on stonework, and the types shown are those grown in Peru today. By the time of the Spanish conquest, the Peruvians were in fact probably the most skilled cultivators of maize in America, and it is reasonable to assume that by then they had much experience in selectively breeding only those varieties which they found of special value as food. The Maya, no less than the Incas, were dependent upon agriculture for existence, and it is likely that, as among the Maya Indians today, maize was the prime foodstuff.

Maize has also been made into a variety of drinks, most of them with some alcohol content. For ritual purposes, the Incas produced a blood pudding, which was made up of maize mixed with the blood of sacrificed llamas.

Although arguments have been put forward for pre-Columbian maize in Africa, the testimony is far from satisfactory and it seems likely on present evidence that the crop was brought to
115 Africa in the early years of the sixteenth century. It is possible that there were two routes of movement; firstly, from the West Indies to Spain and thence to North Africa; secondly, from Brazil to West Africa. It is mentioned in Chinese writings as a court tribute as early as 1550, showing that it achieved rapid 'dispersal' in early post-Columbian times.

Chapter VII

The Vegetables

PULSES

THAT THE PULSES were used as food, and possibly even cultivated from very early times is supported by archaeological finds from many parts of the world. Like cereals, they keep very well when dried and therefore we are able to prove their use in ancient times by the actual discovery of remains and do not have to rely on texts and pictures. In the Near East they were certainly eaten, if not cultivated in the sixth or seventh millennium BC, as is proved by finds of field-peas, lentils and blue-vetchling at Jarmo. Indeed these as well as beans, vetch and chick-peas were long ago established in this area. Finds in Palestine dating from 4000 BC at the latest show that the chick-pea was definitely used as a food at that time.

From Hittite texts we know that peas and beans were included in their agriculture, and excavations in Anatolia have brought to light actual containers storing lentils. These were grown in Assyria, and are also included in the lists of vegetables of the garden of King Merodach-Baladan of Babylon (eighth century BC).

There seems to be some uncertainty about the use of pulses in Egypt. Peas were found in Twelfth-Dynasty tombs as also were quantities of beans, and lentils are said to have been a common dish there. One of these tombs, at Thebes, yielded a sort of paste made of cooked lentils, and an even earlier find places lentils back in Predynastic times. However, despite these discoveries, it has been suggested that peas and beans were not commonly cultivated in Egypt, and Herodotus mentions the fact that the Egyptians 'never sow beans, and even if any happen to grow wild, they will not eat them, either raw or boiled'. Perhaps this taboo was a more recent innovation and need not necessarily have applied to all sections of the community.

45, 90 Food remains from the Swiss prehistoric lake-sites have also provided evidence of beans, peas and lentils, while beans and peas have been found at the Glastonbury 'lake-dwellings' of Iron Age date, though the peas are not thought to be cultivated ones. It is interesting that the beans from both sources are identical—a small variety, which appears to have been cultivated and eaten in considerable quantities.

The Greeks made great use of the pulses in their diet, indeed they even had a God of Beans, and held a 'bean feast' in honour of Apollo. Pea soup was made and could be bought hot in the streets. As supporting evidence for early Greek writings, archaeological finds of beans, peas, lentils and vetch go back to the Early
107 Bronze Age. Late Bronze Age excavations in Crete have yielded beans, peas, vetch and chick-peas, often stored in large pithoi, and it is very likely that these legumes were known and used in this area in Neolithic times, though archaeological proof is still lacking.

According to Herodotus, the lentil was also a major food of a Graeco-Scythian tribe, the Callipidae, who grew it along with grain, onions, leeks and millet.

In Italy, pulses were widely used and cultivated and Roman literature contains many references to them, though one is left with a feeling that they were considered rather more as a food of the proletariat. Indeed, they were undoubtedly an important constituent of the poor man's meal; Horace in describing his well known 'economical diet' refers to his 'onions, pulses and pancakes'. Chick-peas and lupin seeds were sold hot in the streets, providing a nourishing cheap meal for the poorer people, and Pliny, always ready to condemn the extravagant tastes of his time, highly recommended the latter food.

Even Apicius devotes several pages to recipes for peas, beans and lentils. Beans were perhaps slightly more favoured than peas, as the growers of Baiae had evidently taken the trouble to develop a superior variety for which Apicius gives a special recipe. However, he gives many varied methods of cooking peas, one which he honoured with his own name. Lentils could be cooked with chestnuts or with mussels and a recipe for barley-broth contained lentils, peas and chick-peas.

The importance of beans of the *Phaseolus* and *Canavalia* (Jack bean) genera, is shown by remains found at various New World
sites; these take the history of the use of *P. vulgaris* back to about 105
5000 BC. Early stages of the site at Huaca Prieta in Peru show that the lima bean (*P. lunatus*) was already cultivated, the green or common bean (*P. vulgaris*) appearing in later levels. The Jack bean is also much in evidence at Huaca Prieta, where coprolites containing identifiable remains of beans, gourds, peppers and
sea-foods were also found. Furthermore, at a level representing 15, 16
approximately 1500 BC was found a skeleton in whose abdomen were the remains of a meal eaten probably two days before death. Analysis showed clearly that the man's meal had consisted of vegetables (including the kidney or common bean), fruit and sea-food.

Mexico has furnished us with evidence of a similar kind, this
time in caves dating back to 7000 BC. In the oldest cave, the refuse 15
from the floor contained a certain amount of vegetable matter—including beans; but as yet, the coprolites found there have not revealed bean contents. However, in more recent levels (about 4000–2300 BC), beans are still found in the floor refuse and this time coprolite analysis showed remains of the kidney bean.

Finally, mention may be made of the soy bean; the many different names given to it in the Orient and also its many varieties and uses show it to have been in use for a long time. Not only is it eaten as a vegetable but, having a high oil content, butter oil and cheese of a kind can be prepared from it. It is still to be found growing wild in China. There is a reference to the soy bean in Chinese literature which takes its history back at least as far as 2800 BC.

ROOTS AND TUBERS

ONION, LEEK, GARLIC

The praises of the onion have been sung throughout historic time, except perhaps in India where onions and garlic were never really regarded as quite respectable. This aromatic vegetable must surely have been equally attractive to prehistoric peoples. The Turks have an old story which places the onion and garlic right at the beginning of time; it relates that when the Devil was sent out of Paradise and first set foot on earth, on the spot where he placed his right foot there grew the onion and in the place of the left sprang up garlic!

However far back one searches in available historical records, the onion is already well known. In Egypt, according to various Roman writers, the onion was regarded as a deity. Pliny makes this apply to garlic as well and says they were both sworn-by when oaths were taken; but the use of garlic in Egypt is in doubt, as archaeology has revealed neither inscriptions nor actual finds relating to it. Juvenal in his *Satires* mocks at Egypt as a country where 'onions are adored and leeks are gods'.

The onion was indeed of major importance there, and, eaten with bread, formed the basis of the Egyptian every-day diet. The priests did not eat it but it appears on the altars of the gods, as is shown both in reliefs, and in actual finds from Hawara. In details of funerary offerings in Old Kingdom chapels bread heads the list, followed by baskets of onions, and Herodotus records that it was on a diet of 'radishes, onions and leeks' that the labourers built the Great Pyramid. Leeks do not appear in inscriptions but some are said to have been recognized amongst Egyptian funerary offerings; Pliny, for his part, declared that the finest leeks of his day came from Egypt.

Bread and onions also formed the basic diet of the people of Mesopotamia. Here again the onion was regarded as a peasant food. Accounts dating from the Third Dynasty of Ur (early second millennium BC) state that on one day each month various persons received a ration of about a 'gallon' of bread and some onions. They were usually eaten raw with bread and were sold in strings. Gardens in fertile Mesopotamia flourished, and onions leeks and garlic were amongst the most frequently cultivated plants. They were grown in the gardens of King Merodach-Baladan II of Babylon, and Ur-Nammu of Ur (2100 BC) records that by constructing a temple to Nannar he saved his garden, wherein grew onions and leeks.

Archaeological surveys have not as yet brought to light any material proof of this type of vegetable in Greece, although linguistic evidence suggests that leeks and garlic go back to at least the Early Bronze Age. Theophrastus (*c.* 372–*c.* 287 BC) was acquainted with a number of varieties of onion and garlic and both were undoubtedly used particularly in sauces and dressings to which the Greeks were very partial with their meat, fish and game. One particular kind of garlic was the Cyprian, and this was not cooked but used as a dressing for salads. 'When pounded,' says Theophrastus, 'it makes a foaming dressing,' obviously comparable with the 'aioli' of modern France.

Unlike the Greeks, the Romans did not favour garlic. Apicius mentions it only twice, and even then recommends only small quantities which would barely be noticed. Nor does he give a prominent place to the onion. Although it occurs in many dressings and as an accompaniment to meat, it is not mentioned as a vegetable in its own right. This suggests that here again one is faced with class differences in taste, as onions were in fact very widely grown in Italy. Pliny gives a number of varieties in order of pungency, the African ones first, followed by those from Gaul, Tusculum, Ascalon and Amiternae, and he recommends storing them in chaff. Pompeii was also noted for its onions, which Columella recommends should be preserved, after being first dried, then pickled in vinegar and brine. Horace puts the onion in a key position in his 'economical diet', so it would seem that here as in Mesopotamia and Egypt, onions were poor man's fare along with the pulses.

Leeks, however, were not. The Emperor Nero himself ate quantities of leeks to keep his voice in trim, and thus earned himself the nickname 'porrophagus'. They were used in many ways: the green part as a salad, the bulb cooked as a vegetable, and as a seasoning. Apicius gives four recipes for leeks as a vegetable on their own, so they were obviously appreciated by rich and poor alike.

A very important group of vegetables are the root crops. Their present-day cultivation is undoubtedly a very much diminished relic of the use formerly made of roots. Many may well have passed into oblivion without leaving even a trace; we know of others that have gradually disappeared, ousted by those which flourished in developing market gardens; nevertheless a number still used regularly in our own kitchens and all over the world have been grown and eaten from remotest times.

RADISH

The radish is a very long-established plant and has been cultivated all over the Old World as far as China and Japan. It is of such antiquity and so many varieties have been established from the Mediterranean to the Orient, that its true origin is very obscure. We do know, however, that it was formerly grown to a very large size, intended as a food and not just a mere salad decoration or hors d'oeuvre. The leaves also might well have been eaten as greens.

The Greeks knew the radish well and Theophrastus lists five varieties, declaring the Boeotian kind to be the best and sweetest. Pliny confirms the popularity of the radish in Italy and says that it was grown very widely there for its yield of oil from the seeds, but as a general food he considered it a 'vulgar article of diet', noting that radishes 'have a remarkable power of causing flatulence and eructation'.

TURNIP

Turnip varieties appear to be indigenous to the area between the Baltic Sea and the Caucasus, where they were presumably first eaten and later cultivated, subsequently spreading to Europe in general. At all events the cultivation of the turnip is older than recorded history and because of its excellent storing qualities, it must have been a good stand-by for the winter months, both for a man and cattle. The Greek and Roman writers leave us in no doubt that it was a food for the poorer classes and country folk. Theophrastus notes several varieties and Pliny and Columella both speak of two roots, *rapa* and *napus*, but the terms seem to be interchangeable and identification is not easy as they are almost always referred to together. Columella points out that they are a filling food for country people and therefore must not be overlooked; he also gives a recipe for pickling them. Apicius recommends preserving them with myrtle berries in honey and vinegar. Pliny regards them as the third most important plant north of the Po, and confirms that the leaves of root crops were also eaten, but particularly interesting is his remark that turnip tops were enjoyed even more when they were yellow and half-dead!

SWEDE

The swede was a much later development, first used on the Continent in the seventeenth century.

CARROT

The carrot, unquestionably one of the most-used vegetables in the Western World today, has an obscure history, and certainly did not acquire much importance until quite a late date. It is indigenous in Europe and parts of Asia, and remains have been found in the Swiss prehistoric lake-dwellings. In its wild form it is somewhat thin and wiry, and one cannot imagine that it would have been eaten regularly in this form. It responds quickly to cultivation, however, with a great improvement in quality, and indeed it seems to have been known in cultivated form in the Mediterranean area for several centuries BC. It has been recognized as one of the plants in the garden of King Merodach-Baladan, but is placed among the scented herbs along with fennel, which suggests that the root was discounted. Pliny refers to a plant grown in Syria resembling a parsnip, called in Italy 'gallicam' and in Greece 'daucon'. It is mentioned only briefly by Columella, who talks of the 'field parsnip and the cultivated variety which bears the same name and which the Greeks call "staphylinos" (carrot)'. He gives no recipes for storing it, which suggests that it was not a very common vegetable. The mention of the same name for both carrot and parsnip is recalled in the recipes of Apicius for '*Caroetae seu pastinacae*', in one of which the carrots were fried and served with a dressing. They have only a brief mention, however, which supports the view that carrots were favoured by perhaps a small gourmet section of the community.

PARSNIP The carrot's close relative, the parsnip, is similarly surrounded
45, 90 by doubt and enigma. Remains of *Pastinaca sativa*, the wild parsnip, have been found at both ancient Glastonbury and the Swiss lake-dwelling sites, but one cannot say whether they were cultivated or merely gathered wild; the latter seems more likely. The parsnip is indigenous in the Mediterranean area and north-eastern Europe including the Caucasus; but since it, the carrot and another root called by the Romans 'siser' and translated by some as skirret have often been confused, it is very difficult to get a clear picture of exactly what use was made of these root vegetables. Columella mentions both a wild and a cultivated parsnip (*pastinaca*) and we learn from him that the unopened flowers of this plant were collected and stored as herbs. The more civilized early Mediterranean communities, then, knew about and cultivated roots of the parsnip type, but apparently did not think very highly of them. Some of the more northern European peoples may have prized them, however, since supplies were specially imported from Germany for the table of Tiberius. It must be remembered too that parsnips keep quite well and indeed improve by being left in the frozen ground—an added reason for their not being widely cultivated nor preserved, since they could be dug up wild whenever required.

POTATO To the native inhabitants of South America the potato was of
94 supreme importance; it was cultivated and developed by the populations of Chile and the Andes long before the discovery of America by Europeans. It is perhaps the climate of the area that caused the potato to be grown here alone, and not, for example,

Fig. 29 Peruvian pot (Proto-Chimú) representing the twin tubers of a potato

in the warmer maize-growing regions of Mexico, where, though wild species are to be found, the potato was not cultivated until after its introduction by post-Columbian explorers. Since maize will not grow at great heights, the potato along with one or two other of the hardier plants became the staple diet of the mountain-dwellers.

The long-standing importance of the potato in the New World *Fig. 29* is evidenced not only by pottery representations of it which go back at least as far as the second century AD, but also by botanical remains from archaeological sites; these show that the potato was cultivated during the early part of the Formative period of Peruvian agriculture which lasted from about 750 BC until the present era, actual potato specimens having been identified at the site of Chiripa. 105

Archaeology has also revealed prehistoric stories of *chuño or* dehydrated potato. The method of making this seems to have remained unchanged right up to the present, and this product is of great importance to the South-American Indians, as it forms the major item in their winter stores. To make it, they expose the potatoes by night to severe frost, then trample them to extract the juice and expose them to the sun and drying air throughout the day. The process lasts for four or five days. By a slight variation on the method they produce something called *tunta* or white *chuño*, which is made into flour.

Among the many varieties of potato that were being grown when the Europeans 'discovered' America was a frost-resistant variety; it was being cultivated by the Indians living at higher, colder levels. Whether they themselves intentionally developed this kind, which is a hybrid of two wild forms, is questionable, but they were astute enough to select it as being most suitable to their climatic conditions. Three other tubers, less appetizing than the potato, were also eaten, *oca, año* and *ulluco*, the *chuño*-making method being applied to the first two, possibly because it improved their bitter flavour.

SWEET POTATO

The sweet potato is widely grown in South America, in the West Indies and all over the Pacific area. Early trans-Pacific migration most likely caused it to be carried from its home in America by man, resulting in its widespread cultivation under its Peruvian name, *kumara*. Recent studies show it to have been cultivated in Peru during the Formative period of agriculture, and dried remains of it were found in the necropolis at Paracas
79 of about the same date. Columbus, on his arrival in the West Indies, found it very much in evidence. He was given the tubers which he likened to large radishes and also bread which he called *aje*-bread—*aje* or *axi* being the local name for the sweet potato. On Santo Tomé he was received by the king and given a feast at which three or four varieties were served.

MANIOC

At this same feast he also tasted *cassava* bread. If the sweet potato was a mainstay of the diet so also was and is cassava, particularly among the inhabitants of north-eastern South America. Flour is prepared from the manioc root by first shredding and soaking it to remove the toxic qualities, a technique probably already long-established by the time of the Spanish conquest. Indeed, what are believed to be traces of manioc have been detected in one of the levels of the Tamaulipas caves in Mexico dating from about 2300–1800 BC.

YAM

The removal of toxins is also necessary in the case of the yam, a valuable food in three major areas of the world. Different species have been both cultivated and gathered wild in Africa, South East Asia and the Atlantic drainage areas of South America, particularly the Guianas and the West Indies, since pre-European contact times. Even if we concede that Columbus got his botanical names confused, it seems possible that he did recognize the yam there. It has been suggested that the American yam came originally from Africa on the grounds that if people could sail between America and Polynesia, why not, following the Equatorial current, from Africa; a single find of one kind of yam in the 51
Marquesas Islands has in fact been declared a close relative to—if not identical with—the African variety, *Dioscorea cayenensis.*

These are probably the best known edible root plants today in the modern civilized world but there are countless other roots and bulbs which have been more or less popular at different times in different places. As already mentioned, the Egyptians set great store by the white lotus, not only using the seeds in confectionery but also frying, roasting or boiling the root. Papyrus root and stem was much appreciated for its sweetness. Part of the swollen bulb of the 'Barbary nut', the species *Iris sisyrinchium,* was eaten by various peoples of the Mediterranean area. The bulbs of American Aloe, rich in saccharine, were roasted by the Indians as a food. The natives of north-east America probably used what we now know as the Jerusalem artichoke. Refuse from pre-pottery levels at Huaca Prieta showed remains of the rhizomes of the *Canna* lily, cat's-tail, rushes and sedge.

Greeks and Romans seem to have eaten a number of bulbs or roots including the taro or *Colocasia* (which is also used in the Pacific Islands and South East Asia). Theophrastus and Pliny both mention squill and asphodel: Pliny recommends cooking squill in honey, and both refer to 'Epimenide's squill' as the best variety for eating; the Romans also made squill vinegar. Asphodel to the Greeks was a major article of every-day diet. Hesiod speaks of 'Fools . . . who know not what advantage there is in mallow and asphodel', this being evidently a poor man's frugal meal. Theophrastus says the stalk was fried, the seed roasted, and the root in particular cut up and eaten with figs. The gladiolus is stated by both him and Pliny to make bread more wholesome if boiled and pounded and added to flour. The Greeks and Romans also probably consumed the roots of pursetassels, rampion, salsify, madder and elecampane. The last-named is described by Pliny as being distasteful when eaten alone but quite good when mixed with sweet things. Columella, who sheds more light than most writers on the diet of the country people, gives three methods for preserving it, one being to cook it in vinegar, dry for three days, then store in *passum* or *defrutum* in a pitched jar.

Muscaria, Star of Bethlehem and the Spanish Oyster Plant have all been eaten with relish, and lily bulbs were especially popular in China and Japan. Alexanders or horse parsley seems to have been popular too; not only does Columella give a recipe for pickling it but Apicius gives several recipes for it including a cream of alexanders and a purée made from it. 'Scythian root' or licorice was also known as a thirst quencher.

Scirpus tubers were found at Çatal Hüyük, and in Neolithic Denmark bistort was eaten. This is yet another root which requires expert removal of toxins before it can be cooked and eaten.

Though not exactly a 'root', the water chestnut may perhaps be mentioned here. It grew wild over Northern and Central Europe and has been found in the Swiss prehistoric lake-dwellings. A quantity of specimens, mostly split open were found at a Finnish site of Late Stone Age date, suggesting an even wider use then than is common now. Pliny and Theophrastus both mention its use as a food.

GREEN VEGETABLES

Unfortunately archaeological excavation has revealed little concerning green vegetables and here again it is necessary to rely mostly on written records.

BEET

The beetroot as we know it today is a comparatively recent variety, propagated in Northern Europe in about the sixteenth century. Prior to that the plant was grown mainly for its leaves, hence its inclusion in this section.

Beet probably originated in the Mediterranean area, growing wild from there as far as the Caspian and Persia. Red beet and white chard (now the only one grown for its leaves) were both known to the ancients, but the leaves only were used for culinary purposes while the root was employed medicinally. Thus, what was called *beta* was in fact chard or leaf beet. Aristotle mentions red chard, while Theophrastus knew black (or dark green) and white, preferring the white. Pliny says it was made into a salad with lentils and beans and served with a dressing as for cabbages, but he does not recommend it to people with weak digestions.

Apicius, listing the ingredients for barley broth includes *beta* among the *viridia* or greens. It is said to have featured among the plants of the garden of King Merodach-Baladan of Babylon, but of the Roman horticulturists only Columella takes the trouble to give instructions about cultivating it.

CABBAGE

In Europe many different varieties of cabbage were developed though we cannot tell from the writings just which were eaten where. The cabbage of the Greeks and Romans was certainly one with a stalk and it is thought that the headed varieties were developed in more northern areas probably by Celtic people, for Celtic words can be traced in its names. The Mediterranean peoples probably ate types of kale and broccoli. Theophrastus mentions three kinds known to him, the curly-leaved, the smooth-leaved, and the wild cabbage. Cato refers to it just as *brassica* and *brassica erratica* (the wild variety); he is full of praise for its virtues as a medicine and gives a great many details as to its uses for promoting good health. He says it surpasses all other vegetables and can be eaten raw or cooked; if eaten raw he recommends dipping it in vinegar. Raw cabbage was well-known as a remedy for drunkenness and Cato suggests eating as much as possible with vinegar before a feast, and still more afterwards. However, the Romans seem to have been chiefly fond of what they called *cymae* and *cauliculi. Cauliculi* have been interpreted by some writers as Brussels sprouts but this is obviously incorrect, as Brussels sprouts were not known until about five hundred years ago. Pliny probably gives the best definition of them as growing in spring on cabbage stalks after the first sowing, and says they are very delicate and tender. He quotes five cabbage varieties including one from Aricinum with particularly tasty sprouts. He also gives a variety called *halmyridia* which grew on the sea coast a special mention. *Cymae* is generally taken to refer to sprouting broccoli and it was sold in bundles for no mean price, as can be gathered from Pliny who comments: 'Growing cabbages is also one of the ways to supply table luxuries.' Again one is conscious of the perennial class difference in eating habits, for after Cato there is little mention of the ordinary *brassica* and everything is centred upon the production of young tender shoots. Apicius does not once mention anything other than *cymas* or *cauliculos* and the impression is that plain cabbage was a country food or a poor man's dish. This is borne out by Juvenal's satire describing the differences between the food of the patron and that of his poor client—the patron has olives to garnish his excellent fish, the client finds cabbage is his 'nauseous dish'.

ASPARAGUS

Asparagus, as a vegetable, has a somewhat confused history. The very name is of Greek origin and implied originally all kinds of tender shoots picked and eaten whilst very young, no doubt a most welcome food after the winter months spent eating preserved vegetables. That one of these 'asparagus' shoots was no other than the sprouting broccoli just mentioned, is demonstrated by the fact that when this was introduced into England much later, it was known as 'Italian asparagus'. However, what we now know as asparagus grows wild in Europe, the Mediterranean area and Asia Minor and is thought to have been recognized in Egyptian representations and among funerary plants of some of the Memphite Dynasties.

Asparagus received much attention in Roman times. Pliny deplores the efforts spent at Ravenna on producing heads weighing three to the pound, when 'nature made asparagus grow wild for anyone to gather at random'. This of all plants, he says, needs the most delicate attention and Cato had already given full details of how to succeed in growing it. Nevertheless, some of the recipes of Apicius hint that at first the name, now applied to one expensive and highly cultivated vegetable, had its origins in a humbler context, for after two recipes for '*patina* of asparagus' he continues with a similar '*patina* of wild plants' and includes as possibilities *tamnis* (black bryony), *sinapi viridi* (mustard leaves), *cucumere* (cucumber) and *cauliculis* (cabbage shoots). Columella also includes asparagus in a long list of shoots and stalks for preserving in brine and vinegar; this contains, among others, sprouts and stalks of cabbage, butcher's-broom, white vine, charlock, and tender little stalks of fennel. Very many others were gathered too: gourd shoots, strawberry, rue, house-leek, and the wild-hop which even now is called in France 'wild asparagus'.

MUSTARD

Undoubtedly many leafy vegetables other than those of the cabbage family were eaten. Mustard was certainly used as a green vegetable. Pliny comments that it grew in Italy without sowing, which suggests that it was just gathered wild. Remains of what is
thought to be mustard were found at the Glastonbury 'lake- 90
village'. Dock and nettle leaves made dishes of greens too; Pliny considered the latter pleasing fare when gathered in the spring, and although it was undoubtedly a peasant dish, Apicius gives a recipe for a *patina* of nettles (a sort of purée) which sounds something like a dish of spinach with the addition of eggs. Mallow was a popular plant with the Greeks, and the Romans also ate it. Chervil was known to the ancients as a food and according to

Pliny the Syrians ate it both cooked and raw, whilst orach, practically unheard of today, was familiar to both the Greeks and Romans who called it *atriplex*; it also appears in Ancient Egyptian texts. Still more interesting is the actual recovery of orach seeds among others from the intestinal area of the Early Bronze Age
109 skeleton found at Walton-on-the-Naze. They also feature among the finds at ancient Glastonbury. Many other plants, today unheard-of as food, must have been used as greens. Who for instance in Britain would consider the hollyhock as a vegetable?
SEAWEED Yet its leaves feature in Egyptian cookery. In some coastal areas, great use has been and still is made of certain types of seaweed (a valuable source of iodine). The Japanese feature it among their delicacies, the native inhabitants of Chile enjoy a particular variety, whilst in Britain laver-bread is eaten. Lake algae were dried and made into cheesy-flavoured cakes by the Aztecs, and the North American Indians in particular found lichens of many kinds a valuable food source especially when times were hard.

SPINACH Spinach appears to be indigenous to the Persian area. It was quite unknown to the Greeks and Romans and did not make an appearance in Europe until about AD 1100, whilst the earliest mention of it seems to be a Chinese one stating that it was introduced into Nepal in AD 647.

ARTICHOKE The globe artichoke we eat today is a comparatively recent development. The early Mediterranean peoples ate a plant called the cardoon, a large thistle which they eventually cultivated especially for its young and tender leaf stalks. The earliest known mention of the plant comes from Hesiod who merely comments on its flowering time but gives no indication of whether it was a food plant or not. The Romans used both the stalks (*cardui*) and the flower receptacles, which they called *sponduli* or *sphondyli*, and according to records the *cardui* were more expensive.

Pliny remarks rather ironically that thistles were forbidden to the lower classes, and says that he cannot speak of them without feeling ashamed at the high prices asked for certain types; 'we even turn the monstrosities of the earth to the purposes of gluttony', he comments, adding sarcastically that, by preserving them in honey and vinegar, there is no need for any day to go by without having thistles for dinner.

SALAD PLANTS

Almost any non-toxic green leaves with a palatable flavour could be made into salads but certain ones have no doubt always been preferred and therefore have come under more serious cultivation. The lettuce has undoubtedly been prized as a food from very early times. Most probably it grew wild all over temperate and southern Europe and in temperate East Asia before being brought into cultivation; but its history in China is more recent. It was grown in ancient Egypt and has been identified amongst funerary plants, its seeds have also been discovered among plant remains in some of the tombs. The fertility god Min had lettuce offered to him, probably because its milk was believed to possess aphrodisiac qualities. The Assyrians also believed in these properties, and the lettuce grew in the garden of King Merodach-Baladan of Babylon.

LETTUCE

In Greece the lettuce has long played a leading dietary role, being mentioned by Hippocrates and Aristotle, and later by Theophrastus, who lists four kinds known to him: the white variety, which was sweeter and tenderer, and then the flat-stalked, the round-stalked and the Laconian. Pliny tells us that the Greeks called the white lettuce 'poppy lettuce' because of its soporific white juice, and that formerly this was the only kind known in Italy where this 'milk' led to its being named *lactuca*. Lettuces, he says, are cooling and very pleasant to eat in summer, as well as being good for the stomach and for promoting an appetite. Columella leaves a record of how it was preserved: the leaves were stripped off and soaked in brine, this was then washed out and the lettuce pickled in vinegar and brine. He mentions a number of different varieties, but, as with the cabbage, all these were of the stalky kind, as hard-headed varieties were not developed until much later. Although lettuce was mostly eaten as a salad with a dressing, Apicius also gives a recipe for a purée of lettuce leaves and onions.

In Apicius too we find the instruction: 'Use endive in place of lettuce in winter with a dressing or with honey and strong vinegar.' The endive certainly tolerates the winter weather better than the lettuce, and frequently replaces it still today. Apicius calls the plant *intuba*, which suggests that it may have been the wild chicory or *Cichorium intybus*; this is a perennial which, as well as being cultivated, grows wild in most of Europe and in the Punjab, Kashmir, and Russia. It was no doubt gathered and eaten in all those places but there seems to be no clear evidence as to whether this or the garden chicories, *Cichorium endivia*, were the ones grown by the Greeks and Romans, the latter being less bitter than wild chicory though they are annuals. Pliny described chicory as being in a class of its own and bitter; there are also references to the peasants gathering dark and bitter chicory from the fields, so probably this was the variety cultivated also in the gardens and perhaps bleached to take away some of the bitterness.

Two other salad plants were chervil and purslane. Of the chervil nothing very much is known except that it was used, and Pliny mentions in particular the Syrians who both boiled it as a vegetable and ate it raw. Purslane on the other hand has been known and cultivated from very earliest times, having grown widespread as a wild plant. Traces of its Sanskrit name linger on in other languages, suggesting that it was perhaps transmitted from Asia to other parts of the world. Theophrastus listed it among his plants for 'summer-sowing' in April, and Columella recommended preserving it in a pot between layers of salt with vinegar poured over afterwards.

WATERCRESS

It is recorded that the Romans ate water-cress with vinegar to aid the cure of mental complaints, and it was certainly eaten, if not cultivated, before their time. Garden cress has a long history of cultivation, which is hardly surprising as it is so easy to grow. Its origins are thought to be in Persia; it is listed among Assyrian plants and Dioscorides states that it came from Babylon. It spread through Syria to Greece and to Egypt, where ancient cress seeds have been found. Cultivated in Greek gardens at the time of Theophrastus, it is also briefly mentioned by Pliny.

Other plants known to have been used, at least by early populations of the Mediterranean area, include dandelion, cat's-ear and groundsel. A basic salad recipe upon which Columella made other variations consisted of 'savory, mint, rue, coriander, parsley, chives or green onion, lettuce leaves, colewort, thyme or catmint and green flea-bane'.

CELERY

Celery seems to have started its career as a medicinal herb. It was still mentioned as such when grown in the sixteenth-century gardens of Italy. Theophrastus mentions it as a garden plant and Pliny distinguishes between the wild and cultivated forms. It was probably grown largely as a flavouring, as the recipes of Apicius also suggest. Identified among Egyptian funerary offerings, celery probably had its origins in the Mediterranean area.

TOMATO

Perhaps the only plant of American origin used widely as a salad plant today is the tomato; strictly speaking this, of course, is a fruit, but it is very rarely used as such. The name is of Mexican Indian origin but studies of Mexican cave remains as far back as 7000 BC have as yet produced no trace of it. Its country of origin, Peru, has little to offer, there being no remains from excavations though at least one pot depicting tree tomatoes exists, dated to *c.* 500 BC. One possible reason for its lack of popularity was that it did not keep well; the early inhabitants could preserve their potatoes and their beans, as well as their gourds, but tomatoes soon perish. So perhaps these were simply gathered when in season and no real cultivation was attempted. In the United States, the tomato was grown as an ornamental plant, but for a long time it was believed to be poisonous, so that it was being eaten in Europe much sooner than in North America, where it was not cultivated to any extent until after the Declaration of Independence!

CUCUMBER Of far greater antiquity is the use of the cucumber. It was cultivated very early in Asia and Europe, being known in Sanskrit as *soukasa*, and has been grown in India for at least 3,000 years. Its transmission westwards was fairly rapid but it appears not to have been used in China until the second century BC. Some doubts have been cast on the accuracy of the translation where in the Old Testament, the Israelites are stated to have longed for the food of Egypt including their cucumbers. None the less, it seems fairly certain that they would have eaten the cucumber there, for it was growing round the shores of Lake Karun when the pyramids were being built and remains of it have been found in the Faiyum from the Twelfth Dynasty and until Graeco-Roman times. The cucumber was much cultivated in Egypt in Pliny's day and known in Early Mesopotamia far earlier, being recorded as growing in the garden of Ur-Nammu at Ur (*c.* 2100 BC).

The Greeks of Theophrastus's day knew of three kinds of cucumber, of which, as in the case of lettuce, the Laconian variety was deemed the best. In early Rome, cucumbers were eaten either cooked or raw, peeled or with the skin left on. Apicius cooked them with brains, cumin, honey, celery seed, *liquamen* and oil, or made a *patina* of them. He also served them as a salad with *liquamen* or *oenogarum* or with a dressing composed of pepper, pennyroyal, honey or *passum, liquamen* and vinegar. The Emperor Tiberius was particularly fond of them, and so that he could have them every day, they were grown in movable frames, a method described by both Pliny and Columella.

GOURDS, MELONS AND SQUASHES

80 The cucumber is of course a member of the genus *Cucumis* and this comes within the family *Cucurbitaceae* which contains about 90 genera and 750 species, the three most well-known genera

probably being *Citrullus* (including the water melon), *Cucumis* (including the melon and cucumber), and *Cucurbita* (including marrows and squashes). The *Cucurbitaceae* are spread all over the world with different genera originating in different places and there is a great deal of confusion as to which ones were known to the Greeks and Romans, the translators of whose works refer to them as melons, pumpkins, marrows, gourds, but offer few clues as to what these really were. The *Lagenaria* or bottle gourd was a great puzzle formerly as it occurs wild in both the Old World and the New and appears to have been indigenous in both places. Columbus found it much in evidence when he first visited the West Indies, and remains of it have also been identified from Mexican deposits as early as 7000 BC. It also seems to have been cultivated by the Peruvians from about 5000 to 3000 BC. In East Africa, archaeological gourd finds from Njoro Cave date back to 850 BC; indeed some botanists now regard Africa as the original home of the bottle gourd.

There are contradictory views concerning the ability of the
gourd to withstand long spells in salt water and then to plant 51
itself on a foreign shore. Some experiments are declared to have 52
proved this possible, other botanists cast doubt upon it as the 74
gourd is not basically a shore-living plant, and also because of the action of crustaceans which bore into floating debris and eat the contents. Nevertheless the theory that it floated from Africa has been accepted by some, whilst others believe the gourd may well have been taken there on a craft by man (as perhaps was the yam, which could not have floated), following the same route it would have taken if carried by the currents (see p. 115).

There is little archaeological evidence of this gourd in the Old World though the Sanskrit name for it suggests its use in prehistoric India. Calabashes were found in Twelfth-Dynasty Egyptian tombs, and their use as bottles or containers both for wine and toilet waters was known to early Greek and Roman writers including Theophrastus and Pliny, who says that both the flesh and the stalk were eaten, and that in order to reach the flesh the rind had first to be scraped off. Calabashes could also be preserved in brine like cucumbers or kept green in shady trenches floored with sand and covered with dry hay and earth. Theophrastus and Pliny both described the bottle gourd, but clear identification is by no means easy for the other *cucurbitae* they discuss. For instance, Pliny also knew of a 'big cucumber' which has been translated as a pumpkin, and Columella, having mentioned the April sowing of the 'gourds with the delicate necks' (*Lagenaria*?), goes on to say that they could be grown large for vessels, like the 'Alexandrian gourd' but when grown for eating they must be longer and narrower, and that these latter certainly fetched a better price. What was this 'Alexandrian gourd' and how many varieties are concerned here? Columella says that growing them for jars or for eating is merely a question of selecting a seed from a certain part of the gourd and planting it a certain way up; for instance, for the edible gourd, one chooses a seed from the neck of a gourd and sows it top-upright in order to make it grow longer and narrower.

Apicius gives many recipes containing *cucurbitas* which are generally translated as marrows, indeed his 'stuffed marrow' would be quite acceptable today. Under the general heading *cucurbitas* he includes one recipe 'in the Alexandrian manner', which suggests that Alexandria was well known for its gourds. However, Apicius also refers twice to something which he calls a *citrium*, evidently a large gourd of some kind but which he differentiated from *cucurbitas*.

While on the subject of large gourds, it may be worth recalling the problematical Hawaiian *ipu nui* which is now extinct. Captain Cook, finding it on Hawaii, declared the gourd to hold 10 to 12 gallons; it was ultimately identified as a relation of the *Lagenaria*. Peruvian archaeology has also revealed remains of very large gourds of a similar nature which were centuries older than Hawaiian agriculture.

In Pliny's time a new plant was developed or introduced in Campania which Pliny calls the *melopepo*; it was, he says, round and golden and did not hang down like cucumbers but trailed along the ground, detaching itself from the stem when it reached maturity. He states that it was developed first by accident, and then seeds from it were taken and planted to propagate more. It sounds very much like a form of melon but again one cannot be certain, although half a melon in a painting from Herculaneum provides some supporting evidence. All one can say for sure is that various types known as *cucurbita, melopepo*, or *citrium* were known at that time in Rome, It is more than likely that the melon had spread to Greece and Rome by then, as it would undeniably have been a most desirable plant. It may well have been the same melon that was known to the Assyrians; indeed there are several carvings depicting Assyrian feasts where the tables display objects very similar to slices of melon. Ur-Nammu of Ur grew it in his garden in about 2100 BC. Other kinds of gourd were probably eaten in those parts too; the garden of King Merodach-Baladan contained 'gourds' and melons, and the Assyrian Herbal refers to the 'desert cucumber' (a species of *Citrullus*), the 'squirting cucumber', and melons.

cf. Fig. 32

The best known species of *Citrullus* is the water-melon which grows wild in large tracts of Africa and is an extremely important source of water in dry periods. Its cultivation is of very great antiquity as can be seen from its many and varied names in different languages. This was the melon for which the Israelites pined in their desert wanderings. It was widely cultivated in Ancient Egypt and its seeds and leaves have been found among funerary offerings in Egyptian tombs.

The genus *Cucurbita* seems to be about as confusing as that of the *Lagenaria*, for whilst many species may be counted definitely American in origin, it seems likely that one, the pumpkin (*Cucurbita maxima*) was already wild in Africa before European or American contact was made there, and indeed some of the

Fig. 30 Chimú pot in the form of Cucurbita moschata, *excluding the spout. (After Vargas)*

Greek and Roman references to *cucurbitas* would fit in well with this genus. Beyond a Sanskrit name, there is little archaeological proof of *curcurbits* having been used in the Old World, but there is plenty from the New. In fact, among the very early inhabitants of Peru and Mexico, gourds and squashes were of primary importance. There is evidence of both winter squashes of the
Fig. 30 *Cucurbita maxima* and *Cucurbita moschata* varieties and summer squashes of the *Cucurbita pepo* kind from very early times, and
15, 16 analysis of coprolites from the excavations at Huaca Prieta and in the caves of Tamaulipas shows much fibrous squash material from which we may conclude that it played a substantial role in their diet. Recent excavations have retrieved palethnobotanical remains which establish without doubt that *C. pepo* was being eaten in northern Mexico as early as 7000 BC, *C. mixta* in southern Mexico by 5000 BC, and that *C. moschata* was being used as a food by 3000 BC. In the United States, three of the species were being eaten at least by 1000 BC.

The nature of this large amount of plant tissue and the relative absence of mature seeds suggest that the squashes were eaten whole and immature. There is also a surprising lack of cucurbit 'pots' from excavations so far, which also suggests that the fruits were harvested before they had grown to full size. Hairs, like those found on all cucurbit plants especially when young, have also been identified from coprolites.

In addition to this, we know that food placed with Peruvian
mummies included pieces of cucurbit with shell, flesh and seeds
still intact. During the Peruvian Period of Incipient Agriculture
(2500–500 BC) *C. moschata* and *C. ficifolia* were cultivated, and 105
continued to be throughout the Formative Period. By the Classic
Period however (*c.* AD 1–1000) *C. ficifolia* had ceased to be
cultivated and its place had been taken by *C. maxima.* Chimú
pottery plant representations include several forms of *C. moschata.*

CHAPTER VIII

Fruit and Nuts

ONE UNAVOIDABLE FEATURE of a broad review of this kind on early foods, is that the evidence varies considerably in its form and extent. In the case of fruits and nuts, we have rather scattered archaeological evidence of actual plant remains, just sufficient to be tantalizing, and far more literary evidence. In this respect it contrasts with the data on cereals, where there is considerably more information on actual plant remains.

BERRY AND TREE FRUITS

On the whole, berries are very palatable, easy to pick and no trouble to prepare, and these wild harvests were almost certainly collected with undiminished vigour throughout pre-agricultural times and into the agricultural phase of human culture, providing fresh food in season and dried stores for winter. They began to be cultivated later than other plants, however, probably because initial concentration would be on plants with a higher yield and better storing qualities.

The very earliest evidence of berry-picking concerns the hackberry. This fruit now grows in North America and Asia and was still used in recent times by the Indians of south-western North America, who sometimes treated it as they would a cherry, discarding the stone, or more often cracked open the stone shell
18 to reach the seed, which they used to flavour meat or bread. The
Plate 46 Choukoutien site revealed that the Chinese variety of *Homo erectus* ('Peking Man') also made much use of these berries, for a layer of broken shells several inches thick was found there. Indeed, it rather looks as if this Middle Pleistocene man may have broken the stone casing for much the same reason as the American Indian. The Ancient Egyptians also made use of fresh berries; a

dish of 'nabk' berries (similar to a cherry) was included in a 33 Second Dynasty funerary offering from Saqqara. Excavations at Plates 48, 49 the Neolithic Swiss and Iron Age Glastonbury lake-sites brought Plate 54 to light further quantities of seeds from berry fruits including those of the service berry, raspberry, blackberry, dog-rose, common and dwarf elder, cornel cherry, strawberry, wayfaring tree, hawthorn, bittersweet and dewberry. The strawberry was the rarest, but berries from the wayfaring tree occurred at more than one site.

A Danish Mesolithic site of the Mullerup culture revealed that raspberries, hips, haws, rowan, strawberries, blackberries, currants and bilberries had been gathered. The last-named, in rather more numerous species, featured also as an article of North American Indian diet. 116

Early written works scarcely refer to what were undoubtedly peasant fruits gathered wild, and archaeological discoveries are few. We do know that the mulberry grew in Mesopotamia, where seeds of this fruit have been excavated; it has also been found in early Egyptian tombs. It was introduced into ancient Greece, but into Italy only after Varro's day, since he makes no mention of it; there it was eaten either fresh or as a sweetmeat. Pliny knew several varieties and also mentions briefly a 'similar but firmer berry growing on brambles'. We also find references to brambles in Homer, but these were probably wild plants. The strawberry is dismissed by Pliny, who says he knew two kinds that grew on the ground or on a tree, but that their flavour was not particularly exciting. The myrtle berry was fairly widely known and cultivated but one gets the impression that it was not used so much as a fruit as for wine-making, or for flavouring. From Theophrastus we learn that yew-berries were eaten by some people and that they were 'sweet and harmless'. Columella mentions the use of cornel-cherries in place of olives but this was no doubt a peasant alternative and unlikely to have been acceptable in richer households.

The fact that orchard husbandry began so early in the Near East, probably between 4000 and 3000 BC, can be attributed to the number of tree-fruits indigenous in that area, and also to the climate in which such fruits thrived and yielded good returns for the efforts spent in cultivating them. However, their cultivation did not spread very quickly westwards, so that the growing of apples, pears, plums, cherries and apricots in Europe is comparatively recent. As the Mesopotamians were so concerned with the laying-out of fine parks and orchards, it is very difficult to understand why Herodotus remarks that Assyria is the richest grain-growing country in the world but makes no attempt to grow figs, grapes, olives or *any other fruit trees,* and talks only of the date. Texts of Urukagina of Lagash, who was overthrown in 2400 BC, reveal that here it was not only the rich who had their orchards, for one of his reforms states that a 'priest may no longer go into the garden of a villein and fell a tree or take away the fruits'.

APPLE

Of the tree fruits, the apple is known to have been widely cultivated from an early date. The wild varieties were also much in demand by early peoples, carbonized apples from about 6500 BC having been found at Çatal Hüyük in Anatolia. The Swiss prehistoric lake-dwellings revealed not only large quantities of sour crabs which seem to have been a very important food at the time, but also larger ones which appear to have been of a cultivated variety. These were mainly cut into two pieces, which suggests that they were dried, while the smaller ones were left whole. From Britain, the imprint of an apple-pip on a Neolithic sherd from Windmill Hill suggests that apples were used in this country too. The apple seems to be indigenous mainly in an area extending through Anatolia to parts of Persia, and we know that the Hittites cultivated apple-trees at an early date. Apples were grown in Mesopotamia, and in Egypt; Ramesses II (thirteenth century BC) had apple-trees planted in gardens laid out in the Nile delta and Ramesses III gave baskets of apples as daily offerings to the Theban priests. From Greece we have no archaeological evidence to show how early they were used, but the classical writers make it clear that by Homeric times orchard husbandry and gardening

Plate 53

were well-established. Theophrastus knew two apple varieties, and from then on the number rapidly increased in the Mediterranean area as interest in fruit cultivation and methods of grafting developed, until by Pliny's time about thirty-six kinds of apple were known, and certain long-keeping ones selected for storing.

PEAR

The pear does not appear to have enjoyed the same amount of popularity in ancient times. Remains of wild pear have been found in Mesolithic middens, but at the Swiss prehistoric lake-sites only a few examples have been found. This is perhaps due to its taste, for whilst cooking fairly soon renders hard sour apples edible especially if sweetened, hard sour pears do not respond so readily to this treatment. The wild pear is found all over temperate Europe but, like the apple, principally in the area from Anatolia to northern Persia, and here once again the Hittites seem to have brought it into cultivation in their orchards. There is no evidence of the pear in Assyria, and the Chinese claim the credit for its introduction into India in the first century AD. It was brought to Egypt fairly late by the Greeks. Excavations at Dimini (Early Helladic) yielded wild pear specimens, and it was certainly an orchard fruit by Homeric times. Once cultivated by the Greeks and Romans, varieties rapidly increased; Cato names five and says there were many others, whilst Columella declares them too numerous to catalogue. The fruits were dried, stored in must, made into a conserve with boiled-down wine and water, as well as being eaten fresh.

QUINCE

The quince, a sour fruit, is similar to the apple and in the past was sometimes referred to as a 'golden apple'. In its wild state it is found in Persia, near the Caspian, in the Caucasus and Anatolia. The earliest evidence of its cultivation is in Mesopotamia and after this, mention of it is made by the Greeks. Pliny states that the tree was brought into Italy from Kydron in Crete and mentions particularly the Mulvian quince which he says is the only one which can be eaten raw. It must have been introduced some time before 220 BC, for Cato already knew of it.

Columella refers to three varieties of the Cydonian quince, the 'sparrow-apple', 'golden-apple' and 'must-apple', and classes the Cydonian quince itself among the apples. Quinces were preserved in various ways and a sort of quince jam was made, but Columella thought the best way of all to keep them was to place them in a wide-necked flagon, cover with willow-twigs and then to fill up with the best and most fluid honey. The liquid resulting from this process, known as *melomeli*, was considered especially good for invalids.

POMEGRANATE The pomegranate has also been classed as an apple in its time. The Romans called it *malum punicum*, the Punic apple, which indicates its transmission to Italy via Carthage, although its original home seems to be the regions of Asia Minor, the Caucasus, Armenia and Persia. The existence of a Sanskrit name indicates an early cultivation in North India.

17 The Assyrians thought highly of the pomegranate and it figures on many of their monuments; the Assyrian Herbal indicates that two kinds were known, the bitter and the sweet. It was common in Hittite orchards and popular in Persia. In Egypt the pomegranate does not appear until the New Kingdom, its introduction probably being an indirect result of the empire-building Syrian campaigns of Tuthmosis I and III. The funerary garden of Ani, a scribe who died at the time of Tuthmosis I (sixteenth century BC) contained five pomegranate trees, and they feature in representations in the tomb of Akhenaten as well as in the gardens of Ramesses II. It seems that once introduced they soon became established and accepted as regular orchard plants. Strings of pomegranates can be seen in many pictures on tomb walls depicting funerary offerings.

Pomegranates were well-known in Palestine of Old Testament times and carbonized fruits were found in one of the tombs of Bronze Age Jericho. In Italy this was probably not amongst the first fruits cultivated, but Cato mentions it and Pliny knew nine varieties. Columella describes numerous ways of preserving pomegranates for the winter; one method recommended was to tie them together with a rush, put them into hot sea-water until they discoloured and then dry them for three days in the sun. To use them, they were to be soaked in cold, fresh water overnight.

MEDLAR

The medlar, another native of Persia, was also cultivated by the Assyrians. It came early to Greece and Theophrastus mentions three varieties, but we know nothing about its use, and it was not grown early in Italy.

PLUM

Most of the well-known soft tree-fruits are related and come under the generic term *Prunus*. Nowadays we have countless varieties of plum, but this proliferation seems to be a comparatively recent development. The wild or common plum (*P. Domestica*) and the bullace (*P. institia*) appear to be indigenous to regions of Anatolia, the Caucasus and northern Persia, so it seems reasonable to assume that the first cultivated plums were to be found in that area. Stones of the bullace were found at the Swiss prehistoric lake-sites, so they must have formed a useful part of the lake-dwellers' diet. Sloe stones also appear there, but as sloes are very sour when raw, one can only assume that they were cooked and sweetened in some way, used with other fruit or, more probably, they were used in wine-making. Plums were grown in orchard-loving Mesopotamia and the Assyrian Herbal recommends eating them alone with honey and butter.

The Greeks knew the plum and it was also grown in Italy, where, although the varieties appear to be few, it seems that much experimentation was carried out on it: 'No other tree has been so ingeniously crossed,' writes Pliny. Indeed grafting greatly preoccupied Roman horticulturists, for Virgil even speaks of grafting 'nuts on an arbutus, apples on a plane, and cherries on an elm'! As usual the fruit was eaten fresh in season, (very few recipes for cooked fruit dishes are known), but it was preserved for the winter often in vinegar and *sapa* or *defrutum*. The only plum occurring in Apicius' book is the *Damascena* or damson which is an ingredient for a number of sauces.

CHERRY

Cherries have a long history, but which kinds were grown where and when is rather difficult to decide as both the bird cherry (*P. avium*) and cherry (*P. cerasus*) appear to be indigenous to the same region, in Anatolia, though the bird cherry is more common. The Danes of the Mesolithic Period used some kind of cherry and the Swiss prehistoric lake-dwellers certainly used bird cherries to a considerable extent. The Mesopotamian orchards again seem to have been the first home of cultivated cherries. Sargon II (722–705 BC) of Assyria liked their sweet fragrance and the Akkadian name *karshu* has survived into European languages as Greek *kerasos* and German *Kirsche*. Herodotus mentions a cherry from a tree called *ponticum*, and says it was the staple diet of a Scythian race called the *Argippaei* who lived each man beneath his own *ponticum* tree, and protected the trees from winter frosts by binding thick white felt around them. The fruit, he states, was strained to form a thick juice called *aschy*, which they drank, and the sediment was formed into cakes. It may be this variety to which Pliny was referring when he made the rather curious statement that the cherry was unknown until Lucullus brought it back from Pontus after the war against Mithridates (74 BC). It is most unlikely that no kind of cherry was known by then in Italy but this Pontic cherry may have been a rather special one, worthy of introduction, as Herodotus' description suggests.

APRICOT

Although in China, which is thought to be its native land, the apricot was probably cultivated as early as 2200 BC, it seems to have been very slow in spreading. Its progress westwards must have been via Persia and Asia Minor, and we know it was grown by the Assyrians and Babylonians, who called it *armanu*. The Latin term for it, *armeniaca*, has always been understood to imply an Armenian origin but it is more likely that it was first grown in the orchards of Mesopotamia, its name having been subsequently adopted into the language of other countries to which it spread. Apart from the Mesopotamians, there is not much evidence of apricot-growing. The apricot was not known to Theophrastus in

Greece and apparently only reached Italy, where it was sold for exceedingly high prices, in AD 50. It was clearly not fare for the poorer Roman, which undoubtedly accounts for its being one of the few fruits given any particular attention by the gourmet chef Apicius. He incorporated apricots in a fricassée of shoulder of pork and also invented a special sweet fruit dish in which they were cooked in honey, *passum*, wine and vinegar; this, before being thickened, was flavoured with pepper, mint and a little *liquamen*.

PEACH

Like the apricot, the peach probably originated in the Orient where it was cultivated at least as early as the third millennium BC. Arriving in the Fertile Crescent, its cultivation was taken up by the Assyrians and Babylonians and it must have been from this region that the Greeks and Romans came to know of it, for they both call it the 'Persian fruit'. Its introduction into Italy took place during the first century AD, for Pliny tells us it had only just begun to be cultivated there and not without difficulty. Introduction into India took place about the same time, though directly from China. Being exotic fruits, they are accorded a recipe by Apicius, who made a *patina* of them and served them with cumin sauce.

JUJUBE

Another plant seemingly of Chinese origin is the jujube which probably spread into western Asia round about the first millennium BC, though by this time three varieties were already known in India. It was quite probably grown in Assyrian orchards and is stated by Pliny to have been brought to Rome from Syria in the reign of Augustus. The lotus jujube (*Zizyphus lotus*) is the fruit of the lotus-eaters of Libya who are well-known from accounts by Homer, Herodotus, Theophrastus and Pliny. The plant is also known as the African date palm and grows wild in the Libyan region of the Mediterranean. Herodotus comments on the similarity in flavour to the date, and all who mention it say that the 'lotophagi' lived exclusively on the fruit and also made a drink from it.

CAROB The word for 'sweetness' in Egypt is generally associated with the carob or locust bean but apart from seeds and pods found there in tombs as early as the Twelfth Dynasty there is little we can learn about its use. It is thought to have grown wild on the coasts of Syria and Anatolia but there is not much information about its culinary use there either. It is not mentioned in the Old Testament and the locust that St John lived on in the desert, traditionally now implying the carob and giving it the name 'St John's Bread', was probably not a fruit at all but the insect. It does not seem to have been grown in early Greece though Theophrastus does mention it, saying that it was called by some people the 'Egyptian fig'. This name according to Pliny signifies the sycamore fig, which is far more likely, but Columella is the first to talk of growing the carob. It was eaten by the Romans green and fresh, when its taste was sweet; when dried, Pliny says, it should be soaked in water for several days before use.

BANANA The evolution and spread of the banana has recently been
99 discussed in detail by N. W. Simmonds, but although much is now known of the taxonomy, genetics and more recent origins of this fruit, its early domestication is still rather questionable. The wild banana is somewhat unattractive, seedy, and inedible, and has been changed by man from this jungle weed into a large seedless fruit. The wild plants are distributed in tropical Asia and Australasia (with 'outliers' in some Pacific islands), and certainly this area is the cradle of banana domestication. However, the story is not simply one of deliberate selection for larger and larger fruit, and Simmonds has pointed out that in fact the plant may well at first have been cultivated for other reasons. In particular, the sheaths yield valuable fibres, the leaves are useful wrapping materials, and from the point of view of food, the soft inner sheaths, the male buds and flowers, and the immature fruits can all be eaten as vegetables (and still are in South East Asia today). Thus, fruit improvements probably followed long after the plant was cultivated for these other reasons.

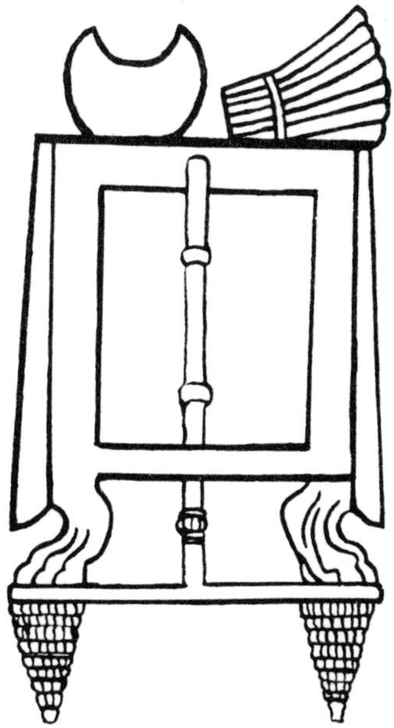

Fig. 31 Dining table with melon (?) and bananas. From an Assyrian banquet scene

Literary and archaeological evidence for the banana is scattered
and as yet very sparse. In India, it is not noted before 600 BC,
although linguistic studies trace its use back possibly to pre-3000
BC. The early African cultivars (cultivatable plants) probably
reached Madagascar from Malaysia late in the first half of the first
millennium AD, and thence spread westwards through Africa.
Possibly many of the Pacific islands were cultivating the banana
by about AD 1000. Claims of a considerable antiquity for the
plant, in two widely separated regions of the world, are still open
to debate. In one or two Assyrian carvings, representing royal 11
banquets, banana-like fruits are depicted. As texts make no *Fig. 31*
mention of the fruit, we only have the art evidence at present, but
it would not be unreasonable to postulate a very early introduction
from India, perhaps by traders wishing to provide special variety
at the royal table.

51 The other instance concerns pre-Columbian America, where it is claimed banana remains were found in early Peruvian tombs. This claim would seem to deserve careful investigation, and if substantiated, would give added weight to early trans-Pacific human movements.

CITRUS FRUITS

58, 83, 104 The citrus fruits were among the later varieties to come into general use in Europe though in some Asian countries they have been known for at least three or four millennia.

Oranges, for instance, were cultivated in China for many centuries before they were known elsewhere. They are mentioned along with grapefruits in a compilation of texts, edited about AD 500, some of which are believed to date back as far as 2400 BC. Another compilation includes the State Ceremonial of the Chou Dynasty (1122–249 BC) in which orange-growing is also mentioned. By the twelfth century AD there was an extensive literature on orange cultivation, one treatise dealing specifically with mandarin oranges. That cultivation remained peculiar to China for a long time is suggested by a gift of oranges to Burma in the third century AD, and in the first century AD they feature among new fruits to come to India.

India had its own citrus fruits, though there is some linguistic confusion about their exact nature. Sanskrit names exist for both lemons and limes, suggesting prehistoric use and an ear-ring of this shape was found at the Indus Valley site of Mohenjo-daro. Oranges and lemons made their first appearance in Europe about the beginning of the present era—they feature in frescoes and
Plate 51 mosaics found at Pompeii—but probably only as exotic fruits brought back by traders who were then developing new and faster trade routes to and from India. By the fourth century AD Roman frescoes depict lemons growing on trees, but there is no actual written evidence of their successful cultivation.

Fig. 32 Stone slab from an early synagogue in Priene, Asia Minor, showing citron to the left of the candelabra. (After Isaac)

The history of the citron is not easy to trace. There are a few Sanskrit words said to refer to varieties of citron, including a sweet one, but South Arabia has also been suggested as the original place of citron diffusion; indeed, in later Indian texts a new word for the citron appears, which has Arabic affinities. Certainly an Arabic citron would account for the fact that it progressed, unaccompanied by Indian limes and lemons, to Mesopotamia and Persia where the Greeks first encountered it, calling it the Median or Persian Apple. Seeds from what is probably the citron were found at ancient Nippur (4000 BC). Whatever its history and however it spread from its original home, it is a known fact that at their religious festivals the Jews cultivated the citron intensively, only the best fruits being used for their Feast of Tabernacles. If we add to this the medicinal powers that are attributed to the citron, it is scarcely surprising that of all the citrus fruits it was the best known to the early Greek and Roman writers. As the Jews dispersed throughout the Mediterranean, so

Fig. 32

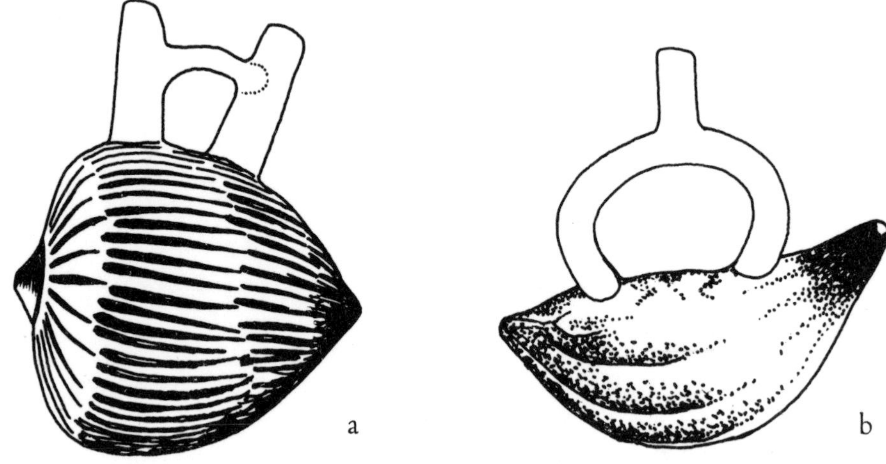

Fig. 33 a, Double-spouted Peruvian jar in the form of a lucuma *fruit. Nazca. (After Towle and Willey); b, Peruvian Nazca pot in the form of* papaya (Carica candicans). *(After Vargas)*

did citron cultivation, and this must have contributed greatly to the development of the Mediterranean citrus industry generally as the areas which now produce the most citrus fruit correspond very closely with the early Jewish settlements.

NEW WORLD FRUITS The fruits indigenous to the New World provided excellent food for early hunting and collecting peoples. The fruit of the prickly pear for instance ranked very high in the diet of the inhabitants of the Tamaulipas caves in Mexico, as early as 7000 BC, as the analysis of floor refuse and coprolites shows. Nor did it early diminish in importance; the prickly pear is thought to have been cultivated in the Peruvian Classic Epoch (first millennium AD), being frequently represented on Chimú and Nazca pots.
15 Another fruit which was equally important to these cave-dwellers is known so far only as 'golden ball fruit', from the appearance of the epidermis found in microscopic traces in coprolites.

The early agriculturists of Peru did not neglect fruit, for it is
105 probable that already during the Epoch of Incipient Agriculture
Fig. 33a (about 2500–750 BC), they cultivated the *lucuma* and *ciruela del fraile*. Archaeological remains show that they gathered wild the

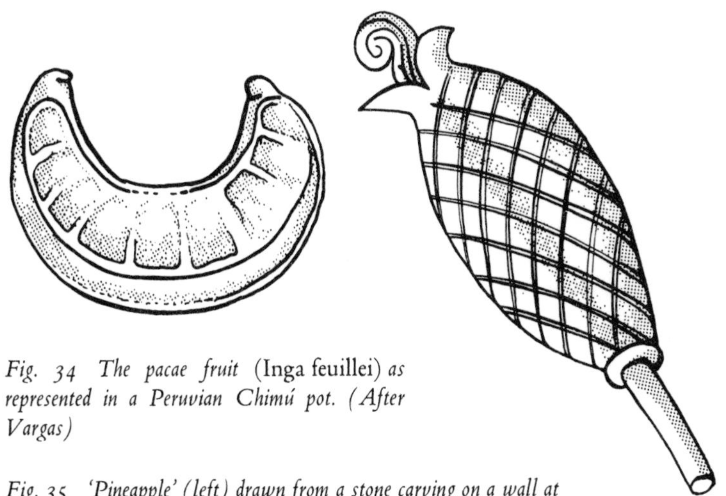

Fig. 34 The pacae fruit (Inga feuillei) *as represented in a Peruvian Chimú pot. (After Vargas)*

Fig. 35 'Pineapple' (left) drawn from a stone carving on a wall at Nineveh. (After G. Rawlinson)

algarroba, which, though strictly-speaking a legume, was eaten rather as a fruit for its sweet pulpy pods. The *lucuma* or 'star-apple' features often in Chimú and Nazca pottery as also does the *pacae*, grown for its sweet, white, fleshy seeds. This was probably first cultivated sometime during the Formative Period of Peruvian agriculture (occupying about the last seven and a half centuries BC) along with other fruits such as the *avocado, guava* and *caigua.* Finds of wild plum and *pepino* dating from the latter part of the Formative Period suggest that these two had then begun to be cultivated. The *pepino*, a succulent fruit, is still grown in coastal regions, and had certainly become a part of the early Peruvians' agriculture by the Classic Epoch, when considerably more varieties of fruit were probably cultivated, including the sweet sop, sour sop and papaw or *papaya,* (all of which are well represented in Chimú and Nazca pottery), the *algarroba, cherimoya, tumbo, granadilla* (these latter two of the *Passiflora* genus) and the pineapple.

Fig. 34

Fig. 33b

Of all these South American fruits the pineapple is the only one which has invaded the modern European markets to any great extent. First seen by Columbus in 1493, its initial home seems to have been Brazil. However, it was used and possibly cultivated in pre-Columbian Peru prior to AD 1000 and some have postulated its spread from there to Polynesia.

It is curious that this unquestionably New World fruit should have been the subject of controversy regarding its purported appearance in Old World artistic representations. First, there was talk of its having been recognized in an Egyptian tomb painting, but doubts were later cast upon this theory. Next, the fruit was believed to be depicted in a carving at Nineveh. Similarly, a
Fig. 35 'pineapple' has been identified in a Pompeian mural, and here again, although the pineapple was unknown in the Old World at that time, the resemblance is striking. At least one botanist has
74 admitted that the picture is certainly based on a pineapple, concluding that Roman traders must have brought it back from one of the Macronesian Islands with which they were possibly acquainted. All these assumptions are still very suspect, and for the present, it is best to consider the Old World appearance of the pineapple as comparatively recent.

DATES, FIGS, GRAPES

The date-palm which grew so abundantly in the Fertile Crescent, even during the early phases of cultural development in that area, was the mainstay of the inhabitants' diet. There is evidence also of its presence in earlier prehistoric times in warm dry places such as, for example, the Shanidar Cave locality in northern Iraq. Middle Palaeolithic layers excavated there show that it was flourishing during that period and it continued into Upper Palaeolithic times, though by the Mesolithic, climatic changes had made the environment unfavourable to the date-palm. Its tremendous value in Mesopotamia is well recorded in Assyrian and Babylonian monuments and texts. A text of Shu-Sin (*c.* 2050 BC) of the Third Dynasty at Ur mentions the yield from the large date plantations and a fresco from the palace of Mari (second millennium BC) shows the familiar method of climbing date-palms to pick the fruit. Herodotus found date-palms growing everywhere, providing the people with sugar, food and wine, in fact everything they needed.

In India, date-stones were found at Mohenjo-daro, and the date always remained among the most popular fruits.

Dates were also an important and commonly used food in Ancient Egypt. They were eaten fresh, dried, or pressed and formed into cakes. Their importance over all other fruits is clearly indicated by the list of fruit-trees for the funerary garden of the scribe Ani of the Eighteenth Dynasty; this included no fewer than 170 date-palms, which is almost twice the number of any other tree mentioned.

It is rather strange that the date, unlike the fig, is scarcely mentioned in the Old Testament. The only reference to it in the Old Testament is contained in a description of Jericho which is called the 'city of palm trees', and indeed the Jericho date was a well-known variety, renowned for its succulence even in later times. Greek and Roman writers knew the date well and it seems that unsuccessful attempts were made to grow it in Greece, but Theophrastus says it either did not bear fruit or the fruit would not ripen. Pliny discusses many varieties known to him and makes special mention of the *caryotae* which he says grew abundantly in Judea, especially around Jericho, and provided a great deal of food. The recipes of Apicius include dates in a great number of sauces to accompany meat and fish, and they were also stuffed as sweetmeats. Here again it is the succulent Jericho date which appears in the majority of recipes.

Figs also constituted a very important article of food in early Mesopotamia, Palestine, Egypt and Greece. Their daily use probably equalled that of the date and even exceeded it in places. Where the fig was first cultivated is not known, though in Egypt its cultivation seems to go back into prehistory. The Egyptians knew and used two kinds: the sycamore fig and the common fig, and of these the former seems to have been the most popular. As well as appearing in art representations, actual specimens have been found in many tombs, as funerary offerings, sometimes threaded on strings and sometimes entire baskets of them. A dish of what appeared to be stewed figs formed part of the Second-Dynasty funerary meal from Saqqara. Figs were both eaten fresh and dried for storing.

In Assyria too the fig was probably a staple item of the diet, although the evidence is unsatisfactory. Sargon of Akkad (*c.* 2400 BC) declared that he brought back figs from Anatolia, but these were probably only new varieties, as earlier texts of Urukagina of Lagash had already mentioned figs.

In Greece and Crete the fig was known from very early times, remains of Neolithic date having been found at Olynthus, and large quantities from the Late Bronze Age at Kakovatos (Pylos). On Crete, figs were found in the palace storerooms at Minoan Hagia Triada and they feature in paintings at Knossos.

In Rome figs were extremely popular with all classes; Pliny states that in their dried state they served the same purpose as bread and other foods, whilst according to Columella dried apples, pears and especially figs formed the major part of the winter food of country people. He suggests various ways of preserving them, one being to tread them, then mix with toasted sesame, anise, fennel-seed and cumin and wrap balls of this mixture in fig leaves. When dried these were then stored in jars. Figs were so important that they were not only cultivated but also imported from Caria, Syria and Africa. Apicius recommended them as an accompaniment to boiled or baked ham.

It was unquestionably man's universal interest in the production of stimulating drinks that led to the vast amount of effort he put into viticulture from late prehistoric times onward. However, wild grapes, which seem to be indigenous to Anatolia and the Caucasus, must have been collected as food along with other berries by the early food gatherers. Finds of grape-stones at the Swiss lake-sites show that they were certainly used by Bronze Age and Neolithic peoples in Europe, and in the New World grape-stones have been found which date back to about 1800 BC. The Indians made use of them, drying and storing them for winter eating.

Exactly when and where man embarked on viticulture is not clear. The Hittites cultivated the grape very extensively, though probably chiefly for wine-production as is the case with other vine-growing countries, such as Assyria, Egypt, Greece and Rome, where table-grapes are of less importance than wine-grapes.

The very earliest tomb paintings, coupled with the fact that remains of grapes occur in innumerable funerary offerings, show vines to have been well-established in Ancient Egypt. The Egyptians must have grown the fine black bunches depicted from at least the fourth millennium BC. Grapes were not only eaten fresh but dried as raisins, and Herodotus tells us that these were used along with figs in stuffing meat.

The Bible is full of references to grapes and vineyards too well-known to need enumeration. At Lachish, archaeological finds from around the beginning of the Bronze Age provide evidence of the use of raisins.

The renown of the vine throughout Classical Greece and Rome is proverbial, but grapes were in use there long before then. Grape-stones were found in Middle Helladic excavations at Orchomenos in Boeotia, and in large quantities at Tiryns, of Late Bronze Age date. We know from Roman writings that certain varieties had been developed for table use and according to Columella the largest and sweetest white ones were selected for drying as raisins, sometimes being rolled in fig leaves first. Indeed, despite the great importance of the grape as a wine-producing fruit, it still remained exceedingly popular as a fruit in its own right and raisins were a major item in the winter store-room.

NUTS

Most nuts are easily gathered and store very well without any special preparation. They are also on the whole quite tasty, high in protein, fat and mineral content and contain certain vitamins. Being generally rich in fats, they provided early communities with a potential source of oil, and nut-oil of one form or another was frequently used even in areas which possessed the olive.

Pollen analyses and actual finds of nuts and other plant debris at prehistoric archaeological sites show that early man had a considerable quantity of nuts at his disposal. For example, the Middle Palaeolithic cave-dwellers at Shanidar (northern Iraq) had available the oak, pine, walnut, and chestnut, and, in later Mesolithic times, though the floral pattern changed, chestnut and pine at least remained. The forests of Europe contained large quantities of oak, and hazel became more prevalent in some places after Neolithic forest clearance had begun. But whatever changes in forestation took place, climatic or through human intervention, nut-trees of one kind or another always seem to have been available in most parts of the world occupied by man.

In the European zone at least, the most widely used nut is perhaps the acorn and it is still used, especially in times of scarcity, to provide meal for bread. There are about three hundred species of acorn, some being more palatable than others. That even bitter acorns can be used is, however, demonstrated by the Yosemite Indians in California, where acorn 'porridge' was the daily food of the majority of the people. The nuts were cracked, pounded into meal, and leached in hot water to remove the bitter taste. This meal was then 'stone-boiled' into a sort of porridge. Acorns were also dried and stored for subsequent use. This treatment was quite satisfactory and possibly bears some resemblance to primitive methods used in other parts of the world. Finds of the fifth millennium BC from Jarmo, and from Neolithic Sesklo in Greece, clearly show their early use as a food. The Neolithic and

Plate 47 Bronze Age lake-dwellings of Switzerland and the Glastonbury

Iron Age site also yielded specimens of acorns, whilst in Germany near Berlin a large Bronze Age storage pit was found filled to the brim with shelled acorns which had apparently been roasted and split in half. The Greeks also knew the value of acorns, for Hesiod writes, 'the earth bears them victuals in plenty, and on the mountains the oak has acorns on top and bees in its midst'.

In ancient Italy acorns were used in times of hardship and the oak was regarded by Pliny as the 'tree which first produced food for mortal man'. Many varieties were known to him, some sweeter than others. In southern Europe and North Africa, the Holm Oak is common and as its nuts are superior in flavour to many acorns, this may have been the kind usually preferred. In Rome, nuts other than the acorn were mostly used merely as condiments in other dishes, or as a part of the dessert.

After the acorn, the most popular nut of Europe seems to have been the hazel, probably from Palaeolithic times onwards. It was certainly a very important food in the Mesolithic period and was among the food remains from both the Swiss prehistoric lake-dwellings and the Neolithic site at Alvastra in Sweden where large hazelnuts were found in quantity. Plate 47 The hazel appears to have come to Greece and Italy from Asia Minor and Pliny refers to it as the 'Pontic nut'. It was cultivated in both countries, some varieties such as the Abellan filberts being particularly well known.

The sweet chestnut was another widely distributed tree in prehistoric times and is unlikely to have been neglected as a source of food. However, it does not often appear in archaeological remains, possibly because it does not preserve so well as other nuts, though some were found together with acorns at an Iron Age site on the Lac du Bourget.

Beech mast, also present at the Swiss and Glastonbury lake-sites, must have been widely used too, for not only are these nuts sweet, but they contain much oil which could be expressed. They are still used in parts of Norway and Sweden to make meal for bread. Theophrastus and Pliny both extolled their sweetness.

In the Near East, the most popular nuts were the almond and pistachio and these are the only two kinds mentioned in the Bible. The almond was not known in Egypt but did grow in Mesopotamia and in Crete and other Aegean lands. An almond seed was found at the Neolithic level below the Palace of Knossos and wild almonds were discovered at the Greek sites of Sesklo and Dimini. Almonds of Late Bronze Age date were also found in the storerooms at Hagia Triada, Crete, and later (fresh or salted) they were a common ingredient of the Greek dessert course. The Romans called the almond the 'Greek Nut' and in Pliny's time several varieties were known. The pistachio, being indigenous to Persia, Syria and Bactria was cultivated widely in the Near East, and still is. It was already appreciated by the inhabitants of Jarmo and later appeared in the gardens of King Merodach-Baladan of Babylon. The pistachio nut was probably exploited for its oil, as well as being eaten fresh and used as it is now in confectionery. It came late to Italy from Syria, and was thus known as the 'Syrian nut', Its price was exorbitant and even Apicius makes no mention of it!

Along with 'Greek', 'Syrian' and 'Pontic' nuts, the Romans also had a 'Persian nut'. This was the walnut, which in fact, was not merely Persian, but far more widespread in its cultivation and use. It occurs in Mesolithic middens and among debris from the Swiss lake-sites. There are about six different species throughout the world growing wild over Greece, Asia Minor, Persia, Kashmir, Nepal and as far as China and Japan, so whilst walnuts were already known in Greece and Italy (as Varro testifies) it was probably a superior kind which came from Persia. These walnuts fetched very high prices in early Rome and were obviously a delicacy, being eaten sometimes as a dessert with fruit. Remains of a variety of walnut were found among the ruins of the Temple of Isis in Pompeii as part of the 'priests' meal', hastily left behind at the time of the eruption in AD 79. Plate 50

There is no evidence before Classical times that pine-kernels were eaten, although this seems very likely. In Classical Greece and Rome, they had become merely an expensive condiment for food designed for the gourmet palate. In recent times, peoples of Russia, India, China and America have all made use of pine kernels as food, a fact which strongly suggests their value to prehistoric communities.

Of other nuts in the Old World, little record remains. One exception is to be found at Isamu Pati, Zambia (possibly AD 900–1300 in date). In his analysis of the food debris from the site, Brian Fagan records storage pits filled with an African species of nut, the Bambara groundnut. These are still cultivated to a considerable extent and are usually soaked prior to cooking in water, or are roasted and then ground into meal.

The New World has its own particular nut varieties. In support of such archaeological evidence of their consumption as exists, it is reasonable to assume that nut-eating among modern Indian groups reflects to a great extent earlier habits. The American beech provides a tasty nut, and the Yosemite Indians sometimes used the Californian buckeye, a kind of horse-chestnut, in a similar way to the acorn, making it into a cake or gruel.

The butternut provides oil and the Narraganset Indians of North America used this oil in their food, as well as the nuts themselves. Hickory nuts of different kinds are widespread over the eastern and central areas of North America and were much appreciated by the Indians who managed to make a sort of milk from them for use in broth, corn cakes, or on roasted sweet potatoes. From the tropical regions, the Pecan nut was an important food to indigenous Indian tribes. Finds of hickory nuts, acorns, butternuts and walnuts in the Upper Great Lakes area prove that their value was realized as far back as about 2000 BC.

Brazil nuts, as their name implies, are indigenous to Brazil, as also are cashews, and these are used in all manner of ways by the native inhabitants. One of the most popular nuts, however, is the peanut, and of its early use in South America there is some archaeological reminder, for peanuts have been found in Ancient Peruvian mummy graves in Ancón and Paracas and they also appear as motifs in Chimu pottery.

The coconut, already established in South America in pre-Columbian times and identified in Peruvian pottery representations, is of Asiatic origin and must have been transmitted by man, first throughout the Pacific Islands and then to the South American continent.

The Sanskrit name for coconut-palm means 'a tree which furnishes all the necessities of life', and this palm must have been to the inhabitants of the Tropics what the date-palm was to the Mesopotamians, for it provides not only solid food but also drink, fibre, and oil.

Fig. 36 Two-handled jar with low projecting spout, from a house at Praesos, Crete. This was probably used as an oil separator. Hellenistic. (After R. C. Bosanquet)

CHAPTER IX

Olives, Oils, Herbs and Condiments

OLIVES AND COOKING OILS

AS PLINY SAYS at the beginning of his chapter on oil: 'There are two liquids especially agreeable to the human body, wine inside and oil outside.' In countries without the olive the place of oil was generally taken first by animal fat. That must have applied to ancient Italy before the introduction of the olive, but we have little direct evidence of this, for once established, the olive became the universal oil provider. Cato, however, suggests its use in making cakes: lard is an ingredient for his sweet-wine cakes and for the doughnut-like *globi encytum*. These were fried in lard and then spread with honey.

Other countries lacking the olive used various oil-producing plants. In Egypt, prior to the introduction of the olive, oil was extracted from radish seed. Indeed, Pliny says that even in his day the people grew radishes in preference to corn because of their high oil yield and the resulting greater profit. The Egyptians also employed the fruits of the *moringa* and it is significant that this is the only kind of oil plant listed for the scribe Ani's funerary garden. The castor oil plant was also widely grown but perhaps not used so much for cooking as for medicine, and Herodotus leaves us in no doubt that its chief use was for lamp-oil and that it had a most offensive smell.

The oil commonly used in Mesopotamia until well into historic times was made from sesame. Tablets of accounts and receipts from Nebuchadnezzar's palace mention the receipt of 'best quality sesame oil'. Oil was evidently very important to the Hittites, as it features to a great extent in their writings; probably this was for the most part made from almonds.

Several early peoples were familiar with flax, and indeed it seems to have been one of the first cultivated plants. It was grown

as early as the fifth millennium BC in Mesopotamia and in Egypt, though it may have been more valued as a textile material than for its oil potential. In Europe, however, the picture is different. Flax was grown in Neolithic Spain, Holland and England, and the Swiss prehistoric lake-dwellings have yielded seeds from the beginning of the third millennium BC. A sort of linseed cake was found at Robenhausen, one of these Swiss sites, which demonstrates clearly that the cultivation of flax was not merely for linen. Finds of carbonized flax together with cameline seed at a Roman
50 Iron Age site in Østerbølle, Denmark, strongly point to flax having been grown for oil-production, as cameline is also a plant with a high oil yield. The two seem to have been cultivated together in both Iron Age Denmark and Germany. A cake of poppy-seeds was also found at Robenhausen, and these were probably another source of oil.

None of these oil-producing plants can be said to have had any great significance as food but in the case of the olive, the fruit was quite as important as the oil made from it. It appears to have originated in Syria and Palestine, whilst a spiny variety may be indigenous to Crete. The olive industry must have played a vital role in Crete and much evidence concerning it has come from that region. Its cultivation there goes back at least to 2500 BC. Olive stores of Late Minoan date have been found and also seeds and an olive press at Palaikastro. A number of settling vats have also been brought to light, and the methods used then for extracting oil must have been much the same as those still employed in modern Crete. This involves drenching the olives with hot water prior to pressing them; the resulting liquid is poured into vats which allow the oil to come to the top, the water being then
Fig. 36 drawn off through a spout at the bottom. The significance of oil in early Crete becomes evident when one considers the vast quantities of pithoi (pottery jars) in the storerooms of the palace at Knossos. Oil seems to have been the king's treasure, and its export one of his major sources of revenue.

Fig. 37 Part of a Greek scene depicting olive gatherers

The inhabitants of Syria and Palestine were not slow to realize the value of the olive which grew wild in their lands and they were the first to cultivate it at least as early as the fourth millennium BC. There are also innumerable Biblical references to olives and olive oil, and Palestine was renowned for its olive groves which even exported oil to Egypt, as well as wine.

Excavations at Lachish showed that the fortress was finally burnt out and that a large proportion of the wood gathered and set ablaze around its walls was olive wood, presumably cut down and taken from the vast surrounding olive groves, for great quantities of charred olive stones were also found there.

Although the wild olive, which does not yield much oil, was known in Greece and Italy and other parts of the Mediterranean region from earliest times, as Neolithic or Bronze Age finds of olive stones attest, it was from Syria and Palestine that knowledge of olive oil and olive cultivation spread. Excavations at the ancient Syrian port of Ugarit revealed stores of jars of oil perhaps intended for export to the western Mediterranean. However, olive cultivation did not reach Italy until the sixth century BC and appears to have come via Greece, where domestication took place considerably earlier.

Fig. 37

Once the olive had reached Italy, its value was quickly appreciated there and with their usual flair for gardening the Romans soon set themselves to work producing fruit and oil of varying kinds and qualities. Even so, considerable quantities were still imported. In Pliny's day this was quite probably to satisfy largely the gourmet tastes of the Romans, for we know for certain from Cato that olives were, along with bread, the staple diet of the peasant and working classes. The rations of his labourers consisted of bread, wine, salt and olives. He recommended keeping for them the windfall olives and later the mature ones with a low oil yield. These were to be distributed sparingly and when used up, replaced by fish-pickle, and vinegar. Each man was allowed a pint of the oil each month. The poor also ate a kind of oil-cake, made from olive-paste. The lower-grade olives having been picked out for the labourers, the rest were made into oil or preserved, and it was these preserved olives which chiefly came to the tables of wealthier classes. All the Roman writers on agriculture give full instructions to be followed when extracting oil. The olives should preferably be fresh when pressed. The first pressing resulted in first quality oil, and two subsequent pressings of the pulp gave second quality and ordinary oil. The oil which the Romans used must have been quite different from that of today, for after the fruit had been briefly squeezed to burst the skins, salt was added to keep the oil flowing. The ancient writers also make it clear that olive oil very soon turned bad, and it was recommended that a store of olives should be kept handy so that oil needed for the table could be produced immediately before use.

Olives for eating were preserved in a number of different ways depending on the variety, but generally they were kept in jars with layers of fennel and mastic top and bottom, and filled with brine, must or even vinegar. A spicy preparation was made from crushed black olives, and olives known as *columbades* were prepared with brine or sea water and used by Apicius in a recipe for a sauce to accompany boiled chicken. Cato mentions a special dish known as *epityrum*; it consisted of stoned green, black and mottled olives chopped and mixed with oil, vinegar, coriander, cumin, fennel, rue and mint, placed in an earthenware dish and covered with oil to serve. These preserves and aromatic preparations were mostly eaten at the beginning of the meal.

HERBS, SPICES AND CONDIMENTS

Though not major articles of food, herbs and spices have none the less long played an important part in making foodstuffs more palatable. There is, of course, less archaeological evidence for seasonings than for other foods but it is reasonable to suggest that anything aromatic which lends its flavour to otherwise ordinary, monotonous and sometimes insipid food, would have been utilized by at least some early peoples. Moreover, it must have been soon recognized that most herbs could be dried and stored without losing their flavour. Poppy seeds and caraway seeds have been found at Swiss prehistoric lake-sites and the latter in particular were most probably condiments for food. Many herbs were brought under cultivation and featured prominently in the early Assyrian and Babylonian gardens which grew amongst others cumin, sesame, mint, basil, coriander, anise, thyme, asafoetida, bay, fennel, rocket, saffron and sage. Many others were known, like mustard seed and capers, as well as the ubiquitous and highly popular leeks, onions, garlic and chives. 82

Egypt too was very fond of its spices, though more is known to us of their use in perfumery than in cooking. However, it seems likely that they used at least sage, rosemary, anise and fennel; moreover, seeds of cumin and coriander have been found in ancient tombs.

Large quantities of spices were imported into Egypt from Arabia and Palestine. It was to Ishmaelite spice-merchants bound for Egypt that Joseph was sold by his brothers, and the Old Testament has many references to spices. In Canaan, saffron grew widely and to supplement this and other indigenous spices and herbs such as cumin and coriander, cassia and cinnamon were imported from India. The seeds of a plant of the ranunculus genus are known to have been used for flavouring cakes.

Finds of anise and coriander seeds of Late Bronze Age date on the islands of Thera and Therasia show that the early Aegean peoples made use of these. Many herbs such as basil, dill, coriander, anise, cumin, fennel, savory and saffron were known and cultivated by the Greeks. Saffron in particular was a favourite, and was believed to grow better when crushed into the earth by the foot. Aristotle speaks of the Sicilian promontory of Pelorus where it grew in such abundance that large waggon-loads of it
Plate 55 could be gathered. It also seems to have flourished in early Crete, as a fresco from Knossos shows. Both the Greeks and Romans highly prized the *silphium*, an umbelliferous plant from North Africa, though by the time of Pliny this was already practically extinct and thus exceedingly costly. Its exact nature is unknown but everything points to its close resemblance to asafoetida which often replaced it. Representations of it occur on Greek coins of the area, to be found in many coin collections. Imported spices in the time of Theophrastus included myrrh, cinnamon, cassia, cardamom, ginger grass and spikenard, and all these could be used for flavouring wine.

The importation of these and other exotic spices became a very important line of commerce and led ultimately to the discovery of new routes to the East. By the time that Rome was at its zenith the list of herbs and spices used in cookery for the upper classes was

Fig. 38 Early Egyptian scene showing the preparation and salting of poultry

formidable. Nothing was eaten without a sauce or dressing of some kind and the making of sauces was an art, as can be seen by the large number of sauce recipes given by Apicius. Though many oriental spices were imported, much use was made of those that could be grown in the local gardens, in particular dill, mint, thyme, savory, cumin, lovage, origan and rue. Rocket, accord- to Pliny, was often blended with lettuce as a salad, and mustard seed was made into a sauce with vinegar. Poppy seeds, sesame, bay, anise and fennel were all used for flavouring cakes and bread, whilst parsley was very popular and a number of different kinds were grown. It was in Pliny's time that pepper began to be used in Italy and he obviously considered it an unnecessary luxury, very expensive and therefore often adulterated. Apicius uses it frequently, but it is interesting that contrary to our present-day usage, it often featured as a dressing to sprinkle over sweet dishes.

One rather interesting result of the Mediterranean taste for seasonings was the invention of *garum* or *liquamen*. This was a standard sauce produced not only at home but in quantity in

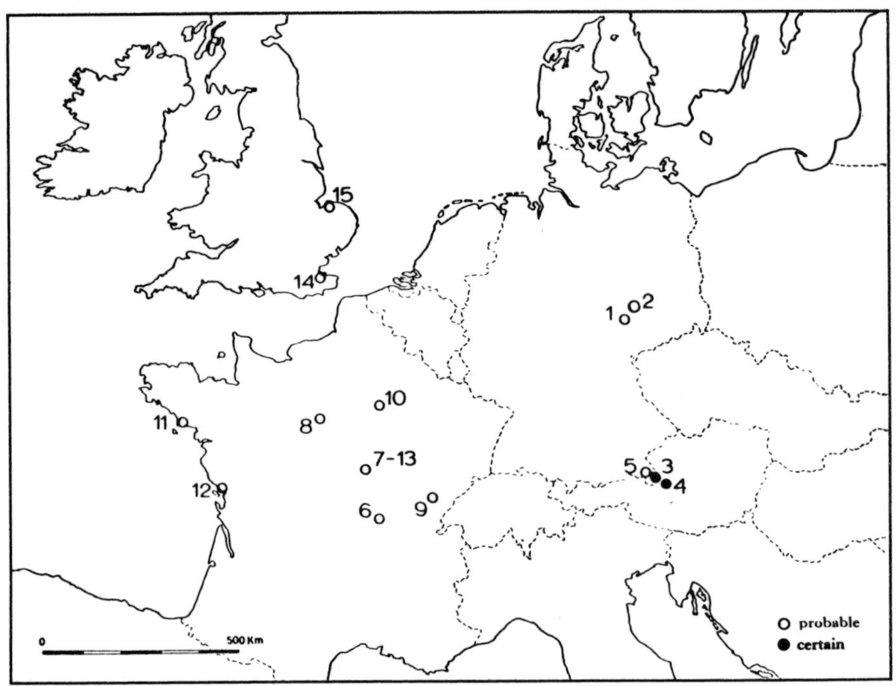

Fig. 39 The salt industry in northern Europe in Neolithic times: 1, Artern; 2, Halle-Giebichenstein; 3, Hallein; 4, Hallstatt; 5, Reichenhall; 6, Bourbon Lancy; 7, Fontaines Salées; 8, Grisy; 9, Lons le Saunier; 10, Montmort; 11, Morbihan; 12, Nalliers; 13, Tharoiseau; 14, Lower Halstow; 15, Heacham

liquamen factories, some of which became famous, and have left their stamp upon jars found during excavations. It was made from the salted-down entrails of fish from which the liquid was strained off and stored in jars. A number of recipes are given for it, but its original fabrication seems to go back to the Greeks of about the fourth century BC. It was not introduced until much later to Italy, where it soon appeared in almost every recipe. From the basic '*garum*', compounds were made: *oenogarum*, with wine and spices, *hydrogarum,* with water, and *oxygarum* with vinegar.

VINEGAR

Vinegar merely as a condiment was not important, but it was a very necessary part of food preservation; 'vinegar and hard

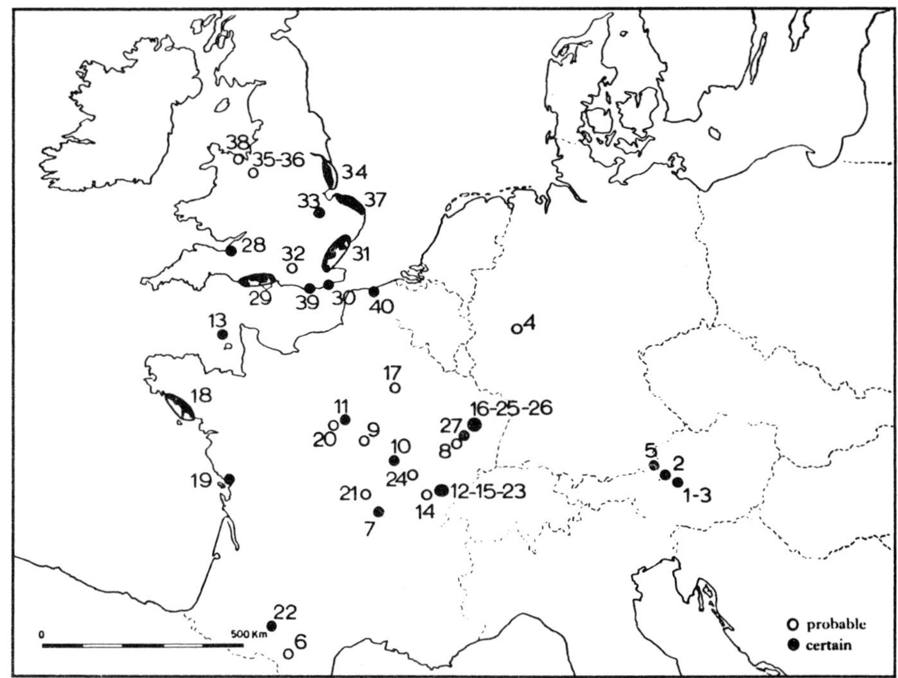

Fig. 40 The salt industry in northern Europe in Gallo-Roman and Romano-British times: 1, Dammwiese; 2, Hallein; 3, Hallstatt; 4, Nauheim; 5, Reichenhall; 6, Ax; 7, Bourbon Lancy; 8, Bourbonne les Bains; 9, Foissy; 10, Fontaines Salées; 11, Grisy; 12, Grozou; 13, Guernsey; 14, Lons le Saunier; 15, Maizières; 16, Marsal; 17, Montmort; 18, Morbihan; 19, Nalliers; 20, Saclay; 21, St Honoré les Bains; 22, Salies du Salat; 23, Salins; 24, Santenay; 25, Seille; 26, Vic; 27, Vittel; 28, Brue district; 29, Dorset sites; 30, Dymchurch; 31, Essex–Kent sites; 32, Farnham; 33, Fens; 34, Lincolnshire sites; 35, Kinderton; 36, Nantwich; 37, Norfolk sites; 38, Prestatyn; 39, Seaford; 40, De Panne

brine', says Columella, 'are essential for making preserves'. In addition, it was commonly used as a drink when diluted with water. This dilution meant that a small amount of vinegar would go much further than the same amount of wine, so it proved to be a useful and refreshing drink to take on long journeys where baggage had to be kept to a minimum. It is not surprising therefore that it figured among the rations of the Roman soldiers when on the march. Vinegar was usually manufactured from flat wine with various crushed ingredients such as yeast, dried figs, salt and honey added. It could also be made from other fruits such as peaches, and squill vinegar is also mentioned.

SALT Probably the most widely-used condiment of all time both as a seasoning and as a preservative is salt. As yet there is no evidence that Palaeolithic or Mesolithic man undertook salt extraction or had any special interest in salt deposits. During the Neolithic,
91 however, there was a systematic and deliberate exploitation of natural salt deposits. Some have seen in this a human reaction to a physiological need for more salt following changes in diet during Neolithic times, but this is a dubious explanation; salt-eating may well have started as a whim, the taste being naturally satisfying. In the train of this prehistoric 'consumer demand' for the luxury salt, would follow the discovery that the mineral was of value in
Fig. 38 preserving other foodstuffs, especially animal tissue. Salt also became more and more involved in national politics and economics, and even in classical texts there is mention of salt-distribution, salt legislation and salt taxes.

76 Returning to prehistoric times and with special reference to northern Europe, it will be seen in the accompanying maps (from
Figs. 39, 40 a detailed study by Jacques Nenquin), that salt-mining expanded noticeably from Neolithic to Roman times. Prehistoric communities clearly made use of natural surface deposits (as found along the Mediterranean shores and in the lands of the Fertile Crescent). 'Salt-pans', resulting from salt-spray and the evaporation of sea-water pools were also an obvious source—as Herodotus and Pliny indicate. Classical writers also mention brine springs, salt lakes and salt rivers, and Strabo goes so far as to say that salt deposits along the river Indus might have provided for the whole of India. Although this receives but brief comment, classical writers did mention the extraction of salt from the ash of salt-plants, a method still used by some aboriginal peoples today.

From the Neolithic onwards, salt consumption clearly continued to increase and large profits must have been made by salt

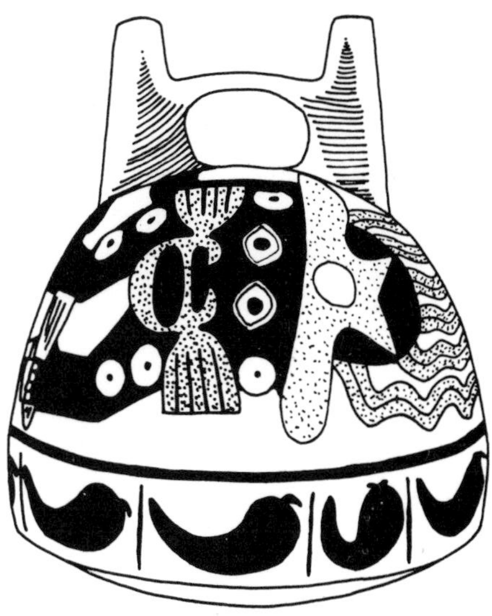

Fig. 41 Double-spouted Peruvian jar decorated with a border of peppers. Nazca. (After Towle and Willey)

traders. The prosperity of the Hallstatt community and the 'salt rajahs' of India (of Pliny's day) is a further indication of the great magnitude of salt consumption by post-Mesolithic peoples.

Finally, one cannot leave this topic without mentioning the best-known spice to come out of the New World, the chili pepper and its many varieties. When Columbus arrived in the West Indies he was able to collect and bring back to the Old World *agi*, which he and his colleagues noted as being very extensively used by the Indians both as a spice to flavour their food, and as a food in itself. The use of chili peppers in South America goes back to at least 7000 BC, for they have been found in both floor refuse and coprolites from the Tamaulipas Caves in Mexico shown to have been deposited then. In Peru, it is possible that peppers were cultivated from the very beginnings of agriculture; certainly they were a major part of the diet of the Peruvian Indians and seem to have been eaten as a food in their young and immature state before the seeds became well developed and thus too 'hot'. CHILI 79 *Fig. 41*

CHAPTER X

Drinks

114 OF ALL DRINKS known to modern communities, water is, of course, the only one necessary for human survival. All others are related to the constant search by man for substances satisfying to the palate, whether the solution has any great food value or not.

On average, about 2·5 litres of water are lost from an individual each day, by moisture in exhaled air, by diffusion through the skin, by secretion of sweat and of urine, and in faeces; in desert conditions, far more is lost. This loss must be replaced at regular intervals if normal body function is to be maintained, and it is thus not surprising that throughout human history availability of water has influenced movement and settlement to an important degree. Moreover, depending on climatic and geological factors, there has been a perpetual readjustment of the settlement of peoples to water supplies. The later technology of water-getting is beyond the scope of this work, but it should be noted that from the original water sources—rivers, springs and lakes—there developed in early urban communities the refinement of wells, conduits and aqueducts. In turn, these have been added to in more recent times by artesian wells and reservoirs. This total complex of water sources has contributed significantly to the development and maintenance of healthy town and city populations.

1, 38 Like so many discoveries, the creation of most fermented liquors probably came about by accident. As certain types of sweet fruit, and also honey, will ferment of their own accord, it was inevitable that any attempts to collect such fermentable substances in containers would on more than one occasion encourage alcohol formation. It is sobering to consider that the neglected jar of fruit juice or pulp, or the half-empty honey-pot left out in the rain, set man along the road to alcoholism and the illicit still. Certainly, the fermented drinks of the Old and New Worlds represent independent discoveries, and it could well be that the development of rice beverages in eastern Asia was quite unconnected with that of the varied cereal and wine concoctions in the European area.

The attractive and 'warming' nature of alcohol would certainly have gained it quick acceptance, and when the 'social' potentialities were discovered its continuing existence was guaranteed. Improved production techniques and experimentation with other liquids must then have followed quickly.

In order to ferment naturally, fruits must have a very high sugar content, which not many have. Few of the wild fruits generally collected by early hunting and gathering communities will have fermented well enough to give a satisfactory liquor; but one food which we know to have been much sought after and used, and which is far more likely to have been stored than perishable berries, is honey. Being pure sugar, it ferments readily and it may well have formed the basis of the first intoxicating drink.

MEAD

The place of honey and mead in the ancient religious rituals of a large variety of peoples shows that they were considered by many to be very acceptable to the gods, and this probably indicates a long tradition of mead-drinking. Indeed, Plutarch states that before the advent of viticulture mead was the drink offered to the gods and that foreign peoples, lacking the vine, still drank mead. Pliny and Columella also state that mead and beer were drunk prior to wine in Italy, and Pliny adds with disgust that beer was imbibed 'neat', not with water as was the practice with wine. Nevertheless, despite improved hivekeeping, honey always remained a precious and quite expensive commodity, so that when the early agriculturists began to produce cereals and fruit (including the grape) in quantity, mead did not stand up to such competition. Wine and ale could be produced on a much larger scale and without using such a valuable product as honey, which, it must be remembered, was the only good sweetening matter then available. The Saxons were renowned mead-drinkers, but although mead may have had a longer life in Britain owing to the lack of grape wine, mead-drinking nevertheless declined. Moreover, it was probably drunk more by the rich man than the peasant.

Even in Ancient Egypt, where bee-keeping was such a thriving industry and where honey was produced in such quantities, the main drinks were water and beer, and wine for the wealthier families. The Romans also retained a taste for honey-wine in their use of *mulsum*, a mixture of wine and honey which usually accompanied the *gustatio* or hors d'oeuvre, but it is clear that it was an expensive drink, for Varro remarks that he could not afford it.

BEER

The brewing of beer may well have occurred soon after the production of cereal crops, and no doubt for a long time beer was home-produced and in the hands of the housewives responsible for preparing the 'gruel' or bread. Malting the grain is the first step in beer-brewing, but malting—that is, allowing the grains to germinate—was initially carried out to make the grains more palatable. After malting, besides being mixed into a nourishing gruel, the grains could also be dried, milled and baked into a more easily preserved kind of bread. Thus, the first production of beer may be reasonably considered as an accidental discovery resulting from the malting of grain for other purposes. When cereals came to be more often baked into bread and less often turned into gruel, malting was not so necessary and became part of the brewer's trade only.

By the third millennium BC, Mesopotamia was already well versed in beer-brewing and old Sumerian texts mention eight barley beers, eight emmer beers and three mixed beers. Aromatic plants were added to the beer to improve the flavour and to assist in its preservation, and extra honey, cereals and malt gave varying added strengths. Up to the third millennium, the grains were de-husked, but husked grains then began to be brewed and beer was drunk through the drinking-tubes to be seen in several relief carvings. Beer-mugs from Palestine, with built-in strainers, suggest that the Philistines were also drinkers of husked beer.

Brewing followed much the same pattern in Egypt, where too it originally went hand in hand with baking. Herbs and spices were also added, but beer was never drunk with the husks; it was always filtered before being poured into the jars. As early as the Pyramid Age five kinds of beer were noted, some of which are described as 'strong'. Indeed, it is considered that the ancient brewers probably made stronger beer than we now know, owing to the wild yeast which caused the fermentation and produced a greater alcohol content than do our modern specially prepared yeasts.

Beer, to the Greeks and Romans, was a barbarian drink, because most of the beer-drinkers with whom they were acquainted were 'barbarians'. The North European peoples of those days such as the Celts and the Germans did not yet know the wine-grape and the art of viticulture, so after the introduction of cereal agriculture their drink remained beer for a very long time. Indeed, beer-making was probably as long-established in these parts as in Mesopotamia and Egypt, for it is most unlikely that brewing, as a logical step resulting from malting grain, would be discovered in one place only and transmitted from there.

The brewing of beer with hops did not become common practice until medieval times, and was a slow but direct result of adding herbs to beer to provide flavour and even more to preserve it. Of all the herbs used, the hop gradually became the most acceptable one but not without strong competition from 'gruits'—herb mixtures used in Germany. Indeed, in 1380, the Archbishop of Cologne became concerned about the decline in use of 'gruits' from his own 'gruithouses' and banned the import of hopped beer from Westphalia.

WINE

All the same, to the Mediterranean wine-bibbers of classical times, beer remained a nasty barbarian drink. Whilst the Greeks

are on the whole responsible for initiating specialized viticulture which ultimately spread throughout the Mediterranean and into France and Germany, the vine is indigenous to Asia Minor and it was probably among the people of that area that viticulture had its true beginnings. We know from their texts that the Hittites were enthusiastic vine-growers and wine-producers. Viticulture was known in Mesopotamia as early as the third millennium BC,
Fig. 42 and was probably well under way in Egypt even before dynastic times. Although the vine is not indigenous there, pictorial representations appear in tombs of the earliest dynasties and the Pyramid Texts indicate at least six varieties. All large gardens grew grapes along with dates and figs, but wine still had to be imported from Syria and Palestine, where viticulture was of primary importance. So wine remained in Egypt a drink for the rich, with beer and water for the peasants, until the arrival of the Greeks in the Hellenistic period.

Mesopotamia too, whilst producing wine from a very early date, did not make sufficient for the masses. Many of the early kings and governors record that they built irrigated vine terraces, and Sargon II had extensive wine-cellars. However, here, as in Egypt, beer was the drink of the common man until cereals came to be of more value as a food. Then dates took their place, and though the Mesopotamians retained the same name, 'beer', it was now rather a date wine, and this became finally the most common drink.

There is some dispute about the antiquity of wine-drinking in Crete and the Aegean, and it has been postulated that beer was probably drunk prior to wine. However, the contacts of Minoan Crete with wine-producing Egypt, and also with the Greek mainland where wine was certainly being drunk in the Later Bronze Age, make it very probable that the Cretans also drank grape wine.

Nevertheless, it was in Greece that the wine-grape really came into its own, and it is significant that in classical texts one rarely

Fig. 42 Egyptians siphoning and mixing wines

hears of the grape being grown solely for eating. Greek legends claim that Dionysus fled thither from Mesopotamia, disgusted by its beer-drinking. Viticulture in Greece probably goes back to the Bronze Age and by the Homeric era was certainly a fine art. Theophrastus wrote that a great many types of wine were known in his day, some with fine reputations: Lesbian, Chian, Thasian. Of the latter, he says that Thasos Town Hall served a particularly delightful wine, its flavour being improved by the addition of a lump of dough kneaded with honey. The wine-trade became so important in Greece, that at one point Attica produced more wine than cereals and had to import grain to keep its people fed.

Wine-production in Italy is thought to have been initially introduced by the Etruscans. Indeed this remarkable civilization with its love of art, music and feasting must surely have enjoyed wine; but again, it was only after the Greek settlements in the south in the eighth century BC that viticulture really took hold in Italy and became a flourishing industry. As more Greek colonies were established so did the trade in Greek wine spread, and with the founding of Massalia an opening was made for wine exports into Gaul and thus through to the Rhine area, as the excavation of vessels from those parts substantiates. However, as the colonies grew, they began to produce their own wines and thus to close the door on Greek imports. Campania, home of the first 'wine settlers' in Italy, was an ideal vine-growing area with the slopes of Mount Vesuvius producing some of the finest wine of antiquity. When the Romans finally overcame the Greeks, they inherited a flourishing wine industry which made Greek imports no longer of importance. Greek treatises on vine-growing had been translated, vines had been imported and wine-making initiated, and from there the Romans took over. Very soon the grand old Greek wines were spoken of with a slight air of nostalgia and the praises of Roman wines such as Aminean, Nomentane and above all the great Falernian were sung. Italy soon had its own writers on viticulture, such as Cato, Varro and Columella who regarded facilities for wine-production as one of the most important items to be considered when buying a farm. Raisin wines were made, spiced wines too, and *thermopolia*, such as those found at Pompeii, were set up for the serving of mulled wine.

The impression gained from the instructions then given for wine-making in Italy is that an enormous quantity of additives were used which must have given some of the wine a most peculiar flavour. Before the invention of cork stoppers there was a danger of continued fermentation after bottling, so various methods were employed to try to preserve the wine. Indeed, it seems that only the finest vintages escaped the treatment and it was recognized that, to use Columella's own words, 'The best wine is that which can keep without any preservative, nothing should be mixed with it to obscure its natural savour.' Then he elaborates on the necessary pitching of the jars and the method of preserving wine with *defrutum*. When this was reduced, by boiling, to one-third, pitch and resin were added, and then spices, including spikenard, costus, myrrh and cinnamon. This spicy *defrutum* was tested by storing it for one year before use, in case it should turn sour. In addition to this, salt was added and flowers of gypsum. 'But,' says Columella, 'care must be taken that the flavour of the preservative is not noticeable.' Whether it was really undetectable or whether the average Roman, unable to afford the finer vintages, was so accustomed to it as to regard it as normal is a moot point. Sometimes, too, unscrupulous traders, particularly in southern France, used to an outrageous degree the *fumarium*, the warm smokey attic area high in the building, for artificially maturing their wines. They were much criticized by the Roman connoisseurs, but managed to foist their 'mellow-looking' produce on to less particular palates.

The Romans were unquestionably responsible for the introduction of viticulture in Britain—vine-stems were excavated on southern slopes near a villa in Hertfordshire—but after the Romans left, vine-growing made slow progress. Bede in the eighth century said that vines were cultivated in several places but wine remained a luxury to the ale- and mead-drinking Britons. As more monastic institutions became established, they founded their own vineyards and after the Conquest wine-growing areas spread, but still wine remained the drink of rich men. However, in the course of time progressively more foreign wines were imported from the Continent and as the British climate and soil are not really conducive to easy vine-growing, home-produced wines became less in demand and the industry failed. Among the early writers one finds mention of innumerable plants which were turned to wine-production. Then as now the cottage-wine industry flourished, though, of course, it receives little attention in the literature. Asparagus, turnip, squill and wild mint all figure among the ingredients, and judging by usages throughout the world today, it seems as if at some time or another almost every type of plant has been turned into some kind of alcoholic brew.

By no means all drinks concocted by man were alcoholic, though most have a certain stimulating effect. The three most popular hot beverages of today, tea, coffee, and cocoa provide further forms of satisfaction for the palate, and infusions of a great many other plants are in use all over the world, even among primitive communities.

TEA *Camellia thea*, the chief ingredient of that so-British institution
78, 96 the 'cup of tea', is indigenous to China, and goes far back into Chinese history and legend. It is related that in the year 2737 BC the Emperor Shen-Nung, renowned for his powers of healing, was boiling himself some drinking-water outdoors, over an open fire made from wood of the surrounding camellia trees. Leaves from the trees fell into his cauldron and the Emperor, attracted by the fragrant aroma which began to arise, poured himself the first cup of tea. India and Japan have different legends. In these, the discoverer is Darma or Dharuma, who during seven years of sleepless contemplation began to grow tired and, in the Indian story, chewed tea leaves and was restored to alertness. In the Japanese version, he cuts off his offending eye-lids and they spring up from the ground as tea plants.

By the fifth and sixth centuries AD tea had become the favourite drink of China, no longer a mere medicinal stimulant, and it was already an article of trade. Its methods of preparation went through a kind of evolution. In the fifth century AD the leaves were made into cakes and boiled with various ingredients such as rice, ginger, salt, orange peel, pine-kernels, milk, walnuts and even onions. Then fashion changed and powdered tea was whipped up in hot water. Ultimately, during the Ming Dynasty (fifteenth century AD) the method of steeping the leaves in hot water was adopted. Tea finally reached Europe via Dutch traders in 1610.

COFFEE The making of a beverage from coffee is of comparatively recent date. The shrub bearing the coffee berry is indigenous to Abyssinia and the Sudan, but the beginnings of its cultivation are obscure. What is certain is that the berries were not at the outset made into a drink, but rather eaten as a paste. The production of the beverage is attributed to the Mohammedans in an attempt to find something to replace wine which had been forbidden them. It was introduced into Cairo in the early sixteenth century and there became a subject of dispute among the Moslems who were suspicious of this stimulating substitute, and for a time the chances of its continued existence as a drink hung in the balance. However, in 1524 it was declared acceptable and from then on its popularity gradually increased and spread throughout Europe and the New World.

It is chiefly to the Aztecs that we owe our knowledge of cocoa. COCOA
These people were very fond of this beverage, and the cacao bean 13
was an extremely important part of their economy, as currency and as a foodstuff. The bean must have been taken to Mexico by the Indians in pre-Columbian times, from the Amazon and Orinoco basins where it is indigenous. It was certainly from the Mexican Indians that the Spaniards and Portuguese learned the art of making cocoa. The Indians roasted the beans in pots, then crushed them between stones and formed the paste thus produced into cakes with their hands. This paste they diluted with water seasoned with pimento, then drank the resulting beverage with relish. The Spaniards found it wholesome enough, but preferred to add other ingredients such as sugar, vanilla and cinnamon to improve the flavour. They prepared the paste with these additions and put it into large moulds for export.

The contents of these moulds might be regarded as the direct forerunners of our present-day bars of chocolate. The Spanish and Portuguese kept the manufacture of chocolate secret for a long time; so secret in fact, that, when Dutch pirates captured a boat with its cargo of chocolate, they disgustedly described it as 'cacura de carneros' and threw it all overboard. Thus, long after chocolate became the fashionable drink in Europe, the Spaniards and Portuguese still held the trade monopoly and were able to charge very high prices. The English were the first to make the drink with milk and occasionally eggs added. A by-product was cocoa-oil or cocoa-butter, which was used in cooking.

During the past ten thousand years, the basic human drive for sufficient water to satisfy physiological needs has been somewhat overshadowed by the constant experimentation with and elaboration of other drinks. Our quest for palatable beverages, especially of the alcoholic kind, must surely rank as an outstanding feature—if not at times a positive determinant—of earlier cultural change. But let Pliny have the last words on drinks, for as he so truly says: 'There is no department of man's life on which more labour is spent.'

CHAPTER XI

Diet and Disease

ANY SURVEY OF earlier diets would be incomplete without some consideration of the evidence for insufficiency of food in earlier times. In view of the prevalence of malnutrition in the world today, it is unlikely that it did not occur in the past, despite the vast increase in world population. But to what extent, when and why? Palaeolithic and Mesolithic cultures were not necessarily more likely to experience starvation than more advanced ones, indeed the evidence available for modern stone-age communities suggests that, compared with advanced agricultural societies, hunting and collecting economies may be far more adapted to adverse conditions.

Communities dependent on natural resources (i.e. pre-agricultural) usually possess far more knowledge of the edibility of a wide range of plants and animals than do settled agricultural peoples. As it is unlikely that we shall ever be in a satisfactory position to assess accurately the average amounts of foodstuff consumed by most earlier populations, it is doubly important to consider any disease aspects which are related to diet, both from historical accounts and the biological evidence revealed by the study of mummies and skeletons. It is fortunate for us that quite a number of food deficiency diseases leave their mark on human remains, and for this reason such abnormalities can be taken into account as well as the evidence provided by ancient literature.

It will also be convenient to discuss here two further aspects concerned with food and health. The problem of infant feeding is really a corollary to malnutrition, but in view of the special time-period involved, will receive separate, but brief, consideration. Food poisoning and its causes will be treated last of all.

To begin with, some mention should be made of acquired tastes, though only in passing. In assessing the food availability of earlier peoples, it is important to realize that civilized tastes in foodstuffs cannot be used as a yardstick. Indeed, it seems likely that one of the results of increasing cultural complexity is a correlated lack of dietary flexibility.

We have no reason to believe that primitive man set much store by food looking nice, or that his taste in any way coincided with ours. The Malayan aboriginal eats durian fruit even though its foetid smell puts most Europeans off. The consumption of the contents of the stomachs of animals killed is not unusual in hunting and collecting communities, even of recent times. The Maori, when in possession of maize, used to pack the grain into fern-lined containers and immerse it for long periods in water, until the decomposing foodstuff (*kanga pirau*) stank badly. In this state, the Maori consumed it. In the case of animal foods, the Eskimo will eat rotting seal meat and fish. Even bad eggs are in some circumstances edible, as the old Chinese liking for them attests. There is, then, a wide degree of taste-tolerance in man, a fact which must be remembered when considering early economies, especially those depending to a great extent on natural resources.

FAMINE

The records show that from the beginning severe malnutrition occurred in widely separated parts of the world. It resulted from one, or a combination, of the following; detrimental climatic conditions, disease, political strife resulting in agricultural neglect, food destruction, or the breakdown of food-distribution. Populations close to, or possibly exceeding, the optimum for the territory farmed were the most susceptible to these factors, though none was immune from major catastrophies. Early Egyptian texts describe quite a number of famines, resulting from under- or over-flooding of the Nile or from the abandonment of the fields and neglect of the dykes in times of war. The emaciated condition typical of severe malnutrition is shown clearly in the famous famine scene from the causeway of Unas at Saqqara. As the 'Stele of Famine' dated to the Third Dynasty suggests, the famines were sometimes prolonged, in this instance lasting for seven years, during which time the Nile did not inundate the land.

In the British Isles more than 200 famines, local or widespread, were recorded between AD 10 and 1850. Similarly, in China between 100 BC and AD 1910, no less than 1,800-odd famines were recorded. The extent to which these earlier peoples had to scavenge for food is shown by a famine which afflicted the Vikings in AD 892, when they were compelled to resort to eating varieties of seaweed, bark and lichen. There is also evidence that the early peoples of the New World were no less affected by cycles of malnutrition; for example, in AD 1451–56, the Aztecs experienced acute food shortage as a result of severe storms and frosts. During such periods cultural activity would presumably have been seriously impeded, as evidenced by the reports of European famines, the various states of torpor being either the result of chronically reduced vigour or the intentional conservation of as much energy as possible.

PLANT AND ANIMAL DISEASES

Famines and loss of foodstuffs are the result not only of bad climatic conditions, soil deficiencies, and political troubles, but also of disease. It is to the credit of the ancient cultivators that they early realized the value to themselves of healthy crops and food animals. Rust diseases of cereals seem likely to have been known as crop killers since the beginnings of cultivation. For these we find collective terms used; thus, for example, the Hebrew term 'yeragon' (yellowing) of the Bible is rendered 'mildew' (British) or 'Rost' (German). From our point of view, it is convenient to continue to use these general terms. Biblical writings clearly indicate how aware men were of these fungal disorders. 'If there be in the land famine, if there be pestilence, smut, rust . . .' (I Kings 8; 37; II Chron. 6: 28), and again: 'I smote you with smut and with rust and with hail in the labours of your hands, yet ye turned not to me' (Haggai 2: 17). There is some evidence that by 700 BC propitiatory prayers and sacrifices (Robigalia) were being made to rust gods, and according to Pliny these ritual feasts took place between the grain festival (Cerealia, April 12–19) and the blossom festival (Floralia, April 28). Such rituals concerned with rust were maintained for some centuries, and Varro (26 BC) mentions Robigus as one of the protecting gods of farmers.

Changes from year to year in the severity of rust were noted by Aristotle (384–322 BC), who attributed the anomaly to warmth and moisture. Theophrastus notes that cereals were more liable to rust than pulses, and that barley was more affected than other cereals. He also related land and climate to rust frequency. Its connection with climate was also suggested by Pliny, who stated that it was more prevalent in valleys and dewy fields, and that it affected some cereal varieties more than others. Surprisingly enough, there was but little mention of it during the Middle Ages.

An idea of the extent of early crop destruction by rusts can only be inferred from data on the extent of damage to recent crops, a method of comparison valid in view of the fact that early losses seem to have shown similar variation to recent ones. As shown by pre-war surveys in parts of America, plant loss may be variable from region to region and year to year, with percentage losses ranging from less than 1 per cent up to 60 per cent or more (usually over 10 per cent). Assuming that a comparable range of plant losses is likely to have afflicted earlier cultivators, we can readily understand this preoccupation with the subject in earlier literature. In the case of the poorer prehistoric agricultural economies where density of population was closely correlated with maximum food potential, losses of from 10 per cent to 30 per cent of the cereal yield would have had a marked effect upon the average daily cereal consumption of each individual.

Although there is no need to emphasize further the importance of plant diseases, it may be mentioned that smut diseases (resulting from fungi of another order to those of rust) must similarly have affected early agricultural communities. Even today, these may destroy one or two per cent of wheat, oats, barley and corn crops.

Diseases of animals, as well as of plants, may, of course, severely affect the economy of a group, especially if the disease is a killer. We have, however, much less to go by when it comes to interest in or attention given to, diseases in animal populations in ancient times. The earliest evidence of veterinary interest is to be found in the writings of the Egyptian temple priests of the Middle Kingdom (2160–1674 BC). To judge by these inscriptions, it seems likely that the Egyptians at least were acquainted with bovine tuberculosis, sheep pox and anthrax. Attempts were even made to control the spread of such diseases, although we have no idea how successful such attempts were. At about the same time as the Egyptians were making their observations, the Babylonians also commented on animal care and sickness—in the code of Hammurabi (*c.* 1792 BC). As one might expect, the Greeks were one of the first people to study animal disease systematically, their descriptions being surprisingly accurate, and rules were laid down for the control of evident animal disorders. Later, the Romans were no less concerned with control of disease, which could strike both domestic farm stock and beasts used for military transport.

VITAMIN DEFICIENCY

Compared with other forms of malnutrition, we have quite a number of references to vitamin deficiency in earlier populations. As the lack of specific vitamins gave rise to very different pathological conditions, which can be distinguished in earlier writings, they will be considered separately here.

Vitamin A is found in animal fats and oils; also it can be produced in the body from carotene which is present in various green vegetables and yellow and red fruits. Although the vitamin is therefore available to predominantly pastoral, fishing, and horticultural communities, there is nevertheless evidence of a deficiency of it, at least in some earlier populations. Although prolonged vitamin A deficiency produces a severe defect called xerophthalmia (affecting the cornea of the eye), it is more common to experience 'night blindness' (nyctalopia)—the inability to see in a dim light. This defect has been very common in the East for many centuries. The earliest reference to the treatment of an eye condition—very probably night blindness—is to be found in the Egyptian medical treatise known as the *Ebers Papyrus,* dated to about 1600 BC. It is a prescription recommending the use of ox liver which, it says, is very effective and quick-acting. Hippocrates and Galen were also well acquainted with night blindness, the former suggesting the consumption of ox-liver (in honey) as a cure. Later Roman medical writings had similar advice to give, and this eye condition was also described in Chinese literature by AD 610.

Vitamins of the B complex include thiamine and niacin (found in the outer layer of cereals, and in fresh meat). Deficiency of the former results in the disease beriberi which may severely affect the nerves or heart. Because of the less distinctive symptoms of this condition it has not been identified with such certainty in early
55 writings, although Chinese literature as far back as 1000 BC refers to a disease which is probably beriberi. What is probably a good example of the widespread distribution of this disease in an early population occurred during the reign of the Chinese emperor Ta Tsung (AD 529) when the city Tsai Chseng was being besieged. As the siege progressed, about nine-tenths of the 120,000 population developed swelling of the body and shortness of breath, with death following. Although the early progress of pellagra is obscure, this niacin-deficiency disease is believed to have been prevalent in the continental zone of the New World, from Panama to Mexico. From prehistoric times there is likly to have

been a deficient diet based upon corn. The Maya and Aztec economies were almost wholly geared to this cereal, and as the prevalent overdependence on this food in some parts of Central America in recent times is linked with a high frequency of deficiency diseases including pellagra, their incidence in these earlier cultures may be inferred.

In view of the considerable variety of plant material available to most hunting and collecting communities, it seems unlikely that Vitamin C (ascorbic acid) deficiency would have occurred commonly before the era of population concentration following upon the Neolithic revolution. Absence of vitamin C—contained in foods such as fresh fruits and vegetables—results in scurvy. The first identifiable description of this disease is that given by Hippocrates. He mentions a distasteful condition which produced frequent haemorrhages, and repulsive ulceration of the gums—both typical symptoms of scurvy. Pliny was also acquainted with scurvy changes (his so-called *stomacace*), and he noted its presence in Roman troops in the region of the Rhine. Definite descriptions of the disease are known from the Middle Ages, and there is no doubt that it was prevalent in parts of Europe then.

Vitamin D is present in fish-liver oils and dairy foods. It can also be manufactured in the body, provided plenty of the skin surface is exposed to sunlight. A deficiency of this vitamin inhibits normal bone growth and composition, resulting in rickets in children and osteomalacia in adults. In both cases there may be marked bone deformity, and bowing of the long bones of the legs is particularly common. As yet, evidence of D-deficiency has been found with certainty only among the early peoples of the Old World. What evidence there is for this deficiency comes from as far south as Egypt and as far north as Scandinavia. Considering the thousands of skeletons excavated in Egypt during the past century and the few even questionable rickets cases among them, the frequency seems likely to have been very low, which is understandable in view of the common use of fish as food and the

Plate 64

prevalence of sunshine. The skeletal evidence in fact rests on a few slightly bowed long bones (a distortion which might have resulted *post mortem* from the burial conditions) and a deformed pelvis of a form not uncommon in severe D-deficiency. A few wall paintings also depict individuals with deformed legs, although this testimony too is controversial.

63 There is some literary evidence for this condition, not all of which has gone unchallenged. A third-century BC Chinese text mentions a disease producing 'crooked legs and hunchback', an association of deformities strongly suggesting rickets. Soranus of Ephesus (AD 98–138) in his writings refers to a rachitic-like deformity in children. Although mistakenly attributing the anomaly to premature walking, he at least records the fact that some children had legs 'twisted at the thighs'. He also states that the majority of children in the neighbourhood of Rome show such distortions. Although this may be an exaggeration, child care in Rome at that time may well have been conducive to the development of rickets. Judging from some recent European communities, there may well have been mothers in ancient Rome who weaned their children on to D-deficient starchy food and kept them indoors out of the sun more than was good for them.

Plates 62, 63 By far the earliest evidence of rickets in man comes from Denmark, namely, Neolithic tibiae from the site of Raevehøj showing marked bowing, certainly not just the result of post-mortem pressure.

OTHER DIETARY DISORDERS

Although vitamin deficiencies and general reports of famine provide us with the best information as yet of nutritional inadequacy in early communities, there is a little further evidence which demands consideration. Iodine deficiency is known from many parts of the world, from the Midlands of England, from Switzerland, the Himalayan valleys, and the South American continent. Surprisingly, however, there is but little evidence from the early literature. It is debatable whether the Greek physicians knew anything about this deficiency, although some of their statements concerning tumours of the neck have been interpreted as goitres. However, some Latin writers, including Pliny and Juvenal, knew of the occurrence of endemic goitre in Alpine areas. Its incidence in parts of central Asia, at least by the thirteenth century was established by Marco Polo.

Anaemia may be caused, among other things, by a lack of iron in certain foodstuffs. As yet, there is no good evidence of its occurrence in antiquity, although by the seventeenth century there are sufficient references to 'green sickness' to suggest that it was then not uncommon.

Certain intestinal worms, only too prevalent in some groups today, may also have encouraged a comparable degree of anaemia in past peoples. Indeed, hookworm and its varied helminth relatives are quite likely to have dogged man throughout his evolution. Direct evidence is scanty so far, and early literary references to worms are very limited. However, in view of the resistance to decay of the eggs of these parasites, and the increasing work now being undertaken on dried faeces and latrine deposits, far more evidence is likely in the near future.

So far we have been dealing with deficiency, but what of over-indulgence—whether in food in general or a particular variety? The fact is that eating too much food—a big temptation in primitive society whenever the resources are plentiful—generally has little effect upon health. One can perhaps speculate on the significance of the fat figurines from Upper Palaeolothic sites of Europe or from Neolithic Malta (and surely an obesity cult is just as likely to represent plenty as a 'fertility' cult), but such art evidence is of doubtful scientific value.

However, one interesting condition resulting from the consumption of too much of a particular kind of food is known. Certain species of pulse contain a toxic (paralytic) factor, so that when any of these make up a large part of a person's daily food over a period of time, a marked deterioration in physical health may take place, the condition being known as lathyrism. Since the seventeenth century, numerous instances of lathyrism have been reported from North Africa, southern Europe and Asia. At times severe epidemics have occurred with many hundreds—occasionally thousands—of people affected, no doubt with considerable socio-economic repercussions in the groups involved. Here again, the incidence of this disease during the past four centuries may be taken as an indication that earlier societies suffered from it to a comparable extent. This supposition receives support from Hippocrates when he comments that 'At Ainos, all men and women who ate continuously peas, became impotent in the legs and that state persisted.'

Fig. 43 Changes in the frequency of dental decay in three populations and through time. Thick line is the British series, thin continuous line the Greek series, and broken line the French series

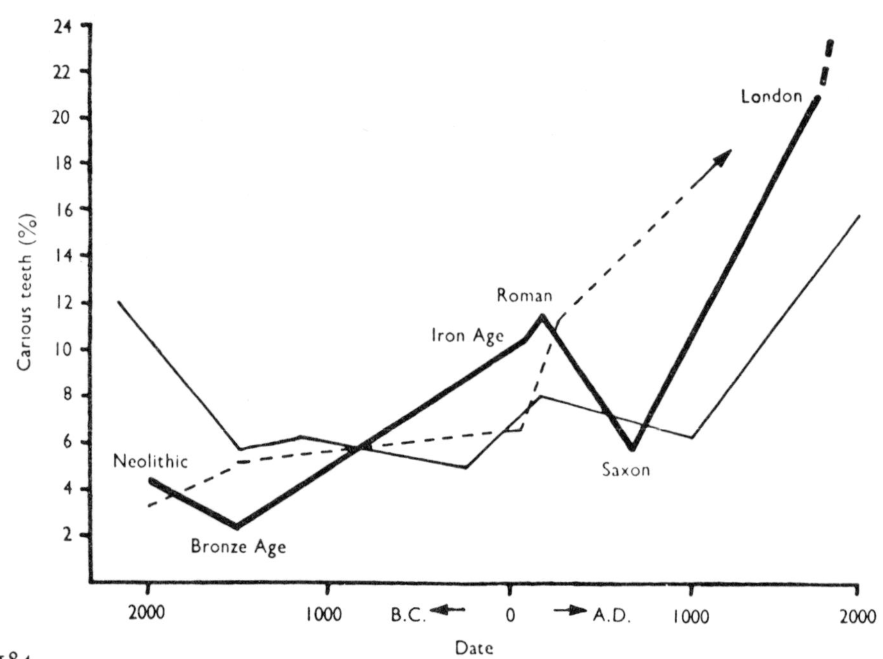

Not only do certain rare skeletal anomalies reveal dietary insufficiency, but there is promise of further and more general information on diet from more common anomalies.

In the case of the long bones, transverse calcified zones—commonly referred to as Harris's lines—have been considered to reflect not only infectious disease episodes in childhood but also periods of malnutrition or perhaps even specific vitamin deficiency. These lines represent minor halts in the longitudinal growth of the bone. As yet, there is no way of distinguishing between lines resulting from dietary upset and those from other causes, but the frequency with which they occur in some skeletal series (over 80 per cent), and within one skeleton, suggests that diet may be a common determinant. Their presence has been noted in Neanderthal man (Tabun I), in Egyptian mummy and skeletal material, in an Iron Age skeleton from Germany, and in British material from Bronze Age, Romano-British, Saxon, and Medieval times. Further studies are needed to equate this interesting anomaly with seasonal malnutrition and periodic famine. This may be more difficult than was at first thought, for recent work has shown that the association between these calcified zones and poor health in childhood is by no means clear-cut.

It is common knowledge that dental decay is related to diet, and although the very high incidence of dental caries in civilized man is not found in earlier peoples, the disease nevertheless occurs,
and can show noticeable differences in frequency from group to 14
group. In the case of early British, Greek, and French groups, not *Fig. 43*
only does the situation change with the passage of time but also the pattern of change is different in each area. The adoption of different ways of living, including food habits, may well account for this. No doubt it was, as now, the increased use of certain starchy and sugary foods which in the past led to a greater incidence of caries, although other variables (such as salivary flow and oral bacteria) may also have played their part. Variations in

Plates 57, 59–61 the wear of the tooth surface have also affected other aspects of oral health. Dental decay is, of course, not restricted to agricultural Plate 56 peoples, and the Upper Pleistocene Rhodesian skull demonstrates the extent to which fossil man could at times be afflicted. In this case, eleven of the upper teeth were carious, but whether the sufferer's poor dental health was the result of a 'sweet tooth' for wild honey or the consumption of too many starchy plant roots we shall never know. The teeth may also be affected during growth, and again infectious disease and malnutrition may be the cause. The condition known as hypoplasia may deform the enamel crowns of the teeth to a very noticeable degree. The anomaly has been noted, for example, in 31 per cent of a small Upper Pleistocene sample (29 individuals), 88 per cent of a Mesolithic sample, and 58 per cent of a British sample ranging from Bronze Age to Plate 58 Medieval times. Again we are left with the tantalizing question as to how much of this hypoplasia in earlier peoples is the result of dietary inadequacy and how much to other causes. There can be no doubt, however, that a not insignificant proportion represents periods of dietary instability during childhood.

Finally, mention may be made of another bone anomaly, known generally as 'osteoporitic' pitting of the skull (though better called symmetrical hyperostosis). Macroscopically, the bone surface may be slightly swollen and display a 'rash' of small pits. It has been Plates 65, 66 noted in numerous skeletal series, from Neolithic times onwards. Again, there is probably a complex of possible causes, with dietary disturbance as a leading claimant.

INFANT FEEDING

The women in all prehistoric—and the majority of early historic—communities probably practised breast-feeding for as long as possible, just as they do in modern primitive and under-developed communities. Again, as modern evidence shows, it is the period just following weaning which may have been particularly critical

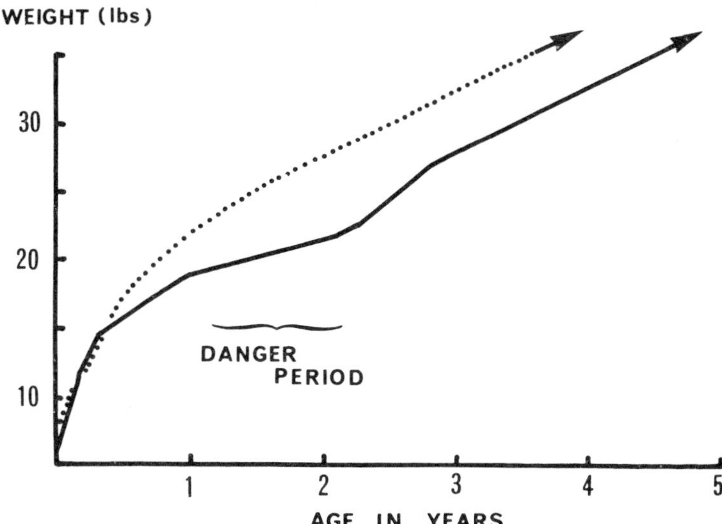

Fig. 44 Weights of modern village children in Uganda (continuous line) compared with English children (dotted line). The danger period between weaning and full adaptation to solid foods is indicated. The village group is most likely to reflect the trend in prehistoric communities. (Modified from H. F. Wilbourn, 1963. Nutrition in Tropical Countries, *O.U.P.)*

to child survival. It is a period when the infant is for the first time chiefly dependent upon solid foods, which can so easily be inadequate or insufficiently varied. A comparison of weights of modern English and African village children demonstrates well the danger period during which disease is particularly liable to strike, either as a direct result of deficiency, or through lowered body resistance. In particular, it is a period of high protein demand often not satisfied owing to the need of a community to resort to a high carbohydrate diet. The result is protein-malnutrition resulting in the unpleasant disease generally known as kwashiorkor. It is quite possible that the high regional kwashiorkor frequencies (over 20 per cent) recorded today among certain African peoples

Fig. 44

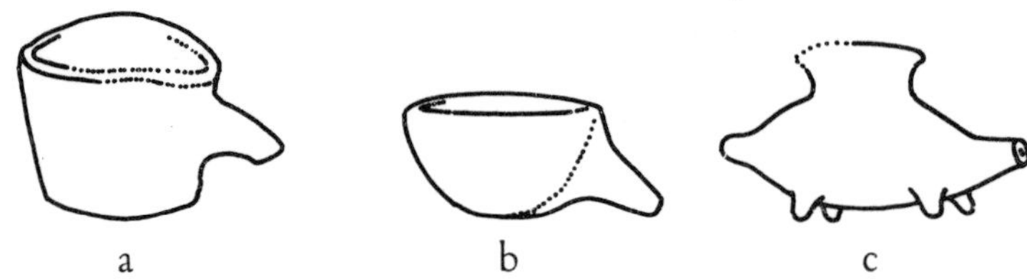

Fig. 45 Early examples of feeding vessels: a, from an infant's grave, Neolithic, at Tours-sur-Marne; b, from the 'twins grave' at Jebel Moya; c, from a Late Bronze Age—Early Iron Age grave at Tulln in Lower Austria. (After Lacaille)

may reflect to some extent the experience of man with this disease during the past few millennia. In particular, the advent of high starch diets, made possible by the domestication of cereals, may well have been responsible for an upsurge in the frequency of protein-malnutrition cases.

Artificial feeding is, of course, not purely a practice of highly civilized society—which is in some respects unfortunate. For, in underdeveloped countries today, one of the great dangers to child health is the uncleanness of feeding containers. The result may be gastro-enteritis, which can be a killer. Once again, it is reasonable to conclude from this modern evidence that in earlier communities also, unhygienic vessels were a constant threat to infant health.

Although the horn of a ruminant may have been used as a fluid container long before the advent of pottery, the earliest likely example of a feeding bottle so far discovered is from an infant's
Fig. 45 grave at Tours-sur-Marne, France, of Late Neolithic date. European Late Bronze to Early Iron Age finds demonstrate even more certainly the presence of specialized feeding vessels. The examples are of fine hand-made ware, ovoid in shape, with a central wide cylindrical neck for filling purposes. A nipple-shaped spout is placed low down on the side of the bottle. Further
Plate 67 good evidence comes from the site of Jebel Moya, in the Sudan, where a number of spouted vessels were found. One notable

discovery at this site was of two small infant skeletons, associated with which were two spouted feeding cups. By Roman times, feeding bottles would appear to have been customary, at least in Europe, and quite a number have been described.

FOOD POISONING AND ADULTERATION

Considering how few plants are used by the great apes (gorilla, chimpanzee and orang utan) as food, in comparison with the very great number eaten by primitive peoples in recent times, the experimental consumption of an ever-increasing variety of foodstuffs may be regarded as one of the important conquests of human evolution. Before the domestication of animals, it is unlikely that potential vegetable food would have been given to any other animal species first, to see what effect these would have (perhaps one of the earliest functions of the dog, besides scavenging, was as an 'experimental' animal to test 'new' foods—a procedure known to have been practised in some recent African communities). Thus, even with the exercise of considerable caution, it is likely that many degrees of food poisoning, from mild stomach disorders to death, occurred before man became fully aware of the limits of his food resources—both plant and animal. It is, of course, impossible to gauge with any certainty at what stage in the million years of human evolution the quest for a much wider food horizon began. Probably the utilization of new vegetable foodstuffs was a gradual development; it would obviously vary according to the plants available in a particular area. Although a simple knowledge of edible plant resources could be transmitted easily enough in Pleistocene times, it seems unlikely that special methods of food preparation were devised before the Neolithic cultural level. In the case of manioc tubers, for example, which are rich in starch, fat and protein, it is necessary to eliminate about 0·1 per cent hydrogen cyanide. In order to render them non-toxic, the roots need to be sliced or pulped, soaked in water for a day and the juice then expressed. Such a long, complicated procedure seems unlikely to be pre-Mesolithic in date, and this similarly applies to the techniques involving the extraction and use of plant poisons for arrow-heads and blow-pipe darts, or as a stupefying agent in water (for catching fish).

Since the beginnings of cereal cultivation one plant disease and
food poison which must have recurrently affected whole villages
and towns is the well-known ergot. Epidemic ergotism results
from the fungus *Claviceps purpurea* contaminating cereal (especially rye) flour. It can thus affect the health of a whole community.
That it was certainly present in the Iron Age grasses and crops of
Denmark has been shown rather dramatically by the palaeo-
50 botanist Hans Helbaek, who found in the stomach contents of
Grauballe man profuse evidence of plant diseases, including
ergot and barley smut.

Some of the malignant 'plagues' which ravaged Europe during the Middle Ages might well have been the result of eating cereals containing undetected ergots. Several possible instances are recorded by chroniclers of the sixth and eighth centuries AD, and it is even more certain that tenth-century French and twelfth-century Spanish epidemics were caused in this manner. We may safely assume that this evidence from the present millennium mirrors to some extent the prevalence of ergotism at least since the beginnings of cereal cultivation. Botanically, there is nothing against this supposition, and it is most unlikely that greater care would have been taken in earlier millennia to eliminate patches of poor quality and diseased cereals from the harvest. One or two early writings definitely suggest the occurrence of ergotism. A Babylonian tablet (*c.* 2500 BC) mentions 'women who gather noxious grasses'. An Assyrian tablet (*c.* 650 BC) also refers to a 'noxious pustule in the ear of grain'. Allusions to it are also to be found in Theophrastus, Hippocrates, Pliny and Galen, the first clear account of ergot and its properties being given by the Perso-Arabic physician Muwaffak (AD 950).

That meat in certain states was not healthly to eat was clearly appreciated by the early Biblical scholars, and in Deuteronomy (XIV, 21) it is stated that 'Ye shall not eat of any thing that dieth of itself.' The early use of food preservatives similarly implies not only the desire to store food for a time, but also to protect it against unhealthy forms of decomposition.

Any consideration of inedible meat would be incomplete without a mention of the classic quail poisoning, as related in the Bible. During the lean days after their departure from Egypt (*c.* 1400–1300 BC), the Israelites were able to catch a large number of these birds during their spring migration. It is related, however, that 'while the flesh was yet between their teeth, ere it was chewed, the wrath of the Lord was kindled against the people and the Lord smote the people with a very great plague' (Numbers XI, 33). Now it is known from modern observations that the birds have plenty of access during the autumn migration to cornfields, but during their spring movements the food resources are very limited, and can include poisonous plants. Such plants include hemlock, which contains the quickly acting poison conine, and it seems highly probable that this or a similar fast plant poison was responsible for the Israelite 'plague'.

Surprisingly enough, honey may also contain poison sufficient to kill, not through decomposition or fungal growths, but again through plant poisons. This abnormal honey is mentioned by a number of ancient writers, including Strabo and Pliny. The honey of Pontus was well known for its poisonous properties, and Xenophon relates that those who ate the honey became mentally disturbed, were not able to co-ordinate physical movements and suffered from vomiting and diarrhoea.

Food is defined as adulterated 'when any substance other than that which the article purports to be is mixed with, or added to it, either to increase the bulk or weight or apparent size, or to give it
a deceptive appearance'. The temptation to adulterate food is no 36
doubt as old as the work of specialized food production and

distribution, but in fact it is not until a few centuries before the Christian era that there is written evidence of this practice. In particular, there are a number of Asiatic references to this matter, and during the second century BC, the Chinese work *The Institutes of Chou* stated that the supervisors of markets employed agents to check on the authenticity of products and prevent fraudulent sales. From the ancient Indian Sanskrit text, the *Arthasastra* (*c.* 300 BC) we learn that the adulteration of grains, oils, alkalis and salts was punishable by a fine. Similarly, another Indian text dated to *c.* 200 BC states that 'one commodity mixed with another must not be sold (as pure), nor a bad one (as good)'. Unlike fruit and vegetables, flour was an obvious and easy material to adulterate. The serious contamination of flour with alum, chalk and bone-ash, although reaching its peak in the eighteenth century, extends back over many centuries, and indeed inefficient early corn milling may well have been an important factor in producing unintentionally adulterated flour.

It is scarcely surprising that fluids such as wine and beer were early contaminated by adulterants. At times, wine appears to have undergone very considerable dilution, and it is difficult to see how such weakened drink could have got by unrecognized unless 'strengthening' adulterants had also been added. Although more substantial evidence is necessary, it does seem quite likely that the addition of lime, chalk, gypsum, and even lead, for the counteracting of acidity was known to the Greeks and Romans. Probably the depths of alcoholic adulteration were not reached in Europe until comparatively recent times. One early eighteenth-century recipe will suffice to illustrate the extremely unhealthy nature of some of the concocted alcoholic drinks; the constituents were sulphuric acid, oil of almonds, oil of turpentine, spirits of wine, lump sugar, lime water, rose water, alum and salt of tartar!

Bibliography

As many of our references include aspects of 'palaeo-dietetics' pertinent to more than one chapter of this work, they seem best arranged in simple alphabetical order. Well known classical authors such as Pliny, Cato, Columella, Varro, and Theophrastus, have not been included. They are all easily available in the Loeb Classical Library series. The literature on the food (and food debris) of earlier populations is now vast—and continues to grow. The following list is meant to give a select review of the publications, but we hope that its brevity will not obscure the great breadth of archaeological and literary sources now available. The plain numbers appearing in the margins of the main text refer to the numbered entries of this bibliography.

1 ALLEN, H. WARNER, *A History of Wine*, London, 1961.

2 AMBRO, RICHARD D., Dietary—technological—ecological aspects of Lovelock Cave coprolites, *Reports of the University of California Archaeological Survey*, *70*, 1967, Berkeley, 37–47.

3 ANDRÉ, J., *L'Alimentation et la Cuisine à Rome*, Paris, 1961.

4 ANGRESS, S., AND REED, C. A., *An Annotated Bibliography on the Origin and Descent of Domestic Mammals, 1900–1955*, Chicago, 1962.

5 APICIUS, *The Roman Cookery Book*, a Critical Translation of the Art of Cooking by Apicius, translated by FLOWER, BARBARA and ROSENBAUM, ELISABETH, London, 1958.

6 ARRINGTON, L. R., Foods of the Bible, *Journal of the American Dietetic Association*, *35*, 1959, 816–20.

7 BIGGS, H. E. J., Mollusca from Prehistoric Jericho, *Journal of Conchology*, *24*, 1960, 379–87.

8 BILLINGHAM, J., Snail haemolymph, an aid to survival in the desert, *Lancet I*, 1961, 903–6.

9 BODENHEIMER, F. S., *Insects as Human Food*, The Hague, 1951.

10 —, *Animal and Man in Bible Lands*, Leiden and New York, 1960.

11 BONAVIA, F., *The Flora of the Assyrian Monuments and its Outcomes*, London, 1894.

12 BOSWELL, VICTOR R., Our Vegetable Travelers, *The National Geographic Magazine, Washington, 96,* 1949, 145–217.

13 BROOKS, R., *The Natural History of Chocolate,* London, 1725.

14 BROTHWELL, D. R., Teeth in earlier human populations, *Proceedings of the Nutrition Society, 18,* 1959, 59–65.

15 BROTHWELL, D. R. AND HIGGS, E. S. (Eds.), *Science in Archaeology,* London and New York, 1963. (See especially papers by Helbaek, Callen, Reed, Herre, Dawson, and Ryder).

16 CALLEN, E. O. AND CAMERON, T. W. M., A prehistoric diet revealed in coprolites, *New Scientist, 8,* 1960, 35–40.

17 CAMPBELL-THOMPSON, R., *The Assyrian Herbal,* London, 1924.

18 CHANEY, RALPH W., The Food of 'Peking Man', *Carnegie Institution of Washington New Service Bulletin, III,* 1935, 199–202.

19 CHAPLIN, RAYMOND E., Animals in Archaeology, *Antiquity, 39,* 1965, 204–11.

20 CLARK, J. G. D., *Prehistoric Europe. The Economic Basis,* London, 1952; Stanford, 1966.

21 —, Radiocarbon dating and the spread of farming economy, *Antiquity, 38,* 1964, 45–8.

22 COLLINS, J. L., Antiquity of the pineapple in America, *Southwestern Journal of Anthropology, 7,* 1951, 145–55.

23 COOK, S. F. AND TREGANZA, E. E., The quantitative investigation of Indian Mounds, *University of California Publications on American Archaeology and Ethnology, 40,* 1950, 223–62.

24 COON, C. S., Race and ecology in man. *Cold Spring Harbor Symposia on Quantitative Biology, 24,* 1959, 153–9.

25 COWAN, RICHARD A., Lake margin ecologic exploitation in the Great Basin as demonstrated by an analysis of coprolites from Lovelock Cave, Nevada, *Reports of the University of California Archaeological Survey, 70,* 1967, Berkeley, 21–35.

26 CURWEN, E. CECIL AND HATT, GUDMUND, *Plough and Pasture: The Early History of Farming,* New York, 1953.

27 DE CANDOLLE, A., *Origin of Cultivated Plants,* London, 1886.

28 DE CASTRO, J., *Geography of Hunger,* London, 1955.

29 DEEVEY, EDWARD S., The Human Population, *Scientific American, 203,* 1960, 194–204.

30 DEGERBØL, MAGNUS, On a find of Preboreal domestic dog (*Canis familiaris* L.) from Star Carr, Yorkshire, with remarks on other Mesolithic dogs, *Proc. Prehistoric Society, 27,* 1961, 35–55.

31 DIMBLEBY, GEOFFREY, *Plants and Archaeology,* London and New York, 1967.

32 DORRELL, SHEILA, The Preservation of Organic Material in the Tombs of Jericho. Appendix L, 704–717, in K. M. Kenyon: *Excavations at Jericho,* Vol. 2, London, 1965.

33 EMERY, W. B., *A funerary repast in an Egyptian tomb of the Archaic Period,* de Buck Memorial Lecture, Leiden, 1962.

34 EWER, R. F., The contribution made by studies of the associated mammalian faunas. *South African Journal of Science, 59,* 340–7, 1963.

35 FARRAR, W. V., Tecuitlatl; a glimpse of Aztec food technology, *Nature, 211,* 1966, 341–2.

36 FILBY, F. A. AND DYER, B., *A History of Food Adulteration and Analysis,* London, 1934.

37 FLANNERY, KENT V., The ecology of early food production in Mesopotamia, *Science, 147,* 1965, 1247–56.

38 FORBES, R. J., *Studies in Ancient Technology,* Vols. II and III, Leiden, 1955; New York, 1964.

39 FRASER, H. M., *Beekeeping in Antiquity,* London, 1931.

40 GABEL, CREIGHTON, *Analysis of Prehistoric Economic Patterns,* New York, 1967.

41 *Geoponika,* [Agricultural Pursuits] *trans.* R. T. Owen, 2 vols., London, 1805.

42 GÜNTHER, R. T., The Oyster Culture of the Ancient Romans, *Journal of the Marine Biological Association, 4,* 1897, 360–5.

43 GURNEY, O. R., *The Hittites,* Harmondsworth, 1961.

44 HEDRICK, U. P. (Ed.), *Sturtevant's Notes on Edible Plants,* Albany, 1919.

45 HEER, OSWALD, Treatise on the 'Plants of the Lake Dwellings', pp. 518–36. In Keller, Ferdinand, *The Lake Dwellings of Switzerland and Other Parts of Europe,* London, 1878.

46 HEIZER, ROBERT F., Analysis of human coprolites from a dry Nevada cave. *Reports of the University of California Archaeological Survey, 70,* 1967, Berkeley, 1–20.

47 HELBAEK, HANS, Early crops in Southern England, *Proc. of the Prehistoric Society, 18*, 1952, 194–233.

48 —, Domestication of Food Plants in the Old World, *Science, 130*, 1959, 365–72.

49 —, *Palaeoethnobotany of the Near East and Europe, in* Braidwood, R. J. and Howe, B., *Prehistoric Investigations in Iraqi Kurdistan.* (Studies in Ancient Oriental civilization, No. 31), Chicago, 1960.

50 —, Studying the Diet of Ancient Man, *Archaeology, 14,* 1961, 95–101.

51 HEYERDAHL, THOR, *American Indians in the Pacific,* London, 1952; New York, 1963. (Part VII on botanical evidence.)

52 —, Plant evidence for contacts with America before Columbus, *Antiquity, 38,* 1964, 120–33.

53 HIGGS, E. S., A Metrical Analysis of some Prehistoric Domesticated Animal Bones from Cyrenaican Libya, *Man,* 1962, 119–22.

54 HIGGS, E. S. AND WHITE, J. P., Autumn killing, *Antiquity, 37,* 1963, 282–9.

55 HOU, H. C. AND YU, C. M., Beriberi in Ancient Chinese medical literature, *Chinese Medical Journal, 58,* 1940, 302–13.

56 HOWES, F. N., *Nuts, the Production and Everyday Uses.* London, 1948.

57 HOUGHTON, W., Notices of fungi in Greek and Latin authors, *Annals and Magazine of Natural History,* ser. 5, 5, 1885, 22–49.

58 ISAAC, ERICH, Influence of religion on the spread of citrus, *Science, 129,* 1959, 179–86.

59 —, On the Domestication of Cattle, *Science, 137,* 1962, 195–204.

60 JENSON, LLOYD B., *Man's Foods, Nutrition and Environments in Food Gathering Times and Food Producing Times,* Illinois, 1953.

61 KELLER, F., *The Lake Dwellings of Switzerland and Other Parts of Europe,* London, 1878; repr. New York, 1963. See sections on fauna and flora.

62 KELLER, WERNER, *The Bible as History,* London and New York, 1956.

63 LEE, T'AO, Historical notes on some vitamin deficiency diseases in China, *Chinese Medical Journal, 58,* 1940, 314–323.

64 LORET, V., *La Flore Pharaonique d'après les documents hiéroglyphiques et les spécimens découverts dans les tombes,* Paris, 1892.

65 LUCAS, A., *Ancient Egyptian Materials and Industries,* London, 1934. Fourth edition, revised and enlarged by J. R. Harris, London and New York, 1962.

66 MACADAM, W. E., On the results of chemical investigation into the composition of the 'bog butter', and of 'adipocere' and the 'mineral resins'; with notice of a cask of bog butter found in Glen Gell, Morvern, Argyllshire, and now in the Museum, *Proc. of the Society of Antiquaries of Scotland, 4,* 1882, 204–23.

67 MANGELSDORF, P. C., Reconstructing the Ancestor of Corn, *Smithsonian Report* for 1959, Washington, 1960, 495–507.

68 MANGELSDORF, P. C., MACNEISH, R. S., AND GALINAT, W. C., Domestication of corn (Zea Mays), *Science, 143,* 1964, 538–45.

69 MARTIN, PAUL S., AND SCHOENWETTER, JAMES, Arizona's oldest cornfield, *Science, 132,* 1960, 33–4.

70 MEDWAY, LORD, Food bone in Niah Cave Excavations (–1958). A preliminary report, *Sarawak Museum Journal, 8,* 1958, 627–36.

71 —, Niah Shell—1954—8. *Sarawak Museum Journal, 9,* 1960, 368–79.

72 MEIGHAN, CLEMENT W., The Little Harbor Site, Catalina Island: An Example of Ecological Interpretation in Archaeology, *American Antiquity, 24,* 1959, 383–405.

73 MEIGHAN, C. W., PENDERGAST, D. M., SWARTZ, B. K., AND WISSLER, M. D., Ecological Interpretation in Archaeology: Parts I & II. *American Antiquity, 24,* 1958, 1–23, 131–50.

74 MERRILL, ELMER DREW, *The Botany of Cook's Voyages,* Waltham (Mass.), 1954.

75 MOURANT, A. E., AND ZEUNER, F. E. (Eds.), Man and Cattle. *Proc. of a Symposium on Domestication,* London, 1963.

76 NENQUIN, JACQUES, *Salt, a Study in Economic Prehistory,* Brugge, 1961.

77 OAKLEY, KENNETH P., Fire as Palaeolithic Tool and Weapon, *Proc. of the Prehistoric Society, 21,* 1955, 35–48.

78 OKAKURA, K., *The Book of Tea,* ed. E. V. Bleiler, New York, 1964.

79 OLSEN, J. E., AND BOURNE, E. G. (Eds.), *The Northmen, Columbus and Cabot 985–1503* in *Original Narratives of Early American History,* gen. ed. J. F. Jameson, New York, 1934.

80 ORGAN, J., *Gourds,* London and Newton Centre, Mass., 1963.

81 OSTOYA, PAUL, La préhistoire révèle l'origine du Maïs, *Science Progrès, 3353,* 1964, 329–35.

82 PARRY, J. W., *The story of Spices,* New York, 1953.

83 PRAKASH, OM., *Food and Drinks in Ancient India,* Delhi, 1961.

84 RADCLIFFE, WILLIAM, *Fishing from the Earliest Times,* New York, 1921 London, 1926.

85 RAMSBOTTOM, J., *Mushrooms and Toadstools,* London and New York, 1963.

86 REED, CHARLES A., Animal Domestication in the Prehistoric Near East, *Science, 130,* 1959, 1629–39.

87 —, Osteological evidences for prehistoric domestication in southwestern Asia, *Zeits. für Tierzüchtung und Züchtungsbiologie, 76,* 1961, 31–8.

88 —, Snails on a Persian Hillside, *Postilla, 66,* New Haven, 1962, 1–20.

89 REED, WILLIAM, *The History of Sugar and Sugar-yielding Plants,* London, 1866.

90 REID, C., Plants, wild and cultivated, in Bullard and Gray: Glastonbury Lake Village, Vol. 2, 1917.

91 RIEHM, KARL, Prehistoric salt-boiling, *Antiquity, 35,* 1961, 181–91.

92 RITCHIE, J., A keg of 'bog butter' from Skye and its contents, *Proc. of the Society of Antiquaries of Scotland,* 75, 1940, 5–22.

93 ROLFE, R. T. AND ROLFE, F. W., *The Romance of the Fungus World. An account of Fungus Life in its Numerous Guises, both Real and Legendary,* London, 1925.

94 SALAMAN, R. N., *The History and Social Influence of the Potato,* Cambridge and New York, 1949.

95 SAUER, CARL O., *Agricultural Origins and Dispersals,* Bowman Memorial Lectures, 1952, New York.

96 SCOTT, J. M., *The Tea Story,* London, 1964. Published as *The Great Tea Venture,* New York, 1964.

97 SHÊNG-HAN, SHIH, *On 'Fan Shêng-Chih Shu' an agriculturalistic book of China written by Fan Shêng-Chih in the first century* BC, Peking, 1959.

98 SHEWELL-COOPER, W. E., *Plants and Fruits of the Bible,* London, 1962.

99 SIMMONDS, N.W., *The Evolution of the Banana,* London and New York, 1962.

100 SOYER, A., *The Pantropheon or History of Food, and its Preparation, from the Earliest Ages of the World,* London, 1853.

101 STORR-BEST, LLOYD, *Varro on Farming; M. Terenti Varronis Rerum Rusticarum Libri Tres,* London, 1912.

102 STANTON, W. R. AND WILLETT, F., Archaeological evidence for changes in maize type in West Africa: an experiment in technique, *Man, 63,* 117–23.

103 STEARN, W. T., The Origin and later development of cultivated plants, *Journal of the Royal Horticultural Society, 90,* 1965, 279–341.

104 TOLKOWSKY, S., *Hesperides. A History of the Culture and Use of Citrus Fruits,* London, 1938.

105 TOWLE, MARGARET A. AND WILLEY, GORDON R., *The Ethnobotany of Pre-Columbian Peru,* Chicago, 1961.

106 VARGAS, CÉSAR, Phytomorphic representations of the Ancient Peruvians, *Economic Botany, 16,* 1962, 106–15.

107 VICKERY, KENTON FRANK, Food in Early Greece, *University of Illinois Bulletin, 34,* 1936, 97.

108 WAKEFIELD, E. G. AND DELLINGER, S. C., Diet of the Bluff Dwellers of the Ozark Mountains and its skeletal effects, *Annals of Internal Medicine, 9,* 1936, 1412.

109 WARREN, S. HAZZLEDINE, On a prehistoric interment near Walton-on-the-Naze. *Essex Naturalist, 16,* 1911, 198–208.

110 WATERS, JOSEPH H., Some animals used as food by successive cultural groups in New England, *Bulletin of the Archaeological Society of Connecticut, 31,* 1962, 32–46.

111 WHITE, K. D., Wheat farming in Roman times, *Antiquity, 37,* 1963, 207–12.

112 WHITE, T. E., Observations on the butchering technique of some aboriginal peoples, *American Antiquity, 17,* 1952, 337–8; *19,* 1953, 160–4; *19,* 1954, 254–64; *21,* 1955, 170–8.

113 —, A method of calculating the dietary percentage of various food animals utilized by aboriginal peoples, *American Antiquity, 18,* 1953, 396–8.

114 Wilber, Charles G., Water requirements of man, *U.S. Armed Forces Medical Journal, 8,* 1957, 1121–30.

115 Willett, Frank, The introduction of maize into West Africa: an assessment of recent evidence, *Africa, 32,* 1962, 1–13.

116 Yarnell, R. A., Aboriginal relationships between culture and plant life in the Upper Great Lakes region. *Anthrop. Papers, Museum of Anthropology, University of Michigan, Ann Arbor, 23,* 1964.

117 Zeuner, Frederick E., *A History of Domesticated Animals,* London, 1963; New York, 1964.

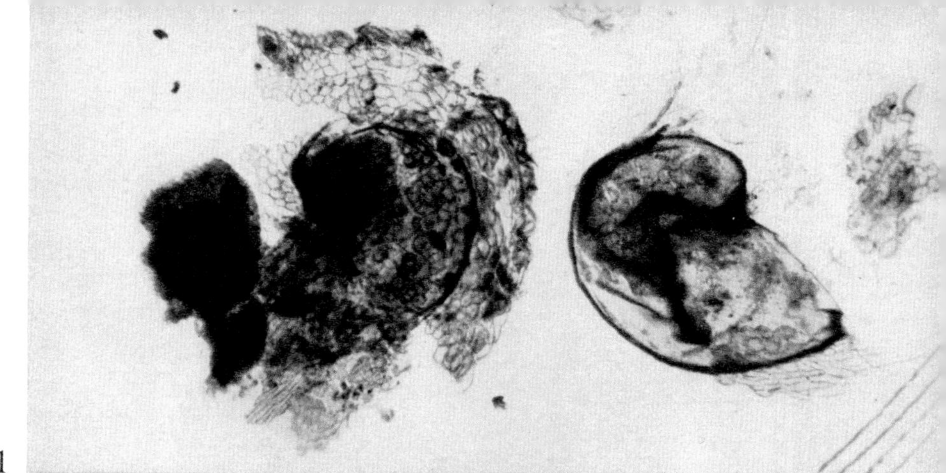

1

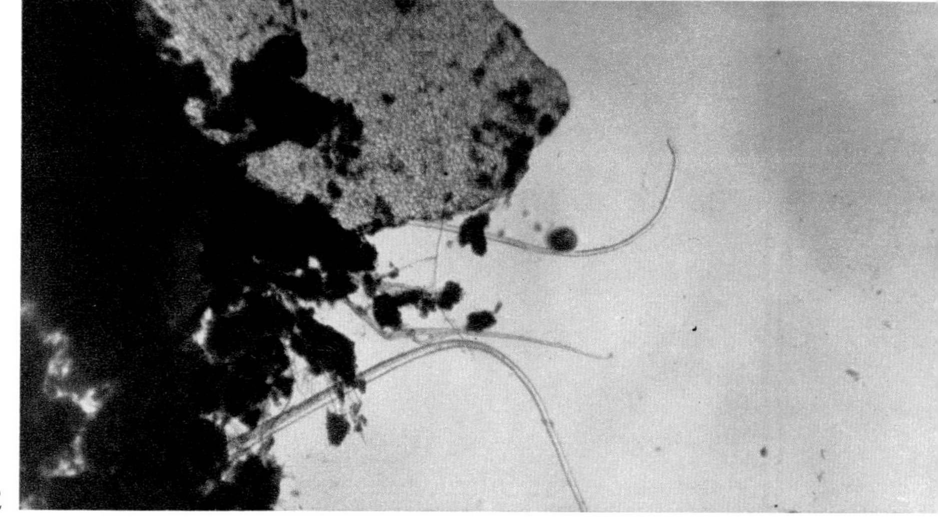

2

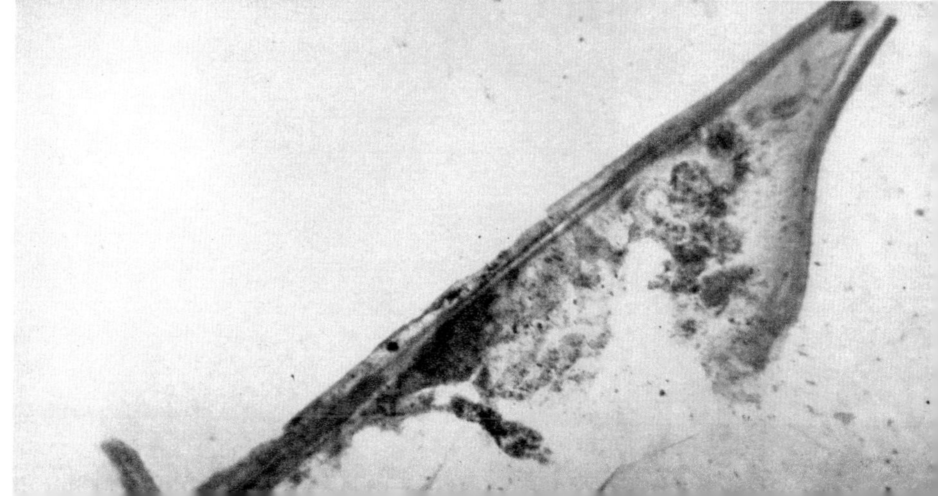

3

4

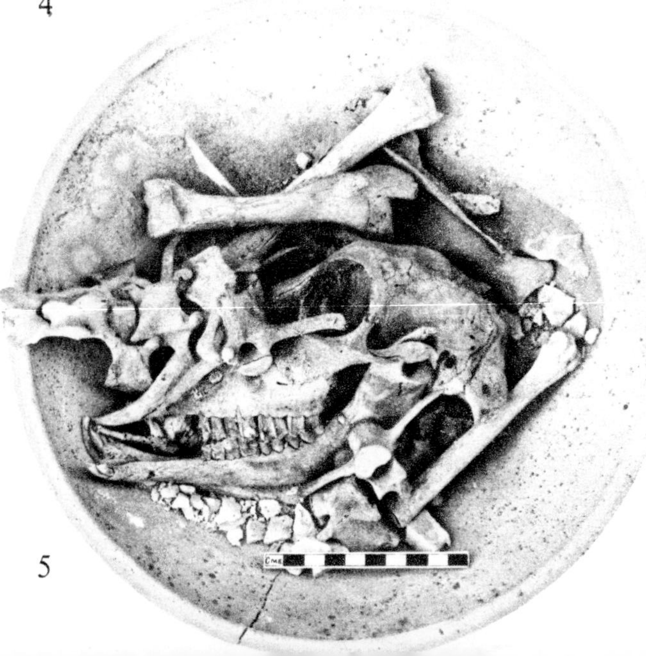

5

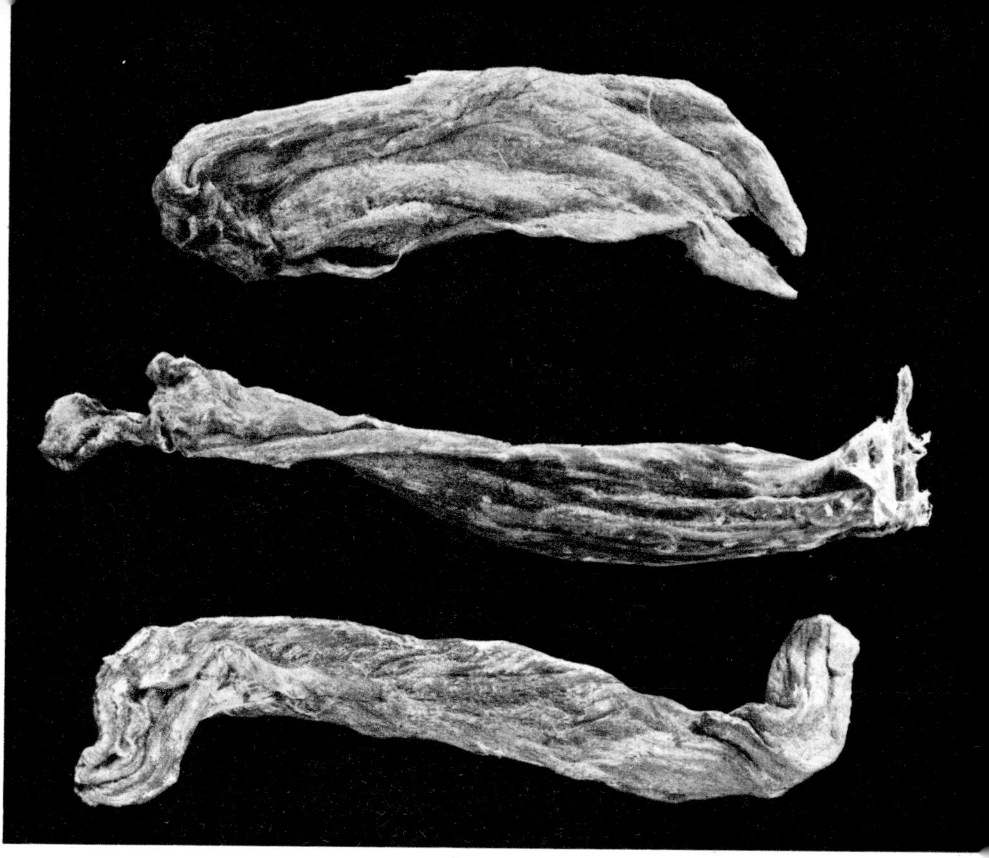

6

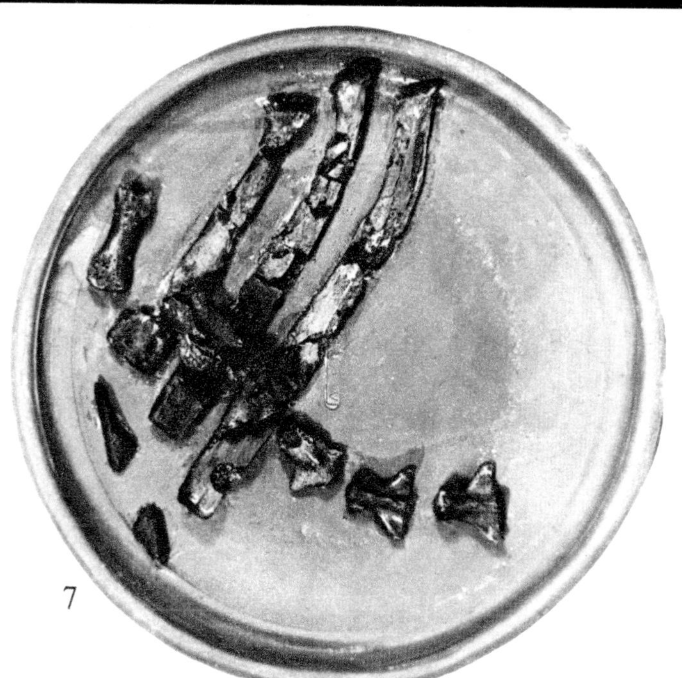

7

8

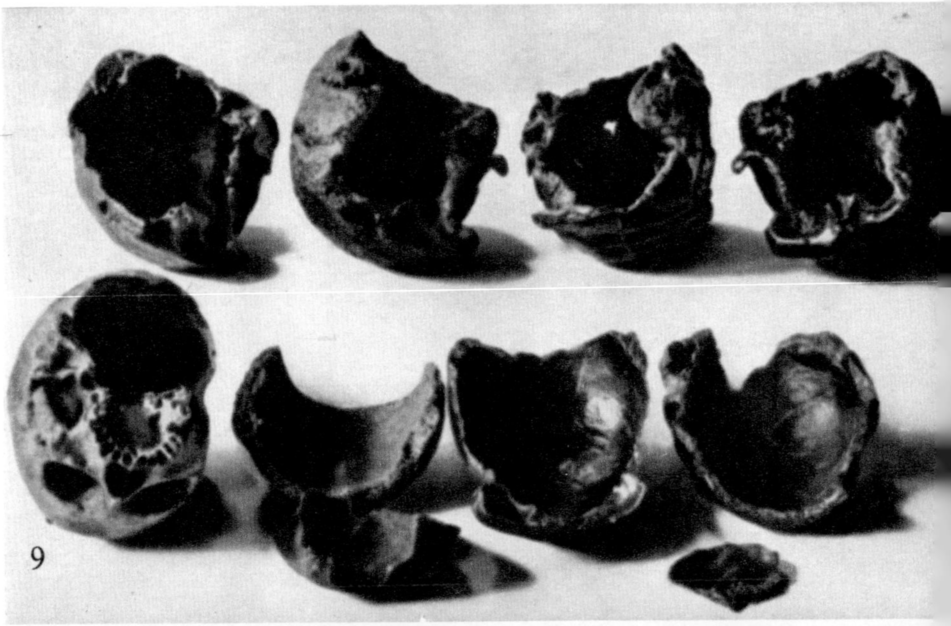

9

10
11

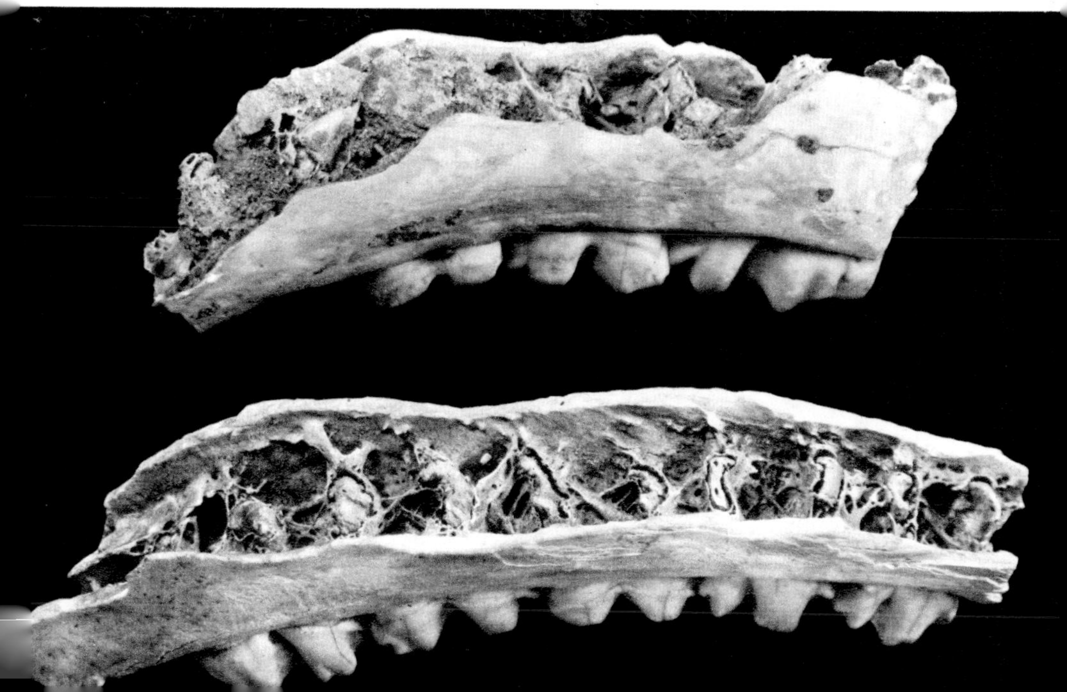

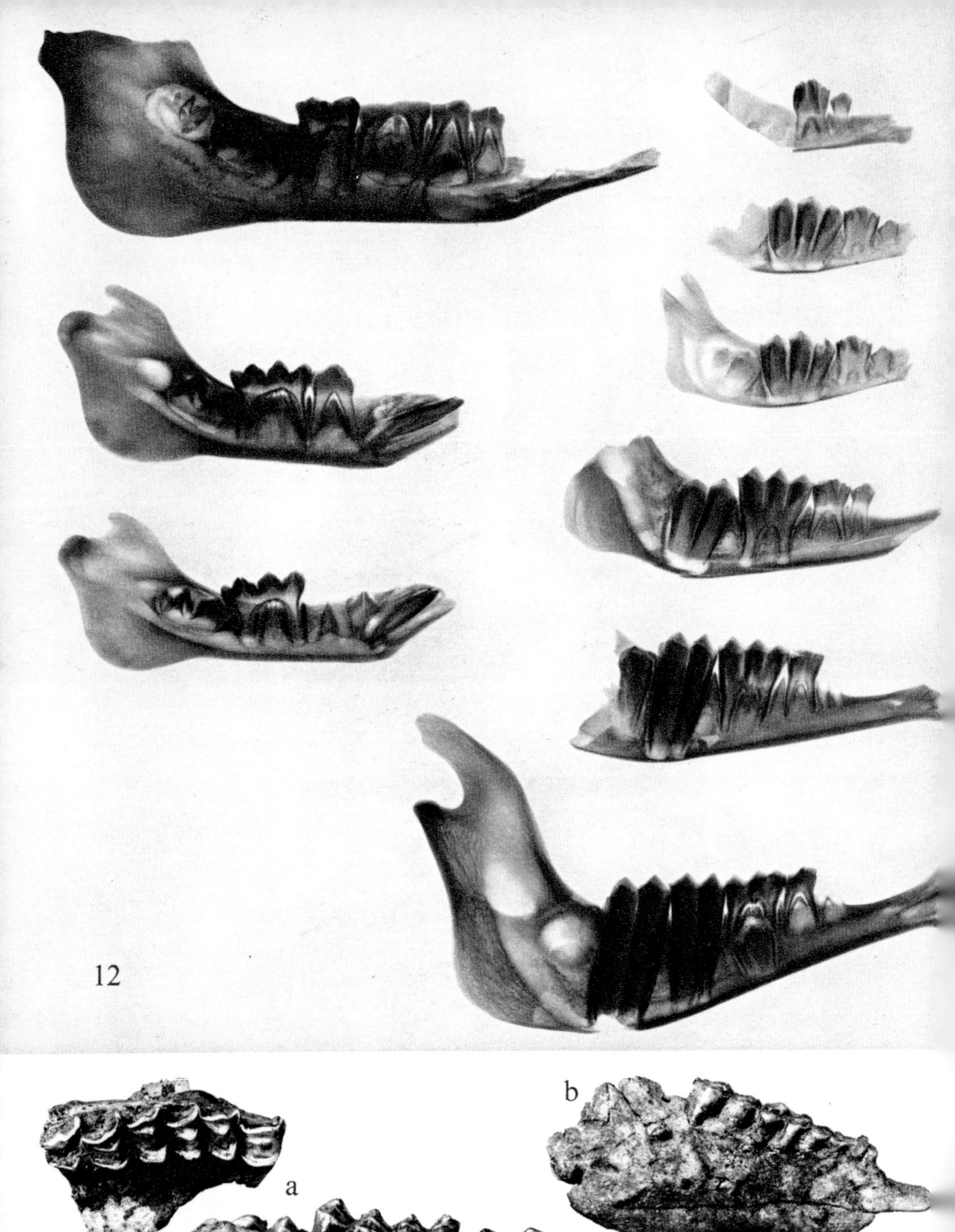
12
b
a
13

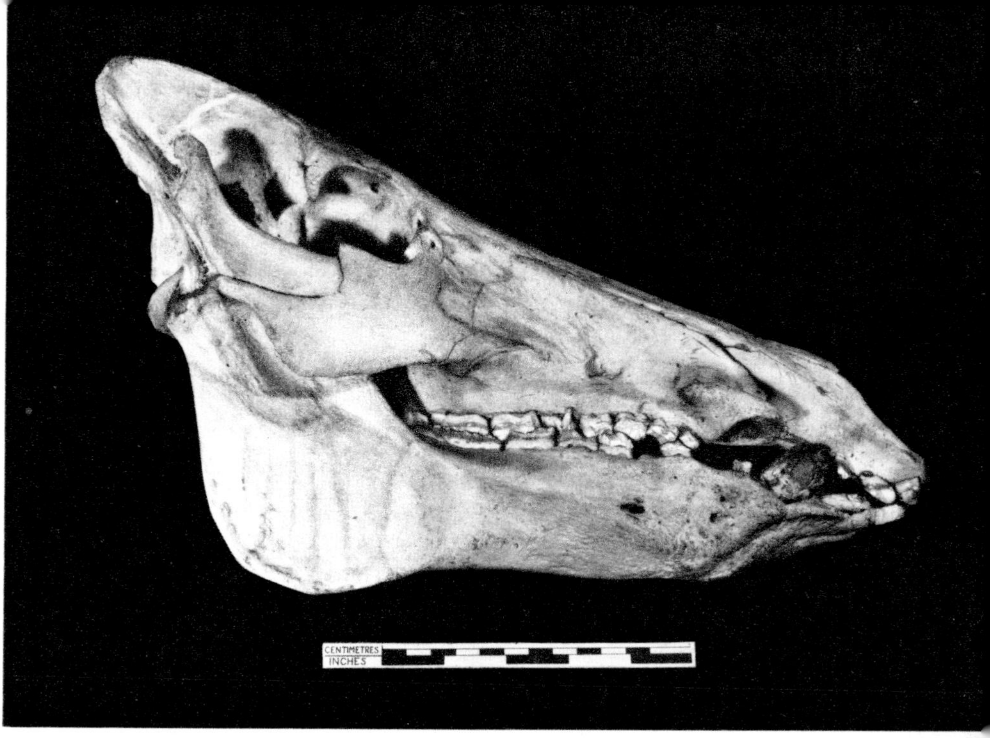

14

15

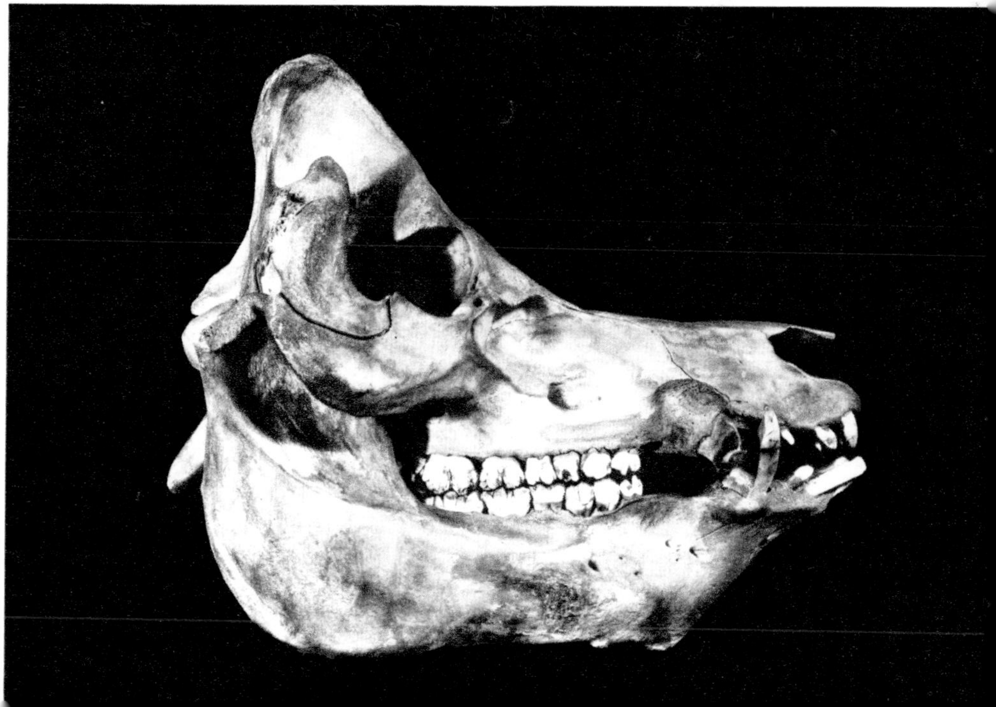

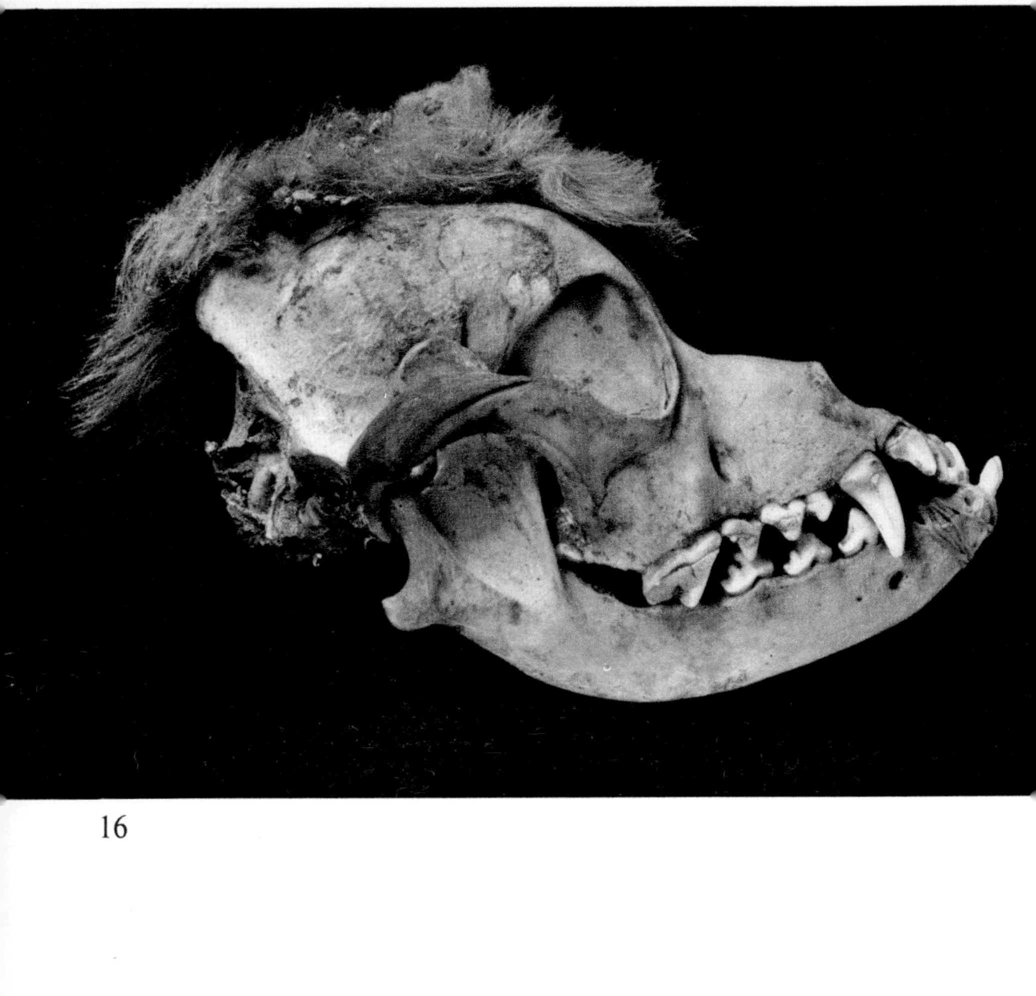

16

18

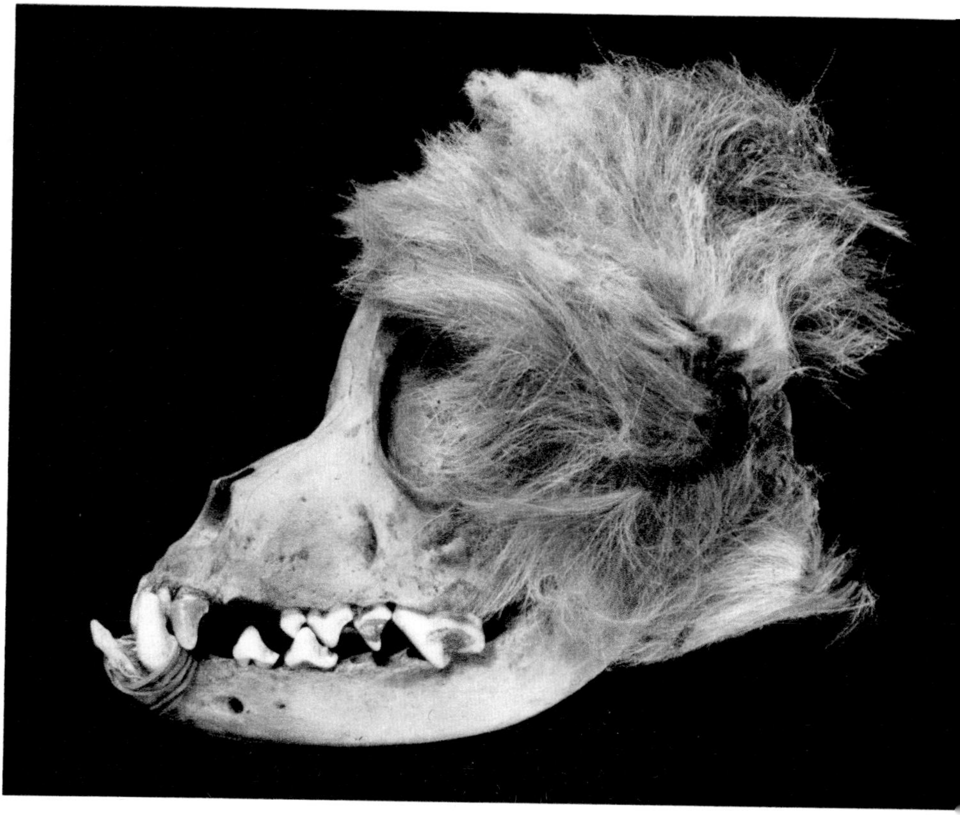

17

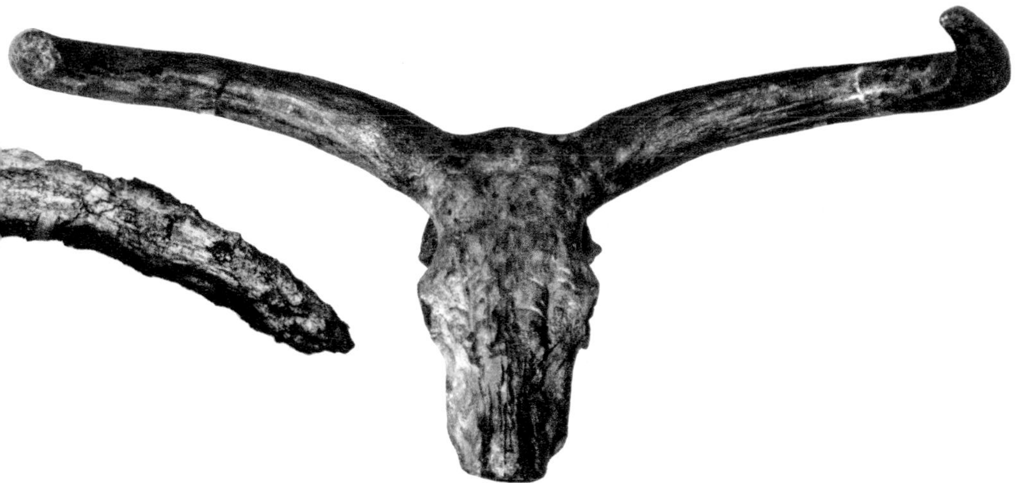

19

20

21

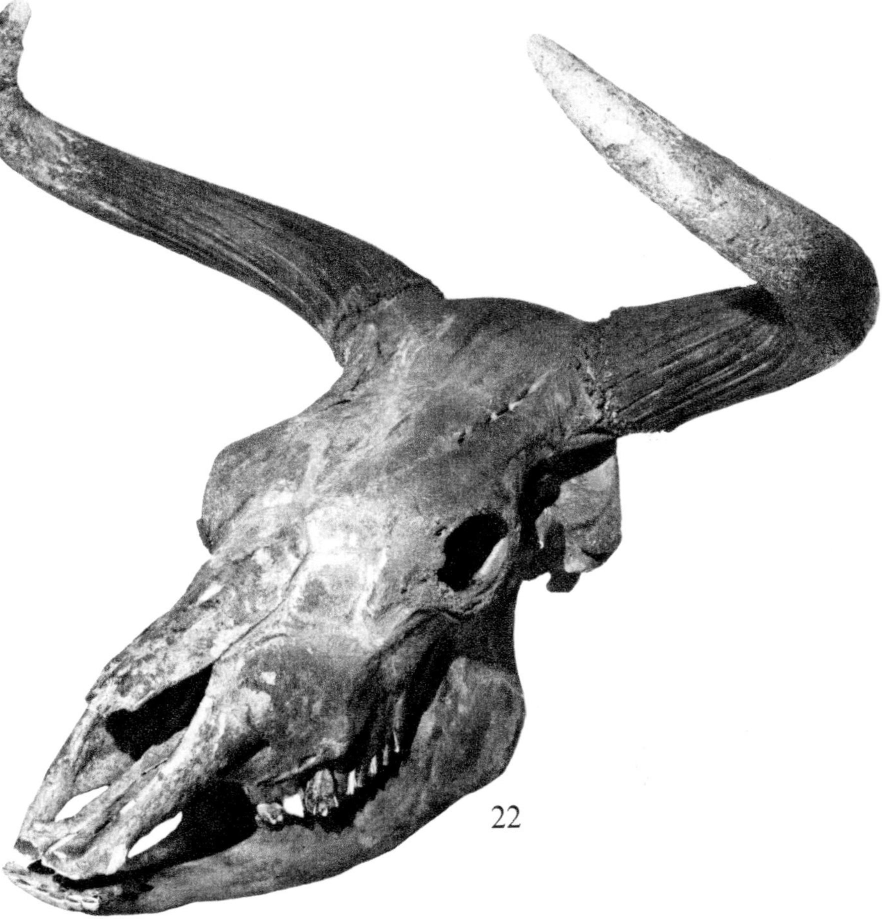

22

23

24
25

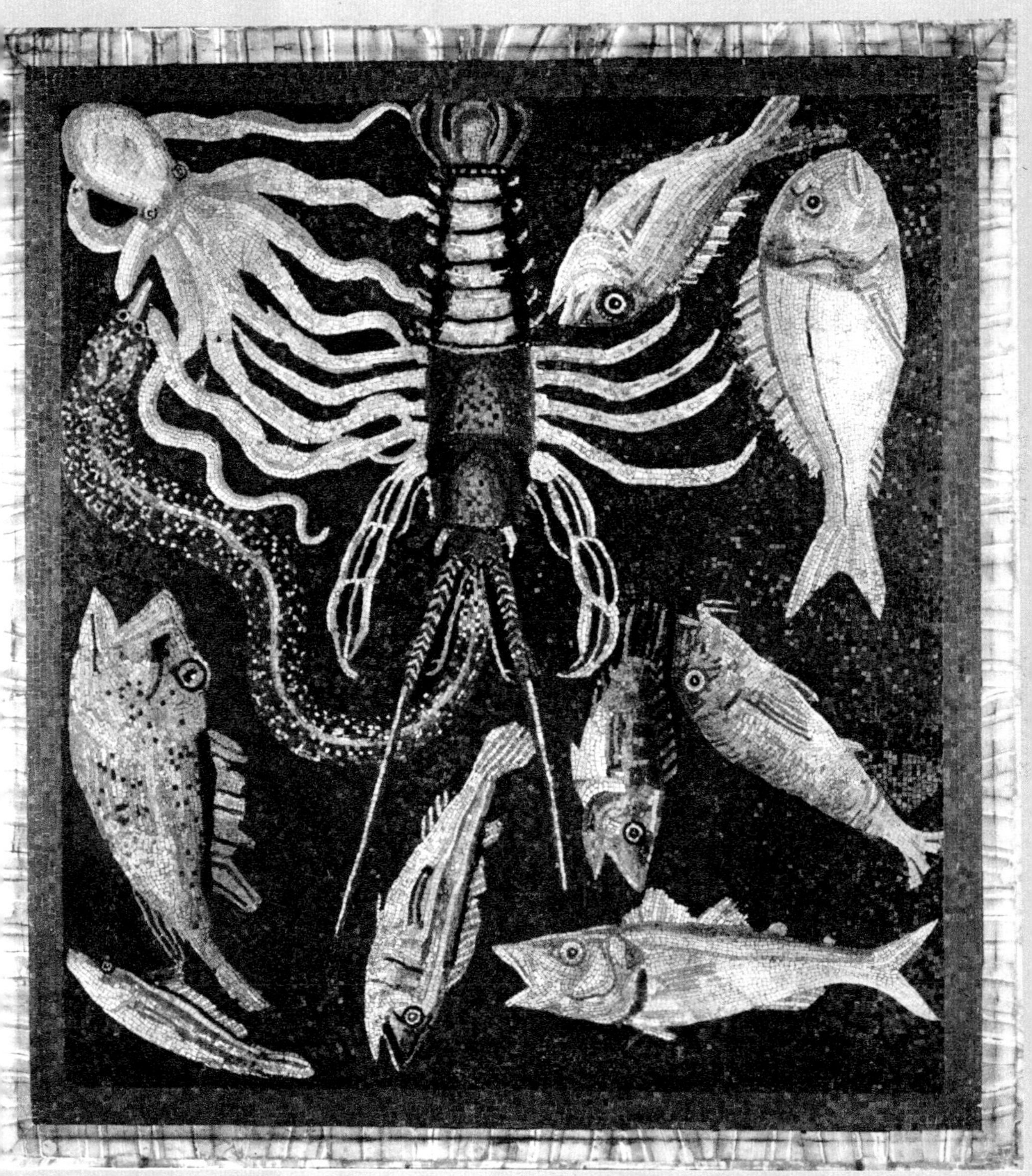

26

a
b
c
27

a
b
c
d
e
28

29

30

31

32

33

34

35

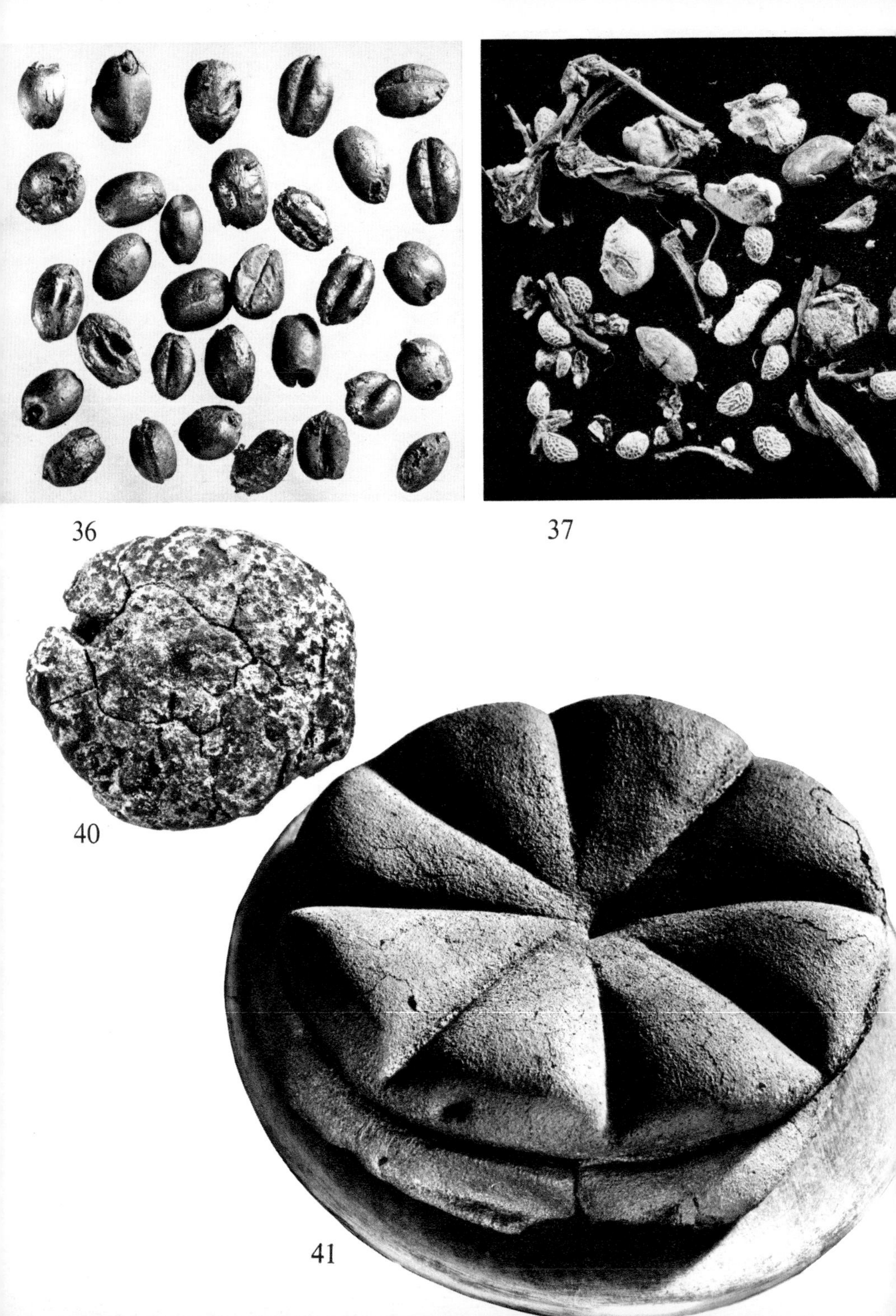

36

37

40

41

38

39

42

43

44

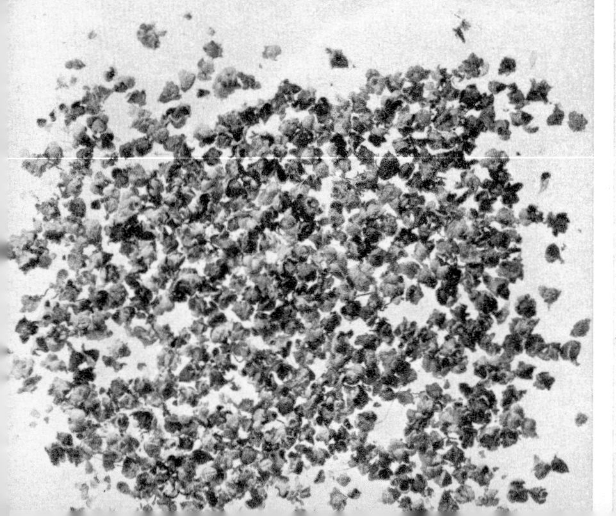

45

46

47

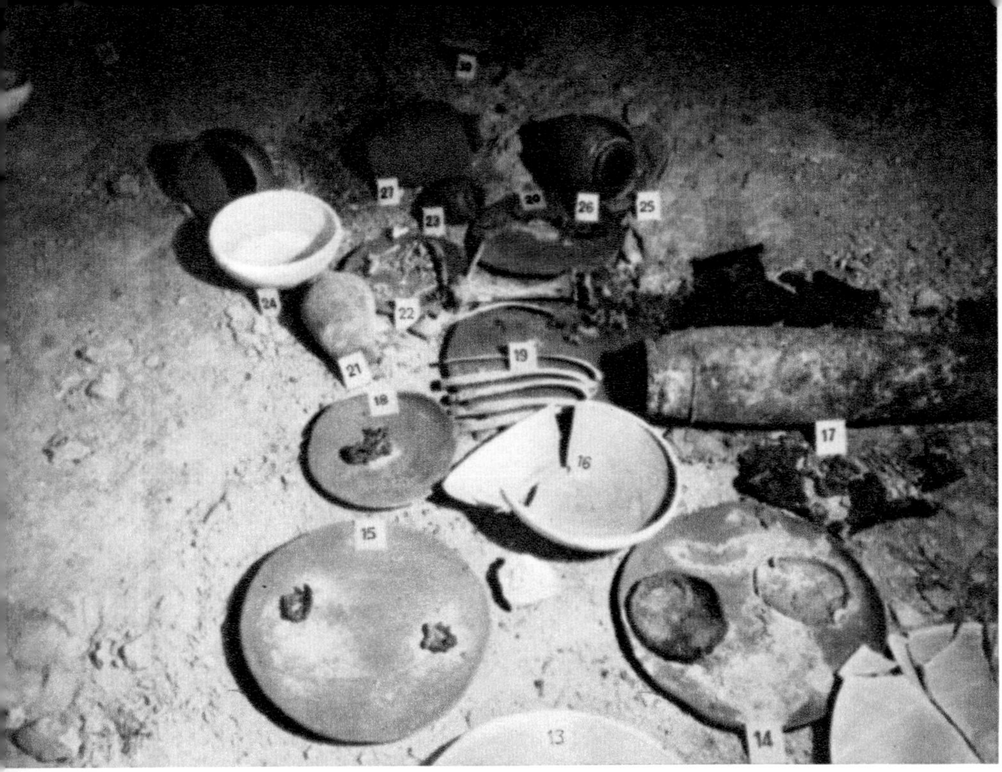

48

49

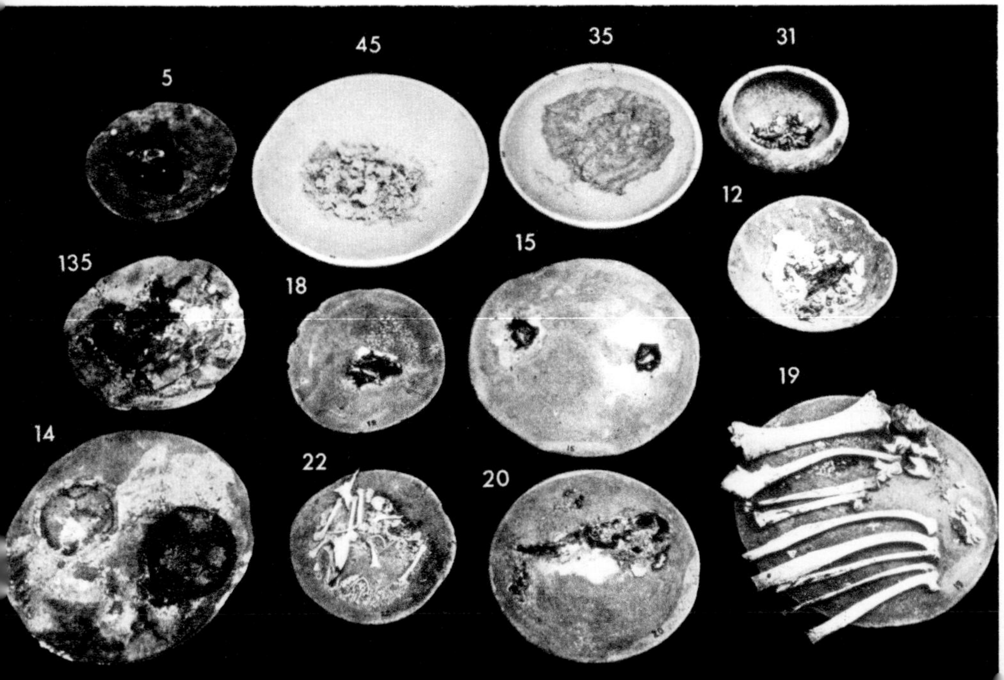

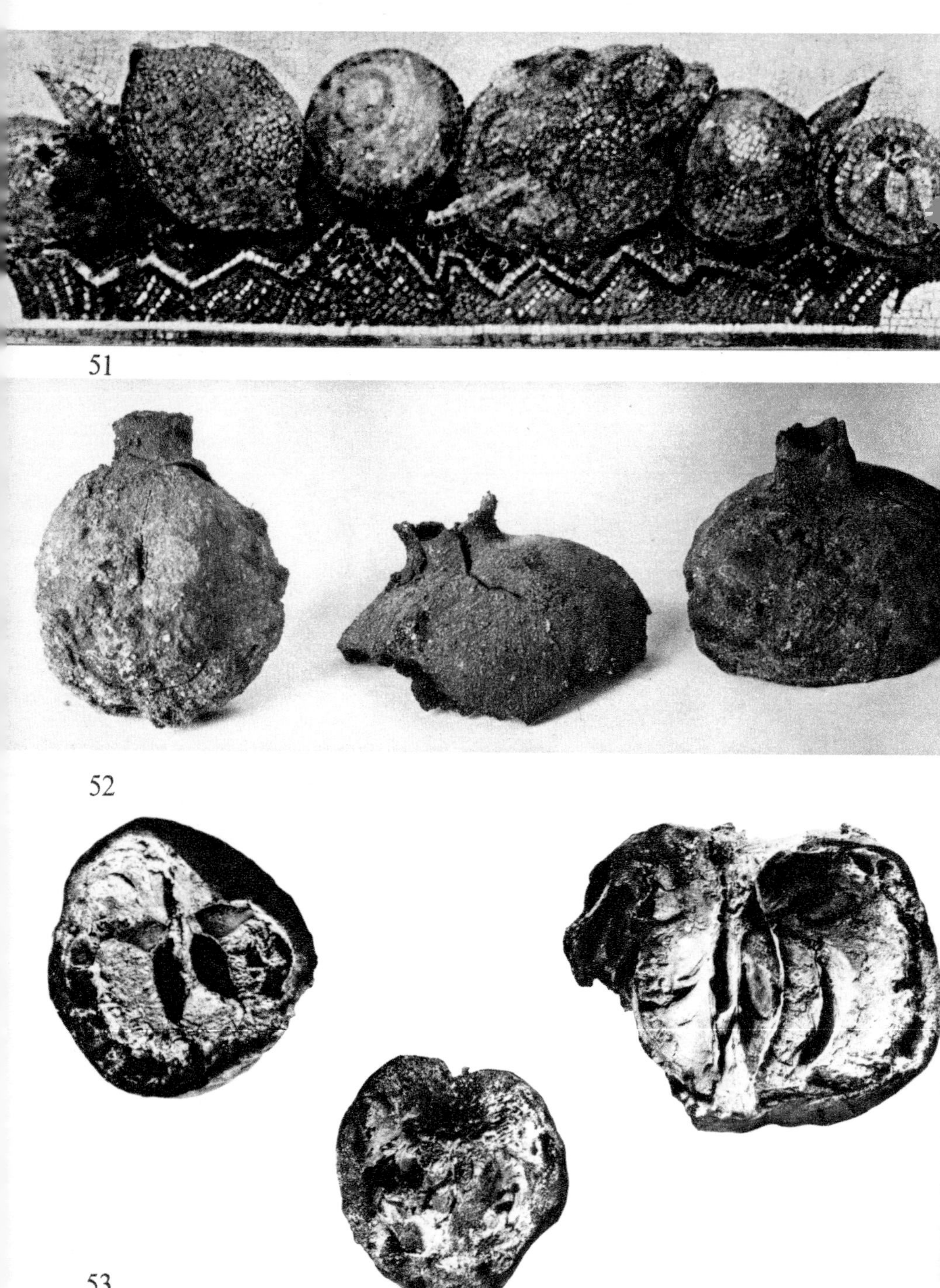

51

52

53

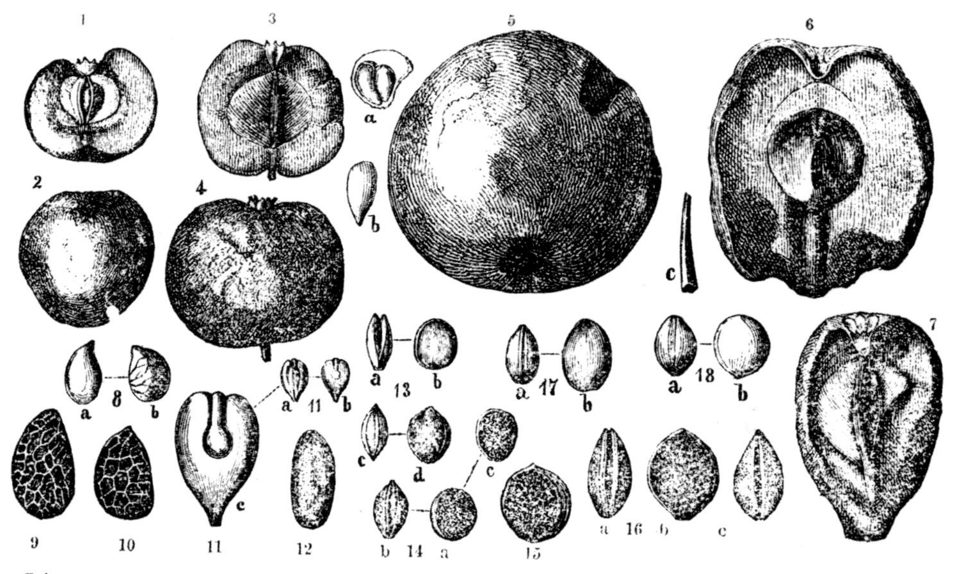
1
3
5
6
a
2
4
b
c
7
a
13
b
a
17
b
a
18
b
a
8
b
a
11
b
c
d
c
c
9
10
11
12
b
14
a
15
a
16
b
c

54

55

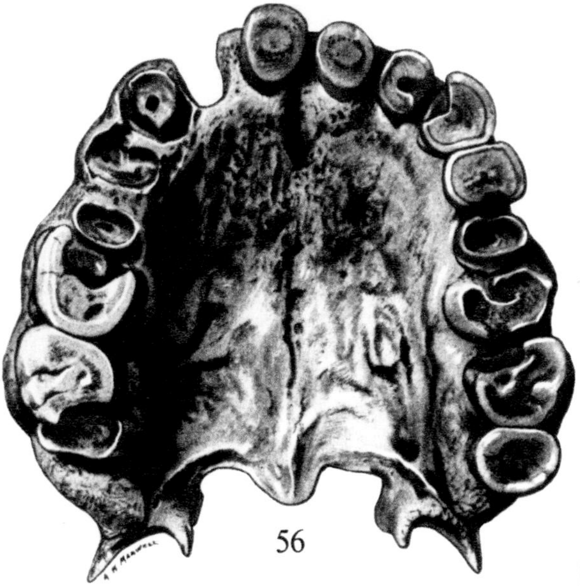

56

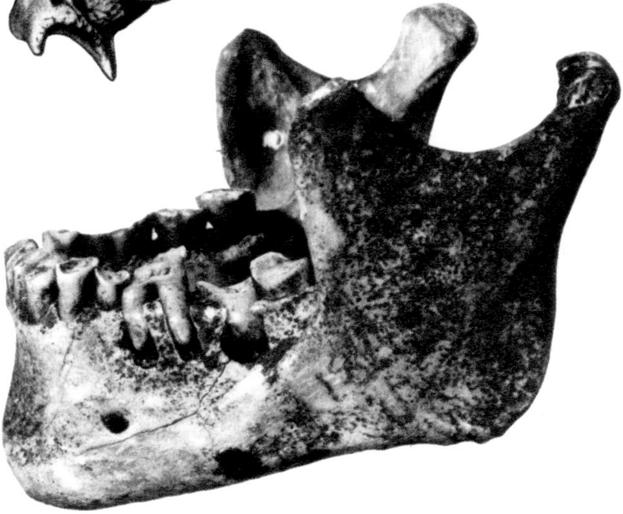

57

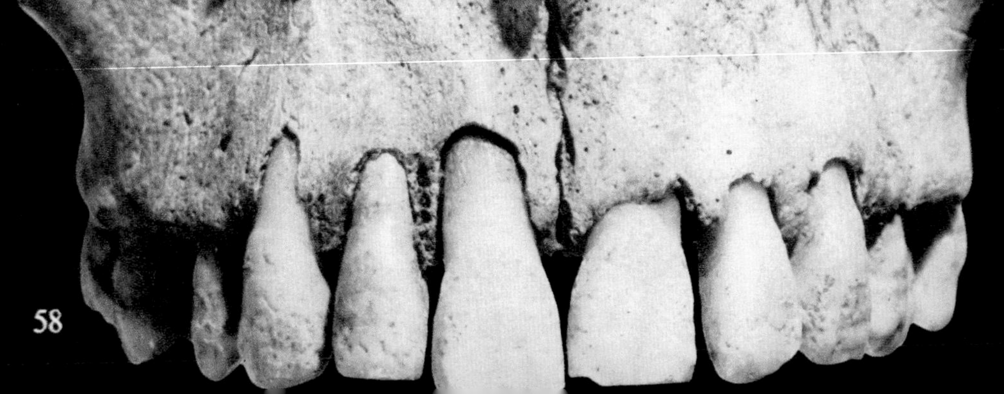

58

59

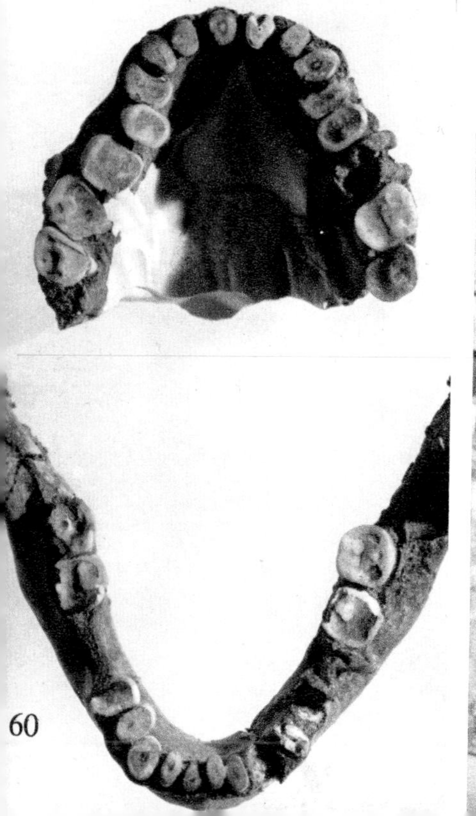
60

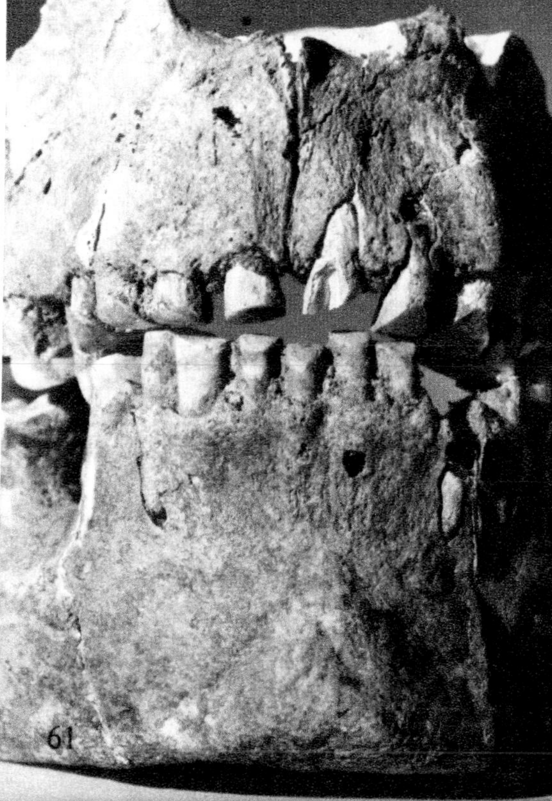
61

62

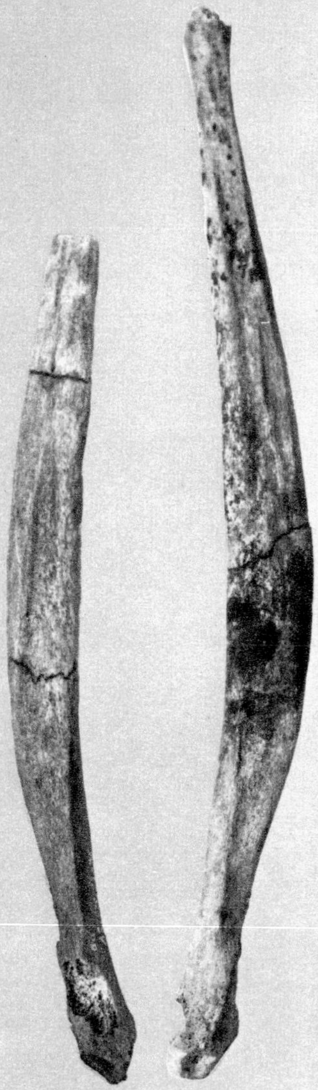

63

64

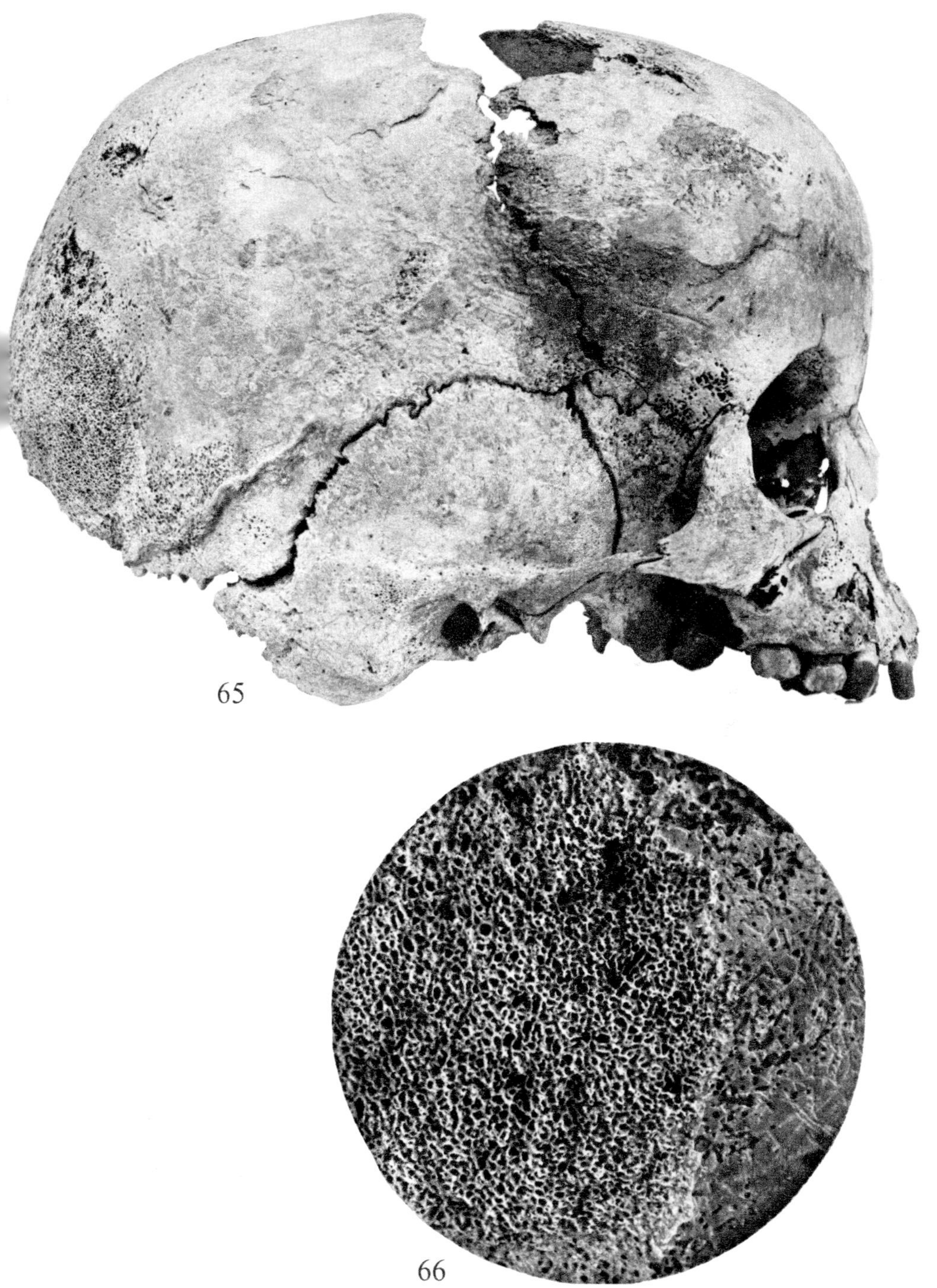

65

66

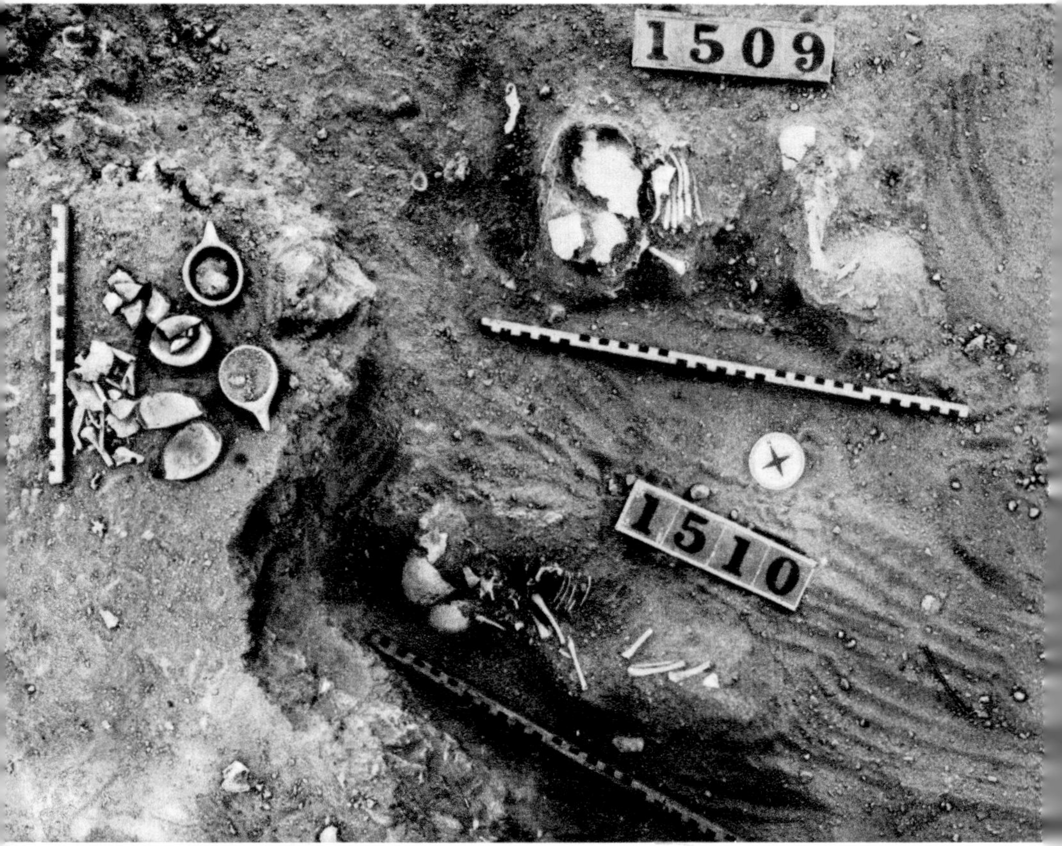

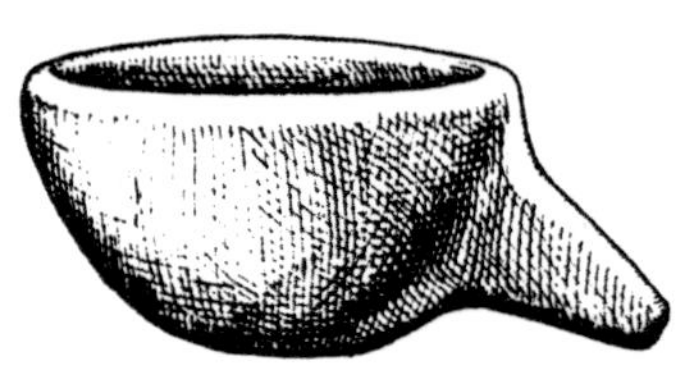

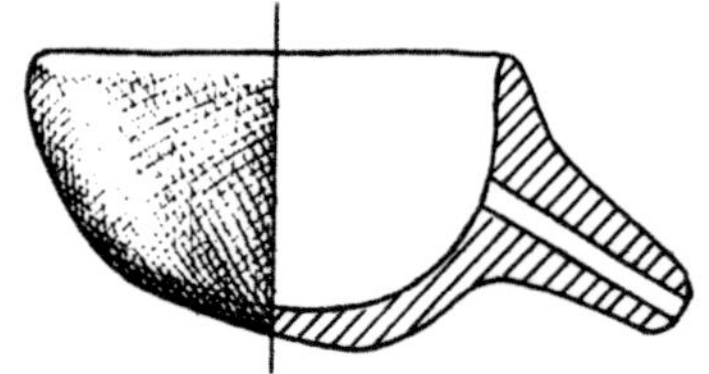

67

Notes on the Plates

1 Coprolite material from Tehuacan, Mexico. The seed is probably 'tuna', that is, from one of the cactus fruits (possibly *Lemaireo ceres*).

2 Rehydrated animal and plant debris from a coprolite excavated at Tehuacan. Meat fibres are present as a dark mass, together with well-defined hairs and an epidermis fragment of *Capsicum*.

3 Portion of a legume pod from a Tehuacan coprolite.

4 Dish containing a large slab of meat, from excavations by Kathleen Kenyon at Jericho. The unusual degree of preservation was related to the nature of the tomb environment.

5 Joints of mutton, including a sheep's head, on a platter found in a Jericho tomb. This direct association between foodstuff and domestic pottery is not common, though examples are known for various regions and cultures.

6 Strips of dried meat (biltong) from Zambia. This recent specimen illustrates the type of dried meat which could have been easily produced by ancient hunters living in hot and dry areas. It could easily be transported back to camp in this form.

7 The Cliffe Dish and its food offering, a Romano-British example in the Passmore Edwards Museum, London. The bones are mutton.

8 Bronze Age storage jar from Jericho, to show the skins left by the evaporation of the liquid. Chemical analysis was undertaken on such food debris, though interpretation proved difficult. 1:5

9 Seven skulls of Upper Pleistocene Solo Man from Ngandong in Java, compared with a modern Dyak trophy (left skull lower row). In each case the base of the skull is seen to be broken, some believe for the purpose

of brain extraction, though this is a very debatable point. After von Koenigswald.

10 Mousterian food remains. Bone breccia from a cavern at La Quina, France.

11 Upper Palaeolithic mammal food debris. Fragments of reindeer mandibles broken for marrow. Magdalenian. La Madeleine, France.

12 Radiograph of immature mandibles of Neolithic pig and sheep/goat from Egolzwil 4 (Canton Lucerne). By this technique, age assessments can be made on the developing unerupted teeth.

13 Pre-pottery Neolithic food animals from Jarmo. It is from this type of broken material that identifications must usually be made.
(a) Jaw fragment of sheep.
(b) Lower jar fragment of goat.
(c) Jaw remains of pig.

14 Skull of a wild boar, showing elongated facial morphology typical of undomesticated varieties of pig.

15 Skull of a domestic pig, showing marked structural modifications as a result of selective breeding.

16, 17 Left and right lateral views of a Peruvian dog skull, showing the short-faced type of skull and the long head hair, Forbes Collection (B.M.N.H.), Necropolis of Ancon.

18 Horn cores of *Bularchos arok,* an example of a large Middle Pleistocene game mammal. Bed 4, Olduvai Gorge. Approx. width 1·65 m.

19 *Bos namadicus* skull from the Nabada River, India, now in the Indian Geological Survey collections. Approx. width 1·4 m.

20 White Park Cattle of the Duke of Hamilton's herd at Cadzov, Lanarkshire. Considered by some to be derived from an ancient feral stock.

21 Matching horn cores of an early domestic goat, showing flattened surfaces and an incipient twist. Jarmo.

22 Skull of *Bos primigenius* of Early Bronze Age date from Lowe's Farm site, Littleport.

23 A sixteenth-century painting of *Bos primigenius* found in an antique shop in Augsburg in 1827.

24 Roman cheese bowl, showing widely distributed holes through which the whey drained.

25 A milking scene depicted at Ur.

26 Marine animals on a Roman mosaic, probably from Populonia in the Pontine marshes, and thought to be about second century AD. The identity of all these animals is not certain, but the most likely are as follows. Beginning with the Langouste in the centre, and going anti-clockwise, are the following: 1, Langouste; 2, Octopus; 3, Muraena; 4, Angler fish; 5, Cuckoo Wrasse; 6, Another form of Wrasse; 7, Bass; 8, Sea Perch; 9, Red Mullet; 10, Sea Bream; 11, Gilthead.

27 Examples of mollusc food debris: a, shell of *Saxidomus giganteus,* Pre-Columbian (?), British Columbia; b, *Acavus* sp. (Waltoni), shell midden, Bellan bandi pallasa, Ceylon; c, *Paludomus* sp. (Tanalia), also from Bellan bandi pallasa, Ceylon.

28 Evidence of molluscs used as food at three other prehistoric sites; *a* and *b* are *Helix naegelea* from Jarmo; *c* and *d* are *Helix* from Jericho; *e* is a limpet from Pindal Cave, Spain.

29 North African desert scrub showing scattered shells and living animals of *Eremina* clustered in a bush.

30 Close-up view of an Eremina shell.

31–33 Photographic evidence of insect-eating by a wild chimpanzee. A suitable stick is first selected, then inserted into the termite mound, and then withdrawn and licked clean of termites.

34 Bee-keeping scene from the tomb of Pa-bu-sa, Egypt. Detail of the east colonnade.

35 Roman mosaic of glass cubes, first century BC. Rabbit with mushrooms and a lizard. Judging from the colours of the mosaic pieces, it is possible that the mushrooms are *Amanita caesarea*, the favourite variety of the Romans.

36 Carbonized grain from a Swiss Neolithic site. Originally it was thought to have been barley, but is probably *Triticum compactum.*

37 Part of the residue of stomach contents associated with an early Bronze Age skeleton from Walton-on-the-Naze. The seeds identified were of blackberry, rose and *Atriplex.*

38 Carbonized grain, probably the wheat *Triticum aestivum,* from an Iron Age site at Dunstable. The chalky soil of this locality is not the best environment for the preservation (or identification) of such plant remains.

39 Carbonized grain, probably barley, from an early site at Lewes.

40 Charred Iron Age 'bun' from a Dunstable site. This type of food evidence can easily be missed, especially if mistaken for a lump of earth.

41 Carbonized bread from Pompeii. The segmented form of the loaf appears to be typical of the period.

42 A storage jar full of carbonized grain, from a tomb at Jericho.

43 Whistling jar, Chimú period, Peru. It is in the form of a cluster of ears of corn, topped by a figurine in a corn-covered costume.

44 A very early example of popcorn, found in a bag attached to the belt of a mummy from Chile.

45 Bag found filled with popcorn. Chilean mummy.

46 Fragment of Middle Pleistocene cave breccia from Choukoutien, China. It shows a quartz implement with a fashioned edge, pieces of charred bone and the shell of a hackberry seed.

47 Hazel-nuts and acorns from Swiss Neolithic lake-sites.

48, 49 Funerary repast of Second Dynasty date at Saqqara, *in situ* (48), and with individual items of the 'menu' set out (49): 5, triangular loaf of bread (emmer wheat); 45, a form of porridge (made from ground barley); 35, unidentified. A liquid containing some sort of fatty substance; 20, a cooked fish, cleaned and dressed with the head removed; 22, pigeon stew; 18, a cooked quail, cleaned and dressed with the head tucked underneath one wing; 15, two cooked kidneys; 19, ribs and legs of beef; 135, identity uncertain, but containing cut ribs of beef; 12, stewed fruit, probably figs; 31, fresh *nabk* berries (rather like cherries in appearance); 14, small circular cakes (sweetened with honey). 23, 26, 27, in the upper photograph, small jars containing some form of cheese; 17 is a large jar which held grape wine.

50 The priests' meal as found in the ruins of the Temple of Isis at Pompeii. It includes eggs, walnut, fish, and cereals.

51 Orange, citron, lemon and other fruit, shown in a Roman mosaic thought to come from Tusculum (*c.* AD 100) and now in the Museo Nazionale in Rome.

52 Remains of two pomegranates (left and centre) together with the lid of a wooden box carved in the form of a pomegranate (right). All are from a Jericho tomb.

53 Dried apple halves from Swiss Neolithic lake-sites, now completely carbonized. Their size range extends beyond that for the wild crab-apple.

54 Plant remains from Swiss and other lake-sites. 1–4, crab-apple; a, b, core and seed; c, stalk. 5, 6, cultivated apple. 7, wild pear. 8a, strawberry seed magnified; 8b, water crowfoot magnified. 9, raspberry seed magnified. 10, seed of the blackberry magnified. 11, grape-stones, a, b, natural size;

c, magnified. 12, stone of the cornel cherry. 13, perfumed cherry; a, b, from Castione near Parma; c, d, from Robenhausen. 14, bird cherry; a, b, round stone from Robenhausen; c, rather a long stone. 15, sloe stone. 16, plum stone; a, furrowed ventral side; b, broad side; c, dorsal furrow. 17, 18, cherry stones. The original drawing in Heer, 1878.

55 The Saffron-Gatherer fresco from Knossos, Crete.

56 The palate of Rhodesian Man showing marked dental decay.

57 Early Dynastic Egyptian mandible showing extreme tooth wear, resulting in pulp exposure and abscess formation. Such attrition results from various factors, including tough foods and accidental abrasives in foodstuffs eaten.

58 The upper anterior teeth of a Bronze Age skull from Cambridgeshire, showing irregularity and pitting (hypoplasia) of the enamel. This may result from phases of malnutrition, as well as infectious disease.

59 Palatal view of the upper front teeth of the Neanderthal adult from Gibraltar, showing extreme wear and apparent exposure at the pulps in a number of cases.

60 The chewing surfaces of the upper and lower teeth of a Mesolithic skull from Gua Cha, Malaya, showing extreme wear.

61 Front view of the articulated jaws of the same Gua-Cha skull showing that the anterior wear has been so great as to cause an open-bite. This anomaly may be cultural but could also have been determined by extreme chewing stress put upon these front teeth, either by tough bony meat or siliceous vegetable matter.

62 Front view of the fibulae of a Neolithic man from Denmark (Raevehøj), showing thinness of shafts.

63 Lateral aspects of the two Danish fibulae, showing marked bowing of the shafts and broadening suggestive of rickets.

64 A seventeenth-century femur from London showing marked bowing of the shaft as a result of rickets.

65 Right lateral view of an Iron Age skull from Kilcornan, Co. Galway, showing parietal osteoporosis (not to be confused with the post-mortem erosion seen in the anterior part of the skull).

66 A close-up of part of the osteoporosis of the Kilcornan skull, showing the honey-comb structure which is not easily confused with erosion.

67 The grave of twins at Jebel Moya, Sudan, showing the skeletons and the feeding vessels above the heads of these infants. Below, details of the vessels, 1:2.

Index